WOMEN'S VOICES, WOMEN'S POWER

WOMEN'S VOICES, WOMEN'S POWER

DIALOGUES OF RESISTANCE FROM EAST AFRICA

Judith M. Abwunza

UTP

Originally Published by Broadview Press 1997. Reprinted 1999.

Canadian Cataloguing in Publication Data

Abwunza, Judith M .(Judith Mae), 1937-
 Women's voices, women's power: dialogues of resistance from East Africa

Includes bibliographical references and index.
ISBN 978-1-44260-114-7
(Previous ISBN 1-55111-132-2)

1. Women, Logooli - Social conditions. 2. Women, Logooli - Economic conditions.
I. Title.

DT433.545.L63A29 1997   305.48'896395   C97-930134-3

North America
5201 Dufferin Street, North York
Ontario, Canada, M3H 5T8

2250 Military Road, Tonawanda,
New York, USA, 14150

Tel: (416) 978-2239
Fax: (416) 978-4738
customerservice@utphighereducation.com
www.utphighereducation.com

UK, Ireland and continental Europe
NBN International
Estover Road, Plymouth, UK, PL6 7PY
Tel: 44 (0) 1752 202300
Fax: 44 (0) 1752 202330
enquiries@nbninternational.com

Higher Education University of Toronto Press gratefully acknowledges the support of the Canada Council, the Ontario Arts Council, and the Ministry of Canadian Heritage.

Table of Contents

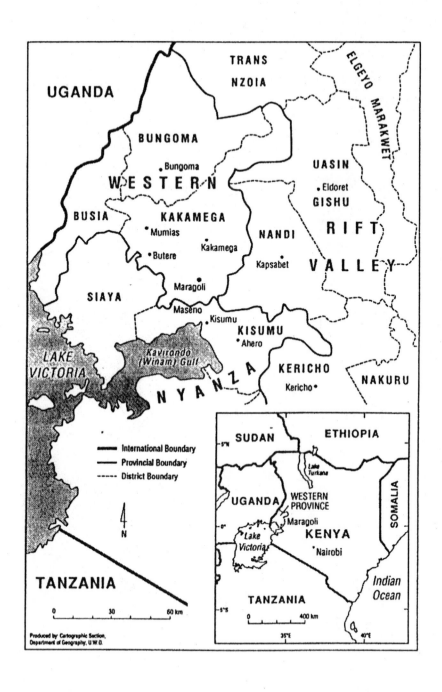

MAP ONE: KENYA AND WESTERN PROVINCE

Legend:
- Locational Boundary
- Sub-Locational Boundary

Regions shown on map:
CHAMAKANGA
KEGONDI
BUGINA
KISATULU
KEDOLI
CHAVAKALI
NORTH MARAGOLI
WEST MARAGOLI
EUSENGERI
VIYALO
BURULUNYA
GAVUDIA
LYADUYWA
MBALE
RIGAMA
MAMBAI
MBIHI
KEGOYE
CHANGO
MAGUI
SOUTH MARAGOLI
MADZUU
MAGOLI
KUMBA
MAHANGA
LUSIOLA
VIGULU
CHAGENDA
MASANA

0 1 2 3 4 5
kilometres

N

Produced by:
Dor J Mulama
Judith M. Abwunza

MAP TWO: MARAGOLI

Part I

UNEARTHING THE PATRIARCHAL WORLD

Introduction to Part I

This book elaborates a single, significant idea: women's power and resistance as they recognise their needs and work to achieve the means to meet those needs. The setting is Maragoli, Kenya, East Africa. The women are Avalogoli, which means "the people of Logoli."[1] Avalogoli are a subgroup of the larger cultural and linguistic ethnic group of Abaluhya. The voices of Logoli women presented in this book contribute both to the anthropology and sociology of East African societies and to feminist scholarship on African gender relations. Most of the contradictions of gender relations and local political economy in contemporary East Africa are played out in Logoli society: through Logoli women, we can examine the increasingly problematic nature of gender relations and reveal the connection of this development to capitalist relations of production. Women's power and resistance in economic, social and political spheres is explored in a way that reaffirms that women's agency continues to exist in East Africa, in spite of the increasingly patriarchal nature of patrilineal societies in the contemporary capitalist state. Through life history and interview material, Logoli women speak for themselves, a technique I believe to be an appropriate methodology for case studies on African women.

I first visited Kenya, East Africa in the summer of 1975 with my husband and our three year old daughter. The visit was personal. George, a Kenyan, and I married in the 1960s and he was returning home for the first time in eighteen years. Culture shock was acute for all three of us as we took up residence in the rural area of Maragoli, my husband's home. Our first small, two-room house, in his father's yard, was newly constructed, built on the day we arrived in Kenya. The mud was still wet. Even though the trip was planned ahead, it was important that we step on Kenyan soil before all the trouble and expense of house building began. We shared this mud hut with the domestic animals from the yard, with only a flimsy wall between us. Facilities are scant in Maragoli. Western Kenya generally is an area populated by cattle-keeping agriculturists, many with few cattle and limited land. Western Province, where Maragoli is located, has a reputation of underdevelopment relative to some other Kenyan Provinces.

My interest in the people I "married to" stimulated me professionally. Although Maragoli people had been written about, they, as they said, had no "book of our own," a book containing relevant historical and current information. Yet other groups around them had received this attention. There is an element of scholarly curiosity about these Western Kenyan cattle-keeping societies. I decided to train in the social sciences in an attempt to fill the Avalogoli void.

Throughout the course of this training another void confounded me and became the significant idea of this book. It did not take long for me to notice that women ran the world in Maragoli, despite an existing patriarchal sentiment. Here is a social world where equality ought to be skewed by a patriarchal ideology. Indeed, I found women posturing an adherence to this ideology. However, this posture stems from their own political decision and is a means to attain their needs. Where in the scholarly work was attention paid to African women, not only to their daily life and efforts, but most particularly to their power and resistance? The processes of gathering and ordering data for my research were influenced by my critique of research on African women.

I recognise the significance of the current literature on women and development, as it represents data on demographic, economic, political and social aspects. Yet, as other researchers note, the indicators which would explain the situation of African women are still not fully understood. Even as we are beginning to have a sense of what day-to-day life is for women in different cultures and the diversity that is likely to exist in their roles and statuses, it seems to me that the women themselves are silent. Their subjective experiences are eclipsed by analyses deaf to their voices. Because their actual experience of daily life is important in any analysis of change, they need to be seen as innovative actors, creative and visionary, surviving their oppressive circumstances, rather than simply as oppressed victims. They need to be given the opportunity to state their own views. In 1986, the CIDA Action Plan (11 June) called *Women In Development* stated that "Women need opportunities not only to participate in development, but to tell their own development story" ("Understanding Women's Role"). More recently this position has been expanded to include gender equity in *Engendering Development* (CIDA, 1995a) and women's empowerment in *Creating a world of equality* (CIDA, 1995b).

I decided on a research that would emphasise Logoli women's views and assessments of their own social reality and their participation in economic, political and social activities. Their views would be discussed in terms of the positive and negative impacts of modernisation and development on their workloads and their lives.

To that end, in 1987 and 1988, my husband, four of our children, and I lived in a permanent house, in a Maragoli yard in one of the Maragoli villages described in Chapter One.[2] One legitimising aspect of my residence stems from my work as a social scientist, yet another stems from a kinship tie, "married to an Umulogoli."

The following techniques were utilised to collect data in the field. Participant observation as recommended by Howell was used in the sense of the four phases he recommends: making friends; being where the action is; putting it all down; and putting it all together (1973, 367). This was accomplished in two ways. First, as friendships and relationships were previously established, I drew upon these to extend the area of participant observation and gradually increased my involvement with families and community affairs. Once my research interest in people was established, most days began with a woman or a group of women calling on me to bring my "hoe" (pen) and join them.[3] Second, I utilised what Staudt has called a "geographically purposive sample" (1985, 63), by which is meant sampling according to the physical accessibility of interviewees to the interviewer. For me, "geographically purposive" meant any Maragoli person within walking or sometimes driving distance who would consent to being interviewed. Thus, a purposive sample for me is better defined as "physically and socially accessible". As a result, in most cases I was party to the action that took place, whether it involved celebration or sorrow, going to market, digging in *shambas* (gardens, Kiswahili), collecting water, firewood, or vegetables, or engaging in long conversations over meals and endless cups of *ichai* (tea with milk and sugar) during visiting.

I had open-ended interviews with 410 women along with varying numbers of members of their families. Three hundred of these interviews took place in the sub-location under study, covering 77% of sub-location yards and 26% of households (each yard averaging about three households).[4] Seventy of the interviews were conducted with women in other areas of Maragoli; twenty were conducted with Maragoli women living in a neighbouring division; and an additional twenty interviews were conducted with Maragoli women living in Nairobi. In these interviews, I collected census information pertaining to all family members: age, sex, place of residence, household composition and relationships (i.e. *inyumba* [house or lineage membership]) within that composition, marital status, number of children, education, religion, land size, occupation and area of occupation. These interviews, which lasted from one to four hours, were conducted two to three times a day. They provide the data which form the background or context for the research.

From these 410 women, some 90 women provided detailed answers on more questions than others. Examples of the topics on which women provided more detailed information are: *uvukwi* (bridewealth) status, amount of land and location, title deed, sex of farmer, hired labour, crops, livestock, government assistance, water supply distance and frequency, fuel supply distance and frequency, commodity purchase, availability and sources of cash, and abuse. I asked questions about attitudes and we discussed perceptions of women, men, and children, government, development, assessments of incentives and rewards, and gender relationships.

A number of government officials as well as educational officials and teachers discussed Kenya, Maragoli, and Maragoli people with me, both formally and informally. I also conducted open-ended interviews with 11 men and had informal conversations with many other men. Fifty-nine families attempted yard budgets over a range of time from one month to six months. Forty-nine of these were from the sub-location (13% of the yards), and ten were from Nairobi households. Nineteen Logoli women gave their time to provide detailed life histories.

In all of these interviews, people were encouraged to provide their own assessment of situations. I kept the criticism relating to our lack of knowledge of African women at the forefront of my thoughts in framing questions. I hope that Logoli women's confidence in the importance of their activities has contributed to a successful collection of textual information. At the outset of every request for an interview, I explained that I would be taking their words "overseas" and writing them down for their children and others to read.[5] In the context of interviews, particularly with attitude questions, I first asked a question and then waited for an answer. If no response was forthcoming, I used the statement, "Say some more, I am telling your story." People usually responded by providing more information or by saying *nindio* (that's all, that's the end of it). Second, I gave them my interpretation of their answer: "I want to be sure I understand, you are saying...?" Agreement or correction followed. I considered agreement tenuous and correction more to the point, although frequently I was regarded by those interviewed as naïve.[6] Logoli women's patience was likely the result of their assessment of their self-importance and their dedication to teaching a relative who was nonetheless an outsider. I have not discussed their corrections of my interpretation with them. Final correction will come about when I read them this book.

Most interviews took more than two hours, and some took up to four. Life histories were collected in one or two hour sessions over differing periods of time. For example, in Florah's case we had six sessions and many hours of spending time together as we engaged in other activities, even interviews with other people. I found the context of other interviews particularly helpful in that Florah or others would say "I believe this to be the case," or "That is not the way I believe this to be."

Archival and statistical research on local and national issues was conducted at the Provincial Commission Library in Kakamega and in various government offices and university libraries in Nairobi. I was not permitted access to the files in the District Officer's office in Vihiga, Maragoli. However, people there, as well as in the Social Service office in Mbale were cognisant of my needs and most gave freely of their time with oral information. Information was gathered on population, unemployment, health care, social services, fertility, development plans, agriculture reports, land tenure records, district plans for rural development, probation, and economic surveys. More intensive investigation, including participant observation, was conducted in areas of health care and fertility in Maragoli at the Rural Health Clinic in Mbale and from women's groups and their leaders. In addition, the 1988 Kenya general elections were held during the time I was in the field, and I was able to collect information on formal policies and procedures relating to that process, as well as on the informal "goings on."

A Note on Language

A glossary of Luragoli, Kiswahili and local English terms used is provided at the end of this book.

Luragoli is the language of the Logoli people. It is a first language spoken by all members of the society. Within Maragoli, Luragoli is the main language of communication. All interviews were conducted in Luragoli unless otherwise stated. In the text, Luragoli words and phrases are italicised and the translation is given in brackets the first time each word is used.

Kiswahili and English are national languages in Kenya. In Maragoli schools, the language of instruction is English and Swahili is taught as a second language. Both languages are, however, used mostly in the schoolroom or in government offices. English or Kiswahili are used more between Avalogoli and others, rather than among Avalogoli. Where Kiswahili terms are used in the text, they are so designated and formatted in the same manner as Luragoli.

Sometimes referred to as "Kenyan English" or "Africa English", **local English** is an adaptation of English words to local circumstances and practices to convey specific meanings to acts that conventional English usage does not. In this book, the apparently idiosyncratic usage will make local English terms obvious to the reader. For example "to provision" or "provisioning" refers to providing food, food-related goods as well as other items: a somewhat conventional translation used as a verb. "Posterity" means children. The words of a childless man lack power and weight: "*Ezingulu zitula ku mwana*" ("Power comes from children"). When a husband or wife separates from a spouse it is said they "walked". Another example is the Avalogoli usage of "dowry." In conventional anthropological meaning, dowry is reserved for the gifts that the bride's father or group pays to the new household. In local English, "dowry" is the term used by Avalogoli for bridewealth, the transfer of wealth from the family of the bridegroom to the family of the bride.

Acknowledgements

The fieldwork during which most of these data were collected took place in 1987 through 1988 and in 1992 and 1994. In 1987 and 1988 support was provided by a Social Sciences and Humanities Research Council (SSHRCC) Doctoral Fellowship, an International Development Research Centre award, and an award from the Centre for International Studies, University of Toronto. In 1992 and 1994, support was provided by a SSHRCC Post Doctoral Fellowship and the Department of Anthropology, University of Western Ontario. The author gratefully acknowledges financial support from the Wilfrid Laurier University Office of Research. Permission to engage in research was authorised by the Office of the President, Kenya, East Africa. Affiliation was provided by the University of Nairobi and the Institute of African Studies, University of Nairobi. In addition, I have spent varying amounts of time in Maragoli during other visits between 1975 and 1995.

Portions of this book appeared in an article entitled "Silika: To Make Our Lives Shine" in *Anthropologica* xxxvii:1; permission from that journal to incorporate that material into this book is hereby gratefully acknowledged.

I have been fortunate in that I have three role models and mentors: Bonnie Kettel, Harriet Lyons and Patricia Stamp have provided assistance and support far above the call of academic duty. My competent Ph.D. supervisor, Michael Levin, and I had a tumultuous few years but our friendship survived. People at Wilfrid Laurier University, University of Toronto and Western were unfailing in their respect and friendship. Michele Amlin and Andie Noack were superb research assistants. Melissa Smith was my copy editor. I thank you all.

Asande muno to Logoli women for narrating their historical and current efforts of solidarity, or as they say, "gathering at the back door"— their concentrated efforts to promote the means in order to achieve their needs. I dedicate this book to them and to my "posterity" (children).

Chapter One
AVALOGOLI

Geography and Description of Place

Maragoli Division is an area of 198 square kilometres immediately north of the equator (see Map 1). The outstanding topographical feature in Maragoli is the Maragoli Hills, which rise to heights of over 6000 feet. The southern boundary of these hills is defined by the Maseno and Maragoli faults. The Vahani River, flowing southward toward Lake Victoria, has deeply incised an area between the peaks of the hills. The northern area forms a peneplain, lying at 4,500 to 5000 feet above sea level (Ligale, 1966, 65; Mmbulika, 1971, 1). Except in zones bordering the hills, where sandy soils and large rocks predominate, the soil from the volcanic rocks is richly red and fertile.

The varied nature of the landscape—steep hill-sides and flat-bottomed valleys—contributes to farming problems. In early days of settlement, prior to population expansion, the hillsides were sources of firewood and when cleared were marked off for communal grazing. Current land scarcity has required the utilisation of this land for crops, leading to erosion. Annual rainfall varies between 40 and 80 inches per annum, with the long rains from March to June, and short rains from September to November. In the past, there was an abundance of surface drainage. Many rivers and streams, most of which were permanent, flowed from the Nandi and the Maragoli Hills. Erosion has reduced these and many are now only seasonally available. Temperatures average between 28 and 42 degrees celcius in the dry season, and 20 and 30 degrees in the wet season.

Today Maragoli is a Division in Vihiga District, Western Province, Kenya. Until recently, it was included in Kakamega District. Maragoli is divided by a tarmac road that runs from Kisumu on Lake Victoria, the third largest city in Kenya, to Kakamega, a Western Province town containing offices of Provincial Government and tourist-oriented businesses. Areas within Maragoli are divided into North, West, South, and Central Locations. Political leaders within the locations include both group elders, determined by descent, and representatives of today's state bureaucratic structures, such as Members of Parliament, Chiefs, Assistant Chiefs, Council Members, and Headmen. Within the locations are further divisions: sub-locations, market towns and villages (see Map 2). One of the larger centrally located markets, Mbale, has recently received the status of "town" and government agencies are being established there. Among other agencies, the court facility and division offices pertaining to agricultural services, social services, and legal services are being moved to Mbale from other market towns. A large central post office and rural health centre have been in place for some time in Mbale, as well as electricity and a central water source. During 1987 and 1988, inconveniences resulting from road paving and construction became a way of life in Mbale. In 1994, the road work was said to be complete. The construction equipment was gone, although there seemed to be little change. However, as one owner pointed out, all the shops had been "renovated"—meaning that their fronts were freshly painted. Expropriation of family-owned land and relocation of people was finished, providing space for Mbale expansion. One hopes the traumatic effect on the families who had to leave their dead behind has somewhat abated.

MBALE MARKET

Mbale is a typical Kenyan market town. It has a mixture of shops made of mud or cement blocks with corrugated iron roofs arranged on both sides of a main thoroughfare. With the exception of two shops owned by Kikuyu, all are owned by Avalogoli. These shops sell assorted commodities: food, clothing, bedding, furniture, general household utensils and supplies, dishes, lanterns, kerosene, as well as agricultural commodities, such as hand tools, seeds and fertiliser. Speciality shops include butcher shops, wholesale commodity shops, supply stores, a grinding mill, carpentry shops, iron works, and bars. Mbale has a printing shop with photocopier (which seldom works), two booksellers, a stationary shop, and a beauty parlour. The recently constructed hotel is large and relatively modern, although it lacks a running water source. Outdoor market tables are also in evidence, supplying fresh vegetables, dried fish, charcoal, chickens, and livestock. Outside market sellers and shops do business on a daily basis, although Saturday is the largest market day in Maragoli. By noon, crowds of people and herds of livestock have raised clouds of red dust that signal convergence. The dust dissipates in the late afternoon, when tired women gather their unsold produce to return home and cook the evening meal. Long lines of children and adults carrying assorted containers form in front of the kerosene pump. Most residences in proximity to Mbale Town and to other market towns are permanent, being made of cement block with corrugated iron roofs. There is little agricultural land in these more concentrated areas, but there are some small domestic garden plots.

Villages in Maragoli are defined by the presence of schools rather than marketplaces. Schools are usually in the centre of a village area and consist of a half-dozen primary and sometimes also secondary school buildings. In some villages a church is dominant. Communal village activities take place in either the school or the church. On Sunday, most people will congregate at church from early morning until early afternoon. Worship takes up part of that time; however, visiting and the arrangement of village communal work are also included in church activity.

In villages, shops are scattered here and there and market sellers sit on the sides of road or paths displaying their commodities on tables or cloths. Scant inventories attest to the fact that the bulk of household needs are purchased at the market towns or Mbale. Most market towns are within walking distance, although the dirt and gravel roads range from relatively good to extremely poor.

Mugitsi, or homesteads (or "yards" as they are called in English), each seen as belonging to a localised descent group, are scattered across what is known as a village area. In the past, a yard had land space for an economic base that supported polygyny as well as patrilocality. Current increases in population and land shortages have created difficulty in permitting a viable economic base to support these traditional structures. Yards still contain extended family groups, some polygynous (usually the ascending generation), with younger men working or looking for work elsewhere. Women attempt to provide for the needs of their family and community from an increasingly reduced resource base. Houses are thatch-roofed, square or round, built of mud, and in some cases are either "semi-permanent" (mud with corrugated iron roofs) or "permanent" (constructed from concrete blocks or yard-made bricks, with corrugated iron roofs). Each wife in the yard should have a house. Livestock (cows, sheep, goats) and fowl (chickens, ducks) share the human living spaces. Outbuildings are also in evidence: "kitchen huts", usually one to a yard, with the required three cooking stones and perhaps a charcoal burner, some granaries, and *ichoos* (latrines). Cemented graves of deceased relatives are in all yards, ideally located in front of houses in which they lived. *Mulimi* (land for crops; Kiswahili: *shamba*), including banana "plantations," are in close proximity. The traditional first task in establishing a yard was to plant "a banana," the second to dig an *ichoo*. The total yard area is usually enclosed by thorn bush fences or trees. Some more fortunate families may have additional agricultural land elsewhere. Water is collected from central, piped spring sources, or when that fails, the rivers. Electricity is not available in village areas. Most villages contain cross sections of family groupings ranging from relatively affluent to relatively poor.

Yards, paths and roads are the usual centre of activity in Maragoli villages. Few aspects of people's lives are private; most are subject to discussion. In the early morning light, in different areas of the yard, men and school children bathe from small basins of water that women have allocated. Women greet one another on the paths as they make their second trip for water. Once men and children leave, the yards are taken over by women washing clothes and spreading them on bushes to dry. Younger children have fun and "assist" by walking over the clothes with muddy feet. Old people sit in favourite spots in front of their houses, caring for children or dozing. People passing by stop to give greetings and visitors may arrive for tea or a meal. Others join in work activities or gossip with those working in the yards or gardens. In the heat of the afternoon, people rest from work, talking or dozing in small groups scattered around the yard or on path-sides. Late afternoons find people moving on the paths, fetching water and firewood or returning from markets to join animated conversations in yards. Preparations for the evening meal take place and noisy children, livestock and fowl are rounded up, escape, and are rounded up again, more times than one would care to count. Children run to shops for kerosene so that lanterns may be lit before it gets too dark. School girls run for a last supply of water. To this outsider, life in Maragoli is active, noisy with conversation, laughter, and sometimes anger, but the tempo is usually slow.

Maragoli is an attractive area when nature cooperates. It is lushly green and interspersed with brilliant tropical flowers in all seasons. It is predominantly agricultural and known for its fertility. The Avalogoli are known for skilful farming techniques and production levels and a phenomenal population growth. Avalogoli are also known for their attachment to "home," where birth gives them membership in a social group and their resting place in death.

Migration and Settlement: Avalogoli History

The history of Avalogoli has been written by both Logoli and non-Logoli people.[7] According to the Avalogoli accounts of migration and descent (Lisingu, 1946 and oral information), "A long time ago" Logoli ancients came from a country called Asia. From Asia they settled for a time in *Misiri* (Egypt), then travelled the Nile and arrived in Congo. From Congo, they travelled overland to Uganda, then crossed Lake Victoria from Uganda in "canoes made from reeds" to today's Kisumu, Kenya. Some forefathers died on the journey: Muyeli in Ethiopia and Nabwege in Uganda (Mwelesa).[8] A strong wind on Lake Victoria is said to have split up the canoes. This resulted in some forefathers going "south" and some going "north."[9] However, "The grandfather of all was the same person, and wherever people went they left behind those who had the same customs and language as Avalogoli" (Lisingu, 1946).[10] The forefathers of Mulogoli, the ancestor of all Logoli people, stayed for some time ("many years") on the shores of Lake Victoria (from about 1250 A.D.[11]). The father of Mulogoli, Andimi, moved farther inland, dying in today's South Nyanza. Mulogoli, "tired of fighting" with the Nandi and the Masai, moved northwest to Seme, then Maseno, and finally to Mwigono (Maragoli Hills) or Evologoli, which is today's Maragoli. His brother, Anyore, settled nearby, in today's neighbouring Division, Bunyore. The Maragoli settlement by the ancestor, Mulogoli, with his wife Kaliyesa, is considered to have taken place around 1700 (Were, 1967b, 7-8).[12] Today's memories say that this land was uninhabited and wars between neighbouring groups, such as the Luo and Nandi, did not begin until settlement was well established (Abwunza, 1985). In the old days, Maragoli was "known in two steps, east and west." For Avalogoli, the east, direction of the sunrise, represents life. The west, direction of sunset, is the place of worship. The Mung'oma Hills (Maragoli Hills) are said to be in the west. The caves of the ancients, where Mulogoli and his people first lived before building houses, are in the Mung'oma Hills. Today, the locations of North and West Maragoli are in the traditional east, and South Maragoli is in the traditional west.

Mulogoli and Kaliyesa had four sons, Musali, Kizungu, Kilima and M'mavi. These four sons make up the *tsinyumba tzinene* (great houses) in the segmentary lineage structure of the people of Logoli. Mulogoli gave his sons land, "as all fathers do." Musali and Kizungu moved north, Kilima went to the west, and the last born, M'mavi, "remained behind" in the south, *yatigala nalinda misango gia Mulogoli* (caring for his father's land). These sons and their children spread over the land, settling in defined territorial segments that for the most part remain today. The sentiment of territorial ownership of land puts the *inyumba* (house) of Musali and of Kizungu in North Maragoli, Kilima in West and M'mavi in South. In terms of authority, the north is the home of the first born son, Musali, and the south of the last born son, M'mavi, which imparts two important hierarchical statuses to these geographical areas.

The names of the sons of Mulogoli, their sons, and their sons' sons are now written for history, as Avalogoli say, "To show the beginning of Mulogoli (signifying people) in the world" (cf. Mulama, no date;[13] Lisingu, 1946). In addition, a further segmentation of 22 (Mulama) or 25 (Lisingu) "little houses"—that is, other grandsons of Mulogoli—are also named, but not designated by specific territorial segments. They live "just anywhere" within the territories of the four sons. Those who trace their relationship from the four sons identify themselves according to descent, showing not only residence legitimisation, but also political authority. Some would say, "We are *avana va Musali* (children of Musali) here." This signifies their relationship to the important first born son of Mulogoli and permits them to live and own land in North Maragoli. In South Maragoli, people say, "We are all children of M'mavi here," or "We are all children of Mahagira here," in a sub-location of South Maragoli. Mahagira was the third-born son of Gonda who was the third-born son of M'mavi, the last-born son of Mulogoli. It is said that traditionally, Avalogoli practised a total exogamy, such that no Logoli person could marry another Logoli person. In recent history, exogamy is practised within the four main lineages. Incest is traced from both the mother's and father's side through at least two ascending generations. As Avalogoli are seen to live in localised descent groups, a man and woman with grandmothers, even great-grandmothers, coming from the same area in Maragoli cannot marry.

Ethnicity

Ethnicity in Africa centres around a common group experience, emphasising the historical underpinnings of group identity that assist in explaining language and cultural attributes. The historical account presented above provides the foundation of Avalogoli collective group experience. Today, 200,000 Avalogoli[14] live in Maragoli. From colonial times they were seen as part of a larger cultural and linguistic Bantu group. This group was first known to Westerners as the Bantu Kavirondo Tribe, a label given by colonial officials. Later, Avalogoli were included in a Luhya Nation. For a time, this indigenous designation served Avalogoli economic and political purposes, particularly with regard to issues of land ownership and independence from colonial rule. In present-day Kenya, they are categorised by the

Kenya Central Bureau of Statistics as a "sub-tribe" in the "main-tribe" designation of Luhya. The Baluhya are second largest in population size in Kenya. Kikuyu are first and Luo are third.[15]

During colonial times in Kenya, all indigenous ethnic groups suffered similar inequalities: alienation from land; conscripted labour reinforced by pass laws; the establishment of reserves or locations; and laws against African cash crop production and trade. Opposition to these inequalities by Western Kenya Baluhya began through voluntary associations introduced by the missionaries, which were later adapted by Africans to serve political ends. One of the most important of these organisations, the North Kavirondo Central Association, was formed in 1932 with the help of the apolitical Society of Friends. It was strongest in the most densely populated areas, Maragoli and Bunyore, and eventually grew until it had membership in almost every location in Western Kenya. By 1938, this Baluhya association had become political, issuing protests against compulsory destocking (slaughter of cattle), demanding payment of war gratuities to dependents of Africans killed in World War I, and campaigning for tax exemptions and lower taxes. Soon, missionaries and settlers were accused of stealing African lands. The Association's gains were few and members often faced persecution from the British; they nonetheless persisted. In 1939, the Association changed its name to the Abaluhya Central Association, by which those people known to the British as the Bantu Kavirondo legitimised the idea of a Luhya Nation. Individual ethnic groups assimilated to advocate reserve ownership of land by title deed and to protest against soil conservation measures within their locations. These were seen as a ploy for further European takeover of African land. By the 1950s, an even broader group identity, the Kenyan nation, emerged in the fight for independence from the British. Eventually the Baluhya Political Union merged with the Kenya African National Union (KANU) to work toward the common goal of *uhuru* (freedom, Kiswahili).[16]

For some time then, Avalogoli ethnic group identity was subsumed into the larger goals of Kenyan nationalism and independence from Britain. An idea of nationalism evolved that stemmed from membership in religious groups, then crossed religious and ethnic lines to a larger group identity of Baluhya, and finally climaxed in a national identity of Kenyans. This is a good example of Weber's notion about opposition generating identity: "a specific sentiment of solidarity in the face of [an]other group" (1958, 173).

Today Avalogoli limit Abaluhya identity to mainly urban contexts. National identity is contextual as well. Although the ideal of national identity in Maragoli—as expressed by the political slogan of *Nyayo*—is one of peace, love, unity, and sharing, the Avalogoli expression of unique ethnicity is still pronounced. Their identity stems from a common commitment to ancestry (Weber, 1968; Barth, 1969; Isajiw, 1975; 1979), their language, Luragoli, and what they characterise as a "proper" Avalogoli way of life, "the Avalogoli way." Thus, their "ethnic cognitions result in ethnic self-identity" (Aboud, 1981). Although their ethnicity emerged from the above characteristics, today it has become an important "objectified principle" (Comaroff, 1987, 313f). As a result, their ethnic identity pervades all aspects of their everyday life, including the political (cf. Patterson, 1977, 102f). This strong ethnic identity permits them to work within collectives for their own interests in order to achieve not merely equality (cf. Comaroff, 1987, 314), but also privilege compared with others in the Kenyan nation. In Maragoli today, privilege means "progress" (development), undertaken by Avalogoli themselves and with government assistance. Ethnicity pervades social, political and economic spheres, as Avalogoli adhere to a hierarchy of contextual allegiance: first among segmentary structures of Avalogoli; second among all Avalogoli; third, Baluhya; and fourth, in Kenyan nationalism.[17]

ARTIFACTS ON DISPLAY: MARAGOLI CULTURAL DAY

Economy

Avalogoli are cattle-keeping agriculturists, who for a long period of time have relied heavily on extra income from wage labour. The segmented lineage structure of their society legitimises ownership and disposition of land and cattle (along with other livestock and fowl) and similarly influences wage labour production.

Today's Maragoli contains people engaged in a mixture of economic pursuits. Some, usually women, engage in farming small pieces of land, usually on one-half or one acre plots, growing the staple crop of maize, along with millet, bananas, sorghum, yams, beans, and green (cowpea) vegetables. A few have coffee; fewer yet have tea "plantations" and the recently introduced, government-assisted, French bean crop. Others, usually men, work or look for work in the wage labour sector, inside and outside Maragoli. Thus, individuals may be farmers, wage earners, or both, and more or less dependent upon one another to survive. Both occupations are nowadays precarious and hazardous, factors which do not allow viable economic expansion.

Economic hardship is common in Maragoli. Few of the potential labour force have been employed in wage labour and there is no indication of improvement. Kenya generally is threatened by an unemployment situation that has reached massive proportions. Agricultural land for personal subsistence is expensive and in short supply. As far back as 1978, a demographic analysis of Maragoli by Ssennyonga called attention to dangerous density levels associated with the agricultural resource base. Population figures then showed a total population of 123,713 in an area of 208 square kilometres, with North Maragoli having the higher density of 614 per square kilometre and South Maragoli next with 542. Ssennyonga pointed out that fertility indices in Western Province generally appeared to be above the national average, at 54.2 as against 50 births per 1000 (population). He observed: "as one narrows the spatial angle towards Maragoli from the national plane, the higher the densities soar" (1978, 5). He assessed the reported rates and figures in Maragoli as "frightening." He wrote of "a total fertility of 8.6 (children per family), and an annual rate of natural increase of 3.52%, in a rural unit where the average density is close to 2500 persons per square mile." In relating this to the resource base and human potential, Ssennyonga said, "Many will doubt whether this rural people has been able to build up a life support system with the capacity to sustain its phenomenal population" (1978, 13, 14).

By 1982, the population had increased to 142,205, and densities ranged from a low of 277 (in a area of very poor land) to a high of 1065. South Maragoli averaged 902, and North 748, increasing the average density to 825 per square kilometre. In the Republic of Kenya *Population Census*, 1982, the area of Maragoli is reported as 198 square kilometres, an apparent reduction of 10 square kilometres from 1978. It was not possible to establish the basis of this revision. There were no reports of Avalogoli "losing land" by boundary revision or other measures. The annual rate of natural increase rose to 4% (Republic of Kenya, 1982), and the increase continued until very recently. In 1988, the population in Maragoli was given as 197,324. A rapid population growth in combination with restricted land resources and limited opportunity for wage employment are the main factors contributing to today's economic difficulties.

Notes on Avalogoli Traditions and Beliefs

IDEAL MARRIAGE OF AVALOGOLI

A marriage in Maragoli ought to be organised and overseen by parents, and ideally by all elder relatives. A request for marriage consideration should come during a visit from one of the parents of either the man or woman. The request is made after the elders have observed the young couple and are able to pass judgement on their appropriateness for each other as well as their "goodness." For a young wife, "goodness" generally means being a "good worker," and for a young husband, the ability to provide his wife with a house and land. At the time of the initial request for marriage, or shortly after, *uvukwi* discussion should be initiated by the young man's relatives. Prior to this discussion, both the young man and the young woman will have an opportunity to discuss the marriage with their parents. If the couple agrees to the marriage, they may also contribute their own ideas as to how much *uvukwi* should be offered and accepted during the negotiation. If the negotiation results in an agreement, at least part of the *uvukwi* should be given immediately in order to assist with wedding expenses.

Uvukwi presentations are cattle and cash. The "first cow" (a bull), important because it starts the uvukwi exchanges and symbolises the relationship, is given by the young man's father. Fathers should have accumulated cattle from their daughters' *uvukwi* in order to assist their sons in providing *uvukwi*. A father will tell his very young son which sister will provide cows for his marriage. All people share this knowledge as the two grow up. The sister takes on the care of this brother while they are in their father's yard, and the brother watches over his sister and is involved in her *uvukwi* discussion. When they marry, their respective children will have a relationship with each other and with their *kotsa* (aunt, uncle and respective spouses) that has more of the qualities of a sibling-parent relationship than the usual relationship between brothers, sisters, and their children. A woman's father receives the cash and cows but a woman's mother should receive part of the cash, as well as "small" gifts, such as cloth, head scarves, tea, sugar, or extra small amounts of cash. The daughter should also provide a small amount of cash for the mother.

Traditionally, two weddings are held. The first is in the yard of the bride. From there, the bride and her female age-mates will walk (nowadays drive) to the second, held in the yard of the bridegroom. In both yards, relatives will contribute wedding gifts and food so that all may "feast." People dance and sing wedding songs. This traditional structure of the wedding opens the way for ongoing reciprocal relations among the relatives of the married couple.

Today's weddings in Maragoli do not often follow the ideal. A few more affluent families attempt it, but for most *uvukwi* presentations are too expensive to consider beginning the ideal marriage transaction. Most young people elope, the woman taking up residence in the man's yard without any *uvukwi* discussion and wedding ceremonies. Frequently, the pressure for *uvukwi* discussion will come later from the woman's relatives. If the negotiations do take place, the initial "payment" is often a token amount. Neglecting a discussion, or the payments following a discussion, creates tremendous dissension within and between entire families. A wife will demand that her father receive his cows: it is a symbol of her husband's and his family's regard for her as a wife. It also opens the way for the reciprocal relations vital to her and her family's welfare in today's situations of economic difficulty.

In my own marriage, which took place in Canada in 1965, the *uvukwi* situation remained unaddressed for some years. In 1976, my women affines in Maragoli insisted that my uvukwi had to be "discussed" and "paid." As my father was in Canada and I do not have any brothers or anyone to be placed in that category, proxies for my father and brothers and a woman "from my husband's neighbourhood" were designated and the discussion took place. After some time, during which totally outrageous figures were tossed around, *uvukwi* was decided upon. The proxies received a share of the cash and the remaining cows and cash were given to my husband to hold "in trust" for my father as he declined to have cows shipped to Canada. Some of the cows died, but they are still "owed" as dead cows have to be replaced. The death of *uvukwi* cows symbolises ill intent, that they were "not sent with a good heart." The remaining cows have assisted my younger brothers-in-law in their marriage arrangements and my sisters-in-law, who benefit from the milk and calves.

IDEOLOGY OF AVALOGOLI PATRIARCHY

Avalogoli are what we would refer to as "patriarchal" in that they believe that all men rule or have the right to rule as *omwene hango* ("commander") over women and children. They have the right to rule if they are honourable and follow custom and thus can be characterised as "good"

Logoli men. Authority extends outward from the rule of the "commander," ideally the eldest man within a yard, and thus throughout Avalogoli society. This authority is age- and context-dependent: elder men are seen to rule over junior men, some elder men are seen to rule over other elder men, but all men have a right to rule over women and children. Men's words and actions are the authority for women. This authority is supposed to saturate all aspects of women's lives, so that their desires and goals are only directed by men's desires and goals. As men see it, their rule allows their ownership over all production and their authority in all aspects of decision-making.

Men expect that women will show respect for their right to rule in all of their words and actions. This respect for men's authority should be evidenced by women's deference to all men, but most particularly to their fathers, husbands, husband's elder brothers and their fathers-in-law. If deference is not maintained, then depending on the context, any of these men have the right to inflict "punishment" in order that women may "learn." However, any of these men, as well as women's brothers and other women, have the right to intervene. "Teaching" women by beating is an institution. According to custom, the left hand should be used, so as not to inflict too much damage, and should not descend upon vital areas of the body, such as the kidney, liver, or heart. Although the ideal instrument for beating women is the hand, *ubangas* (machetes), hoes and sticks are often used. Women may not be beaten when they are "with blood" (pregnant).

Women posture a deference to patriarchy. For example, groups of women and men may engage in animated conversations; however, if any of the men listed above (with the exception of women's brothers) join the group, a woman immediately takes on an attitude of withdrawing from the conversation. She stops talking, lowers her head, folds her hands or arms and looks down. Failure to take on this posture of deference will cause women and men to describe her as "a woman acting like a man," as "too independent," or, as in one case, "computer mouth." Women instruct other women to avoid verbal or physical abuse by assuming this deference to men. Advice runs from keeping quiet no matter the provocation, sitting quietly with legs and arms crossed while absorbing a torrent of abuse, to running to hide in the bananas.

My own relationship, being married to Mulogoli (a Logoli man and thus to all Avalogoli), is an aberration. My husband and I engaged in conversations as a couple, in groups, made eye contact, and often publicly touched one another. On occasion we argued and my husband was disinclined to use institutionalised means to "teach" his *mukali* (wife, usual usage *mukali gwa Abwunza*, wife of Abwunza) the appropriate behaviour. My relationship with my father-in-law, fathers-in-law and elder brothers-in-law was similarly aberrant as I engaged in dialogue with them and all men, in a fashion more appropriate to Western life than Avalogoli life. My relationship with mothers-in-law and sisters-in-law was more characteristically Avalogoli, as I deferred to and respected the former and took on a role of sister and friend with the latter.

Chapter Two

WOMEN'S POWER AND VOICE

The man is omwene hango, the commander, he is the owner, he is in charge.
Although we all have a higher authority who makes the ultimate decisions, it is
a man's duty to be in charge of his home, his wife, his children.
(Barnard, an elder man)

Women have forgotten their place and so have men. When the ancients went to
war it was the men who went first, but it was the women who dragged the rocks.
Without the rocks the men could not fight the war.
(An elder woman)[18]

Patriarchy and Power

The central purpose of this book is to employ a gendered approach to the subtle and complex arenas of women's power as exercised in economic, social and political spheres. It depends on women's voices as they portray their life events. The Avalogoli live in an agrarian society which has been integrated into a market economy of a capitalist state. In this context, women's power emerges as a vital organising principle in Avalogoli society.

Yet patriarchy is a prominent ideology in Avalogoli society. The power of men is taken for granted; both women and men say that it is predominant. This ideology has been reinforced in recent history by a British ideology of patriarchy which transferred to the Avalogoli through missionaries and colonials. The modern Kenyan state also legitimises a patriarchal ideology that is a mix of tradition and capitalism. Women's power is decreased by mutually reinforcing spheres of similar ideologies.

However, the effect of capitalism on women's power has not been entirely negative. In the past, the structural separation of Logoli women's and men's work gave women areas of power outside of men's control. The clear division between men's work and women's work has been eroded by capitalism. Population has increased, land resources have decreased, and there is a heavy dependence on the market economy. Women are required by necessity to confront these difficulties and to participate in what is considered men's work. This extension of their economic activity has increased women's power; they are instrumental in providing necessary goods and services.

Because of Logoli patriarchy, men dominate economically, socially and politically. Drawing on a structure of patriarchy said to be grounded in tradition, but which was also reinforced by colonialism and the Kenyan state, men attempt to impose control over women's production, try to isolate women and subject them to physical violence. The recent economic power of women has weakened many of the behavioural manifestations of patriarchal power, but it has not changed men's words, manners, and attitudes.

Despite the intrusion of capitalism and the increasing expression of patriarchal ideology, Logoli women have considerable power, which is tacitly recognised by both men and women. Like most women in rural East Africa, Logoli women perform physically demanding tasks that are indispensable to their family and the community. Logoli women appear at first glance to be marginal actors in a world controlled by men. Their traditional spheres of power in subsistence production and reciprocal relations have been weakened; the short supply of land and cattle pushes them into reliance on wage labour. There is also the economic burden of the state's emphasis, through *Nyayo*, on individual, community and national *maendeleo* (development: Avalogoli translate *maendeleo* as "progress" in English; cf. Abwunza, 1990).

But these women are goal-setters for both themselves and the community. They are active economic providers for their families, contributors to political and community causes, and economic innovators. Their willingness to divulge their daily lives for inclusion in this research attests to their self-confident assumption of the importance of their activities. Their words contribute insight into economic, social and political issues of women's places in the Avalogoli world. Their successful definition of the world around them permits a recognition of their intelligence in addition to their hard work. As Robertson writes,

> African women have...capacity...to organise themselves and set their own priorities.... The international community, and especially those interested in women in development, are getting wise in terms of attitudes and practices regarding Third World women. The matriarchal[19] attitude that entailed telling such women what to do and predicating that advice on Western norms and experiences is giving way to listening to them and serving as facilitators in terms of resources (1988a, 427-28).

Logoli women say, "today life is not fair for women," with an implied comparison to men. They add, "but that's the way life is." Their comments establish that the gender constructions of their culture—and thus their relationships with men—are increasingly problematic. They are aware that their power is threatened by an increasingly patriarchal ideology and see this as detrimental to family and community survival and progress. To counter this decrease in power, women posture an adherence to men's rule as *omwene hango*, but transform that posture into influence in order to promote their own interests. They also rely on a tradition of women's solidarity in reciprocal relations and "back door decisions." The former is used as a means for social and economic survival. The latter, "back door decisions," facilitates the former and also aids in resistance to patriarchal ideology.

To understand how Logoli women see their relationships with men, the concepts of power and patriarchy and their interaction with capitalism must be examined in the context of Avalogoli life. My use of the term "power" is sex-differentiated. For women, it means exercising their own will despite resistance in a context where the authority of men is normatively structured via patriarchy.[20] For men, "power" is control or influence over all those members in a society who are not considered men: in this case, women, unmarried men and children.

Many writers assume that this approach entails the use of a societal structure model of patriarchy. However, according to this model of patriarchy-as-structure, patriarchy is a monolith, fixed and immovable. For those who are not men, it is a material and symbolic evil, signifying their oppression. Tadesse writes of patriarchy according to this model: "all aspects of peasant life are determined according to the Ethiopian patriarchal family system, which is guided by the principles of domination of old over young and male over female" (1982, 211). Thus, patriarchy is conceptualised as "A system of interrelated social structures through which men exploit women" (Walby, 1986, 51). Patriarchy is "the rule of the father or the domination of women by men" (Vock, 1988, 83); and "The objective of feminism in general has been posed as the establishment of a theory of patriarchy, defined as the rule of men over women" (Stichter & Parpart, 1988, 11). When capitalism is brought into this model of patriarchy, it becomes "capitalist-patriarchy to denote the system which maintains women's exploitation and oppression:"

'Patriarchy' literally means the rule of fathers. But today's male dominance goes beyond the 'rule of fathers', it includes the rule of husbands, of male bosses, of ruling men in most societal institutions, in politics and economics, in short, what has been called 'the men's league' or 'men's house' (Mies, 1986, 37).

This model of patriarchy is insufficient for our purposes.

Criticism against this view, the use of patriarchy as a decisive concept, notes the difficulty in its definition as reified "male power" (Sydie, 1987, 166), fixed and unchanging over time (cf. Rubin, 1975; Brown, 1980; Armstrong & Armstrong, 1983; Burstyn, 1985). Patriarchy is often reified, conceived of as a natural structure. Thus, with its cultural content removed, some writers think of it as timeless and unchanging. In fact, our concepts of patriarchy are not merely structural. For ideological purposes, the term "patriarchy" is used "interchangeably with 'sexism,' a reminder that there is one sex which dominates, another which is subjected." This is equally true for structural purposes, as the "political and social control of women by men" (Coward, 1983, 8).

In discussing "patriarchy," Fox notes the linkage of structure and ideology in that there are "three key paradigms in discussions of 'patriarchy': patriarchy as collective male dominance permeating society, patriarchy as a self-contained system, and patriarchy specifically as the sex/gender system" (1988, 165). All her paradigms are cultural, combining ideology and structure. Fox concludes her discussion of patriarchy by stating that there is a "need to consider *both* social structure and ideology/subjectivity" (Fox, 1988, 177; my emphasis). This is the position I am using. A danger in conceptualising patriarchy as only structure is evident as it is conceived of monolithically, fixed in time as a structure of society; on the other hand, a purely ideological conception of patriarchy will lead to the conclusion that patriarchy is merely "The *feeling* of both men and women that the male's will dominates the female's" (Goldberg, 1973, 31, his emphasis).[21]

Patriarchy among Avalogoli appears to be both distinct from and a part of men's rhetoric and displays of power. It is legitimised by both reified social structure and ideology. Structurally, men are the "owners" of the land that women work. Ideologically, as men see it, their ownership extends to include production from the land, production from the realms of reciprocal relations and production from wage or casual labour. Their ownership further extends to permit them to be "in charge" in all aspects of decision-making. As noted in the first quotation at the beginning of this chapter, men believe they have a duty to "command" women. "Command" is evident as men display their right to rule by words and actions. A traditional military analogy, that men "rule as commanders" is used to express both structure and ideology. The term *omwene hango* or "commander" is used to refer to the senior male in a home, the "owner of the home." The structure and ideology of "male command" are the ideal in Avalogoli society.

Yet the second quotation at the beginning of this chapter reminds us that prior to colonialism and independence, in "the time of the ancients," women did influence men's power. Men's power was qualified by women's cooperation. Both men and women "have forgotten" this. Today, Logoli women's action and resistance remind men and women of women's "place" in Avalogoli society, a place that impedes both the structural and ideological arrangements of patriarchy.

The kind of power of greatest interest in this context is that of women exercising their own will, despite resistance, in a society where men have power over women structurally and ideologically. My purpose in discussing women's power is not to reduce gender conflicts to "myths about male or female rule," but to provide an analysis of "real relationships of men and women" (Sacks, 1979, 122).

The Avalogoli mode of production prior to colonialism and resulting capitalist intervention approximated the "kin corporate mode of production," whereby "People are all members of a corporation with collective ownership of the main means of production and, in one or another sense, are thus political decision makers with respect to the basis of their group's economic well-being" (Sacks, 1979, 115).

Avalogoli speak of collective action through reciprocity and collective ownership in the past as well as today. These ideals are expressed in such notions as men's ownership of land but women's rights to land. In practice, power imbalances interfere with these idealised expectations. For example, both men and women see individual men as current or future holders of the position of *omwene hango*, in this case best translated as "owner" of the land.

Avalogoli land ownership relies on a system of inalienable land rights that are inherited patrilineally. Within the patriliny, ownership of the means of production is today described as "family land," which implies an idealised lineage collectivity: land owned by all for the benefit of all family members—men, women and children. In actuality, the senior male elder controls the land and oversees land distribution. However, acceptance of male elder decisions depends on the power of the elder and the strength of the opposition. Women have rights to land through marriage, and women were and are ("always") the farmers. Men used to be "warriors," "hunters," and "commanders," and they assisted in digging the land and building houses. Today the ideal occupation for men is wage labour. A similar idealisation of the lineage collectivity affects the allocation of products through, for example, reciprocal obligations and benefits in kin and affine networks. Within this collective sphere, men and women lived separate and autonomous lives through the ideals of "women's work" and "men's work," that promoted separate spheres for men and women. Although the separation of men's and women's spheres is no longer as distinct as it once was, the right of appeal against untenable hierarchy still exists.

The Avalogoli kin corporate mode, with its collective underpinning, integrated and articulated with capitalism during British colonial rule. The collective system was affected by the British ideology of patriarchy, which amplified the role of *omwene hango*. Important political changes included the imposition of chieftainship, held by a non-Avalogoli Paramount Chief. This position was replaced in the early 1930s by Avalogoli location chiefs and bounded reservation areas. Avalogoli continued kin corporate relations, traditional landowning practices, and some aspects of reciprocity in these reserve areas. Logoli men began outside wage labour on settler farms to meet new taxes imposed by the British. In men's absence, women added men's labour and managerial responsibilities to their farming duties, and worked to produce and feed the male labour force (cf. Pala Okeyo, 1980, for the Luo; Oboler, 1985, for the Nandi; Nasimiyu, 1985; Abwunza, 1985, for the Avalogoli; Stamp, 1986, for the Kikuyu). Women's responsibilities increased, and women's and men's worlds became more separate. At the same time, however, women were forced to be less autonomous, as the patriarchal ideal of the male owner and breadwinner was imposed by the British. Women's contribution in their own commercial ventures was undervalued, even when they engaged in trade (cf. Ogutu, 1985). The title deed system of land ownership for Kenyan Africans was introduced toward the end of British rule by the Swynnerton Plan of 1954. The British patriarchal system of men as owners of the land and the means of production, and as controllers in relations of production, articulated with the kin corporate mode of production. The capitalist mode of production became stronger as Avalogoli were faced with increasing population and decreasing land sources and the imposition of needed and wanted market goods. The settler need for labour began to decline during and after the depression of the 1930s. The reserves were further exploited by colonial needs for African agriculture as subsidy (cf. Heyer, 1975; Pala Okeyo, 1980; Abwunza, 1985). Colonial attention was directed to men as owners and supposed farmers, reflecting the imposed patriarchal ideology (cf. Davison, 1988).

In independent Kenya, the articulation of traditional patriarchal ideology and the imposed patriarchal ideology perservere. The protective aspects of the traditional kin corporate group appear to be diminishing as the capitalist mode of production further permeates the culture. But the state bureaucracy is schizophrenic in that it promotes sharing and reciprocity while at the same time encouraging capitalism, which entails individual ownership and accumulation. Men are the assumed owners, so development initiatives are directed primarily to men but only rhetorically to women (cf. Staudt, 1985; Nasimiyu, 1985). Women are assumed to be exclusively subsistence or domestic producers, even though it is obvious that providing subsistence today requires women to participate in the capitalist sector in order to maintain a decent standard of living.

To say that only domestic power relations produce value for women is inappropriate in African societies: women participate in both domestic and public spheres (cf. Hay & Stichter, 1984; Stichter, 1988; Stichter & Parpart, 1988; Hay, 1988; Stamp, 1989). Women's power is felt and enhanced through their work in the private and public domains. Making a living necessitates Logoli women's involvement in both private and public domains.

Patriarchy as both structure and ideology is challenged by the working lives of women. Women's participation in the two domains indicates a relationship which "is highly responsive to—indeed, [is] a central part of—changes in the relations of production as a whole" (Leacock, 1986, x). This integration of the two separate spheres of work contributes to the negative consequences for Logoli women and their society, but also provides a location of gender struggles which could re-establish the integrity of power.

Logoli women's integration of work allows criticism to be applied in three areas: an assumed mode of production for women, capitalist labour valuation and a world systems approach. Feminist criticism, taking this integration of work into account (cf. Stichter & Parpart, 1988), is levelled against discussion of a "domestic mode of production" (Meillassoux, 1981), "lineage mode" (Rey, 1975) and "family mode" (Caldwell, 1982) where women's production is seen to be confined to a domestic sphere. Additionally, women's integration of work provides a challenge to the orthodox position that labour valuations in capitalist and non-capitalist modes are absolutely incommensurable. Non-capitalist production is socially regulated and therefore value-creating (cf. Stichter & Parpart, 1988). A "world systems" view describes household production and reproduction strategies as ultimately defined only by capital. It leaves no room for gender struggles within a household and for differing and contesting claims. Ironically, if the "world systems" approach is followed, many of today's African societies are left unanalyzable not only in regard to women's power, but also in regard to the increasingly large informal economy.

In Avalogoli society, people's survival depends upon two modes of production, capitalist and non-capitalist. All members participate in both spheres, because creating and maintaining the Avalogoli "proper way of life" depends upon it.

The Avalogoli way is also connected with reproduction. It is recognised that in any mode of production, domestic labour contributes significantly to surplus value (Gardiner, 1975), and that the labour force is socially constituted (Edholm, Harris, & Young, 1977; cf. Stichter & Parpart, 1988). The danger in conflating human reproduction with the reproduction of the mode of production or with the reproduction of labour power is also recognised (cf. Edholm, Harris, & Young, 1977). But what is important to recognise is that "some part of the multifaceted 'use values' of children must usually be marketed for the family and the individuals to survive" (Stichter & Parpart, 1988, 9). Women's value in human reproduction cannot be discounted in African societies. Reductionism may be overcome in empirical contexts by attention to the value of fertility. Among Avalogoli, "posterity"—having many children—is united with "power:" "power comes from children," as it is connected to the children's labour. Value may be connected with labour and incomes from "posterity" and how these relate to and affect the "rule" of male elders. "Posterity" requires reciprocal relationships between fathers and sons in ownership of land and labour (Abwunza, 1985). Logoli males as well as females use fertility as a strategy for acquiring status and ensuring survival (Abwunza, 1986). Obviously, women figure prominently in this process. "Posterity" is dependent on women's human reproduction.

In a lineage society, there are in a sense only ancestors and children. As long as a person is alive s/he is identified in terms of his or her ancestors, and specifically, his or her parents. One is always a child of the lineage in terms of responsibilities. Women are not only producing the next generation of workers, but also the next generation of actors in reciprocal relations, productive and otherwise, as well as a future generation of ancestors, all of which are vital aspects of Avalogoli society.

Another problematic issue in establishing women's power in situations where patriarchal ideology pervades lies in their consciousness of oppression. Sydie notes that patriarchal ideology discounts any likelihood of men and women acting together against oppressive conditions: "the private, familial exploitation of women that persists under capitalism...nullifies the assumption of a unified class consciousness among men and women" (Sydie, 1987, 120). Balbus concurs in reference to the penetration of patriarchy:

> If there is a domination-subjection relationship based on sexual identity, then there is a structural basis for hostility, rather than solidarity....If the male worker views his wife as inferior, he cannot see her as a "comrade"; indeed he is probably more likely to vent his rage on her than on his capitalist boss. On the other hand, since the woman is oppressed by her husband, she has good reason to view him as an "oppressor", as part of the problem rather than part of the solution (Balbus in Sydie, 1987, 120).

Logoli women identify men as part of the problems they face in their society. Women say, "Men and women should work together to survive and progress:" they recognise that gender cooperation is deficient but necessary. Yet by posturing an adherence to patriarchy, Logoli women are also reproducing the ideology of patriarchy, which is part of their oppression. What is acknowledged in this research is women's consciousness in doing so, and their belief that it promotes their own interests.

The concepts of patriarchy and power and their interaction with capitalism are essential to understanding Logoli women today. However, the conceptualisation of patriarchy continues to present analytical difficulty unless women's interests are taken into account. Recognising differing degrees of power existing in a kin corporate mode of production articulating with degrees of power in a capitalist mode of production only deals with part of the problem. Women's power can only be conceptualised by a further analysis of the pervasiveness of patriarchy as an ideology.

Determining who rules in whose interest is helpful in understanding this situation. As mentioned, Avalogoli socially articulate their lives in terms of an ideal patriarchy. They say that following the "rule" of *omwene hango* is what ought to take place in their society. Patriarchal ideology provides the *vika* (steps) to a "proper Avalogoli" way of life. But reinforcement of this ideology is limited in that the patriarch must exercise his power *in the interests of those he rules*. Without this caution, the patriarch may be replaced. There is a possibility here for transformation of power. Patriarchy loses its effectiveness if the interests of those ruled are not maintained. This principle is important for understanding societal inequality, gender-related and otherwise. Power depends on a continuing fulfilment of role expectations. If expectations are unfulfilled, the power holders can be challenged, leading to change. Among Avalogoli, patriarchal ideology says that "commanders" must be "good" Logoli men in order to receive their authority from those they rule. They must honourably abide by custom, that is, provide women with land (or equivalent production) and bridewealth.

In this research I develop two points. First, structures of patriarchy and ideologies of patriarchy are inextricably linked, but differ in the way each contrasts the actual and the ideal. "The organisation and the experience of patriarchy are different historically and cross-culturally" (Sydie, 1987, 51). Neither are monoliths. Second, we cannot neglect women's power, their own wills and their roles in these processes of change. Women are not merely acted upon; they are also actors. They resist, often militantly, oppressive circumstances. Researchers have recognised for some decades that women do not passively accept a dominated existence: indeed, they act against being placed in this position, overcoming obstacles and actively seeking out opportunities for empowerment (cf. Karl, 1995; Emeagwali, 1995; Blumberg, Rakowski, Tinker & Monteón, 1995; Sylvester, 1993; Young, Samarasinghe & Kusterer, 1993; Wipper, 1985; Newbury, 1984; Mba, 1982; White, 1980; Van Allen, 1976, 1972; Stamp, 1975-76; Bujra, 1975).

Among Avalogoli, in the articulation of the kin corporate mode of production and the capitalist mode of production, women have postured adherence to the tradition of patriarchal ideology to serve their own interests and those of their community. Indeed, an additional part of women's value is in maintaining the ideology that permits patriarchal relations to continue. Ironically, the rule of "commanders" is dependent upon women's interests.

Feminist and political economy scholars have reached no consensus on the theoretical issues of patriarchy and women's power. The term "patriarchy" is so laden with connotations in the feminist literature that it is extremely difficult to contribute to the literature on its meaning. I move between treating it as ideology, or a combination of structure and ideology, and a posture. I prefer to deal with this concept less eclectically and retain it as patriarchal ideology that women may posture if they believe it serves their best interests, recognising their own power in that decision. Today, Logoli women's interests are not maintained by the Avalogoli ideology of patriarchy or the ideology of the patrimonial capitalist state. Logoli women attain power by accruing information and utilising influence to confront patriarchal control. A symbol of women's power is the idea of *vivuni vye chandangu* (back door decisions). Logoli women assist us in relaying their procedure of "back door decisions" whereby they influence local and national events and processes. Theirs is a form of political agency not really accessible via the conceptual approaches previously applied in many East African gender analyses. In this research, there is evidence that women do attain individual power and can influence communal action to promote survival and "progress."

Women's Voices

The recognition of women's action has provided an arena for acknowledging their important—indeed, vital—economic and political participation in African history and current life. In an effort to overcome the former androcentric evaluations that have ignored or undermined women, it is suggested that women speak of and on their own experiences. This approach is an important theoretical contribution. All research—economic, political and social—and its association with "progress" must build on the responses of those who are directly experiencing the situation.

The personal narratives approach is an effort to allow women to represent themselves (cf. Personal Narratives Group, 1989). This method has produced several texts: *Each In Her Own Way* (Levy, 1988), *Three Swahili Women* (Mirza & Strobel, 1989), *Life Histories of African Women* (Romero, 1988) and *Voices from Mutira* (Davison with the women of Mutira, 1989). However, this approach is not without its critics: it has been depicted as "inglorious" in that it is "collecting and publishing what Third World women are saying, as if Western women originated the thoughts or arguments.... Given the monopoly on resources [for African women to engage in research], this is, unsurprisingly, another form of exploitation; it is stealing words from the horse's mouth!" (Amadiume, 1987, 10)

Ideally, however, a personal narrative approach attempts to circumvent the

political and theoretical complexities of trying to speak *about* women, while avoiding any tendency to speak *for* them. Feminist anthropology, unlike the 'anthropology of women', has made some progress in this area, because while it acknowledges that 'women are all women together' it also emphasises that there are fundamental differences between women (Moore, 1988, 191-192).

This book relies on the personal narrative approach while at the same time recognising the imperfections of such an approach. Logoli women are speaking alongside me, while it remains my choice to include or delete their words. As Amadiume has made clear, the ideal presentation of the experience of these women's lives would be entirely their own:

There is a need for material about women, collected and explained by African and other Third World women themselves, from which adequate and suitable theories and methodology can be worked out.... It can be argued that because of their plural and multicultural backgrounds as a result of the colonial heritage, Third World women are best qualified to carry out comparative studies and make generalised statements about women's position in their societies (Amadiume, 1987, 10).

Until that happens, the onus remains on predominately Western researchers utilising case studies. We must recognise that the impact of social change is profound and variable and the risk of overgeneralisation is considerable. Stamp draws on Foucault (1980) in saying, "The task of Western scholars is to take local knowledges seriously: to rescue them from the 'margins of knowledge' and to incorporate them into a scientific understanding of African society" (Stamp, 1990, 133). In this book (cf. Abwunza, 1995), the focus is on Logoli women's voices, providing women-centred discourses that consider Logoli women's own interpretations; a conversation between cultures in which local voices are heard and acknowledged.

Conclusion to Part I

An enduring ethos, "the Avalogoli way," has three requirements for "the good life:" land, cattle, and children. Unfortunately, the availability of these first two requirements is decreasing. An increase in the last, children, has created difficult social and economic circumstances for the Avalogoli. Examination of Avalogoli history and contemporary life experiences provides a framework for the investigation of women's power in light of these demanding circumstances.

A common theme emerges in studies of African women: under most circumstances, the economic and political influences of colonial and capitalist systems have interacted with existing social orders in ways that appear to increase inequality along gender and class lines. If women benefitted from change, it was as a consequence of general conditions which likely benefitted men more, and certainly not as a result of policies or programmes directed at improving the conditions of women's lives. Evidence for this conclusion comes from area studies which found that little or no attempt was made to view women as part of economic situations either during times of colonialism or post-independence periods. There is a further general consensus in these studies: the lack of attention to women's work and their other contributions to their societies has disadvantaged women as well as their communities. A case in point: it appears that the majority of women's lives are made more rather than less difficult by many development processes (cf. Charlton, 1984; Kariuki, 1985) and by economic restructuring. However,

> Women are the majority of the population and form the backbone of the family in Africa....there is a lot of need to focus our attention on their requirements and aspirations. The majority of these women also happen to be residing in the rural areas. Therefore, rural development is actually the development of women (Shitakha, 1985, 1).

The question that comes to mind in reviewing the literature on women's economic and political issues is this: if women are powerless, how is it that so much of the responsibility for family and community well-being hinges upon their efforts? "In many ways, the women perceived themselves as having primary responsibility for the economic well-being of their families" (Kariuki, 1985, 228). Clearly, the enormity of that responsibility does not indicate powerlessness.

Full consideration of the actions and voices of women in the light of women's "own will" or power is required. Some research on African women now centres on interviews with women and on their actual decision-making processes rather than on assumptions about them (cf. Stamp, 1989). In some cases, it is acknowledged that women "subvert the male order of things" (Thomas, 1988; cf. Reiter, 1975) and engage in "guerrilla tactics" against men (Mbilinyi, 1989). Still, in many cases, women's power is not seen as an ingredient of patriarchal and state control; thus, women's power is not considered part of modernising or development processes. This line of reasoning assumes only the structural model of patriarchy rather than acknowledging the possibility of combining structure and ideology that allows contextual change over time. Male power alone is often assumed, and few tests or inquiries are made. This is, in short, a misreading of history in action.

In this study, Logoli women themselves recognise social, economic and political inequality. This recognition contributes to the sense of resignation in their statement, "But that's the way life is." Contrary to this overt statement, the data I collected reveal that women's day-to-day behaviour and their actions in areas of work and decision-making do not demonstrate decisive resignation or deficiency of power.

I recognise the position of power I have taken in this book, as I have chosen which words to include and which to delete. I have tried to compensate for this by framing Logoli women's words with a minimum of discussion and analysis (cf. Amadiume 1987, 10). Their actions and resistance will be evident to readers. In the pages that follow, pages examining both needs and means via Logoli women's voices, I invite you to acknowledge the power of Logoli women.

Part II

WOMEN'S WORK

Introduction to Part II

Question: *"Who works harder?"*
Answer: *"Women work harder."*

Both Logoli men and women agree that women work harder. According to most women, men "only talk and flock to market" or "sit and order women." To be a "good Logoli woman," one must work hard. This sentiment is summed up by Kagonga, a very old woman: "If women don't take care of the entire house and yard, who is going to do it?" Men are ancillary to this productive process.

To understand the magnitude of women's economic role in Maragoli society today, it is important to recognise that women's primary task, "taking care of the entire house and yard," involves a movement across the domains theoretically categorised by Westerners as "private" and "public." Neither men nor women in Maragoli categorise value as "use" or "exchange." Both sexes understand that a woman's role is to "provision" for her family in whatever way is necessary. Avalogoli divide labour tasks into two major domains: "home work" and "outside work." "Home work" is women's work, and entails the production of food and staples from plots of land owned by men. "Outside work" ought to be men's work and entails the production of food and material goods from cash. In fact, the two domains articulate and conflict while sharing a common theme of male elder rule. This structure and ideology requires an unrealistic delineation of labour tasks by gender that contributes to problems between men and women.

Chapter Three

"HOME WORK"

"Home work" is traditionally performed by married women with the assistance of other women and children. Eight school girls, ranging in age from 14 to 16 years, tell of the ways they assist with "home work:"

> We fetch water and firewood around six in the morning. We make tea and wash utensils. If there are fees, we are in school from eight until four. Our work is fetching water and firewood, digging, cooking, caring for the younger children, washing utensils and clothes, cleaning and spreading cow dung. Our main work is fetching water. Boy's work [as they see it] is making fences, building, caring for cows and milking, digging and going to market. Girls don't have time to go to market.

To the question, "Who works harder?" they answered, "Both work hard but girls work harder." In answer to the question, "Is that fair?" they said, "No, it should be equal."

Home work includes digging one's own land. "Digging" is the term for using a hoe to break up the ground, and planting and weeding. Home work also entails "fetching" and "collecting" water and firewood, caring for animals, acquiring and cooking the daily food, caring for children, doing laundry and cleaning the house and yard. Young, single men may engage in some of these tasks on their own or to assist women in the yard. Both men and women may dig on the land, just as both may be involved in entrepreneurial and structured wage activities. For the most part, however, men are only engaged in the heavy work of breaking up the ground for cultivating, and this only occasionally. Although tradition says men should do the initial, heavy work of digging up the ground for planting, in actuality it is usually women who do it. If men are not available, women say, "The land must be dug!" Any task which involves digging is women's work because it involves the production of food, and both men and women agree that women, the farmers, should provide food from the land. This responsibility is extended to digging crops for cash to buy necessities like tea, sugar, cooking oil, flour, condiments, and kerosene at markets.

Unlike women, men do not have culturally-defined roles as diggers, even though they may dig. They are only "permitted" to fetch water if their wives are sick and there is no other woman available. This would be an unusual case, but in its event, a man carries the containers to the top of the hill overlooking the river and convinces a woman to fetch the water for him. That woman then feels it is her responsibility to carry the water to his home. Following that, she returns to the river to obtain her own water. Men seldom clean the night's accumulation of cow dung from the hut, sweep either house or yard, cook, collect firewood, or care for children. This separation of work by gender is clearly summarized in the frequently repeated statement: "Men do not do that, it is women's work." Normative statements about differences between the genders even extend to how items should be carried or how people should sit or converse. Women carry items on their heads or backs; men carry them on their shoulders or in their hands. Men sit with legs crossed, usually on chairs; women sit with legs stretched out crossed at the ankles, usually on the ground. Men may direct their gazes to faces during conversations with either gender, whereas women ought to direct their gazes off to the side and down when conversing with men.

Although cultural expectations prevent men from doing "home work," women are not similarly restricted. A few women are in more structured wage positions as clerks, teachers or nurses, and some do agricultural labour for a wage or for a share of the crop in order to provision for their families. When colonialism brought cash and commodities to the traditional Maragoli economy, a further separation was encouraged between women and men. Relations between them were thus made additionally problematic. Women resent the responsibility of providing more than daily food requirements from "home work" in order to survive. They also resent that there is not enough land to get the cash needed to buy food items and commodities. This resentment is directed at men, who do not or cannot supply land or cash. Men add further to the responsibility shouldered by women by blaming them for mismanagement when the yield of maize from a garden is low or when it disappears "too fast."

The culturally-defined gender categories create difficulties which are only made worse when men and women do not or cannot live up to expectations. Men and women may suffer community disapproval or a loss of social status if they participate in work considered to be the responsibility of the other. This is particularly evident for men who do women's work. This is seen as role confusion:

A lazy woman tells her husband 'go and get water and cook,' and he goes! Or there are women who claim to be sick, refuse to go to hospital, the husband does the work, but she gets up to eat! This is a woman acting like a man and a man acting like a woman (Alfayo, Hannah and Febe).

The implication of this statement is consciously made: men are seen by both genders to play at being sick, or laze around, thus women who do these things are acting like men. When a man engages in women's work, both he and his wife are highly criticised: a man fetching water or cooking suffers ridicule, and his wife is considered lazy. In one case, a sick wife's request to remove the cow dung from the house brought a tirade of overwhelming magnitude from her husband, which concluded with his question: "Do you think I have breasts and a vagina?"

The Daily Routine

A woman's day begins early,[22] somewhere around six in the morning on a sunny day, or perhaps a bit later if it's overcast. *Vuche* (or *vuchee*), the morning greeting, is exchanged with those she meets. It is an important indicator of well-being and sets the tone for the day. *Vuche* means more than good morning. It contains the ingredients of good health and contentment, and really means "It is my sincere wish you have spent a good night and all is right with your world." Neglect to pass this greeting sends a strong message of disapproval with life, or possibly signifies illness.

If there has been no rain during the night and the water containers are empty, a woman's first task is to fetch water for bathing and making tea, providing tea leaves are available. Men and school children bathe in the morning. Collecting water seems the most time-consuming task women face. The number of trips per day and the distance to water were measured for sixty-two yards. A total of 393 trips were made to get water, an average of 6.34 trips per yard daily. In the same sixty-two yards, 531.50 kilometres was the measured total distance walked to water, an average of 8.57 per yard daily. The least number of trips was two, and the most, eighteen. This last was a yard containing over twenty people and a number of purebred cattle which were not grazed. The shortest distance travelled per trip was one quarter kilometre, and the longest, five kilometres. During the rainy season, trips for water are reduced as rain water is collected; however, containers are in very short supply. Thus, even during heavy rains, water will still have to be collected from the springs or river. Only three yards had water tanks, and a number had large (albeit rusty) containers.

Next, a woman will chop firewood and make the fire to heat the water over the traditional three stones. For many, the most frustrating task is obtaining and chopping firewood. In 78 yards, 21 had woodlots. Tree planting was introduced in the 1960s by Sub-Chief Inguya, however many people do not have enough land to plant trees. In four yards, trees were purchased, the cost ranging from 50 to 100 shillings. A tree lasts two to four months, depending on its size. Six yards purchased bundles of firewood, a small bundle costing four or five shillings for a day's supply. Larger ten-, 20- and 30-shilling bundles are also available. In 47 out of the 78 yards, people obtained their firewood "from the garbage"— that is, they (mostly the children) were stealing or scavenging it. (There is little real difference between stealing and scavenging, as all land is owned.) Many arguments and even physical fights ensue over firewood. A further problem develops once the wood is obtained, since many yards do not have axes and must borrow. Because of this, axes are certainly charged with social significance. Often to borrow an axe requires supplying wood to its owner, or at least inviting the owner into the yard where she may chop some of the wood for her own use. A few yards use charcoal if they can afford to buy it. A 50 pound bag was selling for 60 shillings in 1988, plus a ten-shilling deposit on the bag. In 1994, the price had increased to 100 shillings. Charcoal use is of course only an option if women can afford to buy a charcoal burner. Notwithstanding, charcoal making in the area has recently become illegal in order to practice forest conservation, so charcoal is not really a viable alternative to the shortage of fuel.[23]

If there is only one adult woman in a yard, she faces a tremendous burden, as all these tasks and more are her responsibility. Avalogoli prefer to have two or three children assisting in the yard. Ideally, the eldest child should be a girl. An additional source of assistance is sisters-in-law, along with unmarried daughters. Once a daughter-in-law comes into the yard, the assumption is that she will relieve most of the work load from her mother-in-law. Often, young married women with small children will invite a young relative from their natal home to assist them. Ritah and Aggrey saw themselves as "blessed by God, we have the right [ideal] family, a girl first and then a boy. When the girl is older she can collect the water and the boy can care for the cows. When they grow, the older girl can assist in providing dowry for the younger boy, to get a wife." However, Aggrey has a son "outside" this marriage and eventually will be required to provide him with land. They had a third child, a boy, in May, 1988 and a fourth boy in 1990. The ideal is seldom realised.

If older children are in the home, girls will fetch water and scavenge for firewood, and boys will chop it. As cooking utensils are in short supply and not usually washed after the evening meal, they will be cleaned prior to drinking tea and eating any "slept over" food from the night before. Breakfast is not usually eaten as it is in Western culture. If there is flour left from cooking the evening meal, porridge may be cooked for young children, or during the bean harvest, beans may be cooked the night before and consumed in the morning. Tea, however, is almost a necessity. It is served either *itulungi*, "strong" (without milk or sugar), *mukafu* (without sugar), or the preferred *ichai*, "regular". Tea was introduced by the British. Without tea, people are "hungry" or "starving." A man who has to leave his yard without tea considers himself hard put upon and will inform those along his route that he has had to leave home without it. Men often show their displeasure with wives, or inhabitants of the yard generally, by loudly announcing they will leave for their daily activity without taking tea. It is a "bad thing" for a man to leave his yard without taking tea. Reasons for his refusal will be discussed among those left behind, and attempts will be made to correct whatever has angered him.

Cows and other animals are given any leftover water. Women may make an additional trip to the river for them, depending upon the amount of livestock. Following tea-taking, children are sent off to school, and women make another trip for water to wash clothes. Not all clothing is washed daily. Bedclothes, usually rough blankets and rags, get wet through the night with the urine of bare-bottomed children, and are laid out in the sun to dry. They are washed weekly to reduce extra trips for water. Women and children all sleep in one area, usually on the floor. For the most part, men sleep alone, usually in a bed.

The Annual Cycle

Logoli women do not engage in digging, except at peak agricultural periods when the land has to be cleared for planting, or during seeding, weeding, and harvesting. Maize is the predominant crop. Beans are planted after the maize sprouts to provide additional food and put nutrients (nitrogen) back into the soil. The maize stalk provides support for the bean plant. Sorghum, millet, cassava, sugar cane, napier grass for the cows, and green vegetables (assorted cowpea) are also planted if garden space permits. There are two maize crops in a calendar year but the crop grown during the long rains is by far the most productive. Short rain crops are scant, producing smaller cobs. Most people plant beans, but many neglect the planting of green vegetables which make a good addition to the diet. They can stretch the supply of maize flour during the off season, after maize, sorghum and millet have been harvested, but prior to new crop planting. Planting a crop of green vegetables would necessitate digging up the land two more times to plant the seeds. This is additional work and even though everyone "loves" eating green vegetables, many buy them at very high cost rather than engage in the extra work. All Maragoli homes have a banana "plantation." Cooked or sweet bananas provide additional food. If enough are grown, bananas also provide a small cash supply. Cash cropping is limited because land is limited. A few women may plant cabbage, tomatoes, or onions for their own use or to sell.

In Maragoli, most women plant on a quarter to a half acre of land. In fifty-two yards, we measured land size. Nineteen of these yards had one-quarter acre, and 13 had one half of an acre. Only seven yards had one acre. Others ranged from zero in one case to five and one-half in another. Four women in one yard shared a plot of one-quarter acre, and thus had one-sixteenth of an acre each. In Idakho Location, the location west of Maragoli, where some Logoli women in this research have married, average land size was three to five acres. However, agricultural work is difficult there, as soil is very rocky and hilly. In one case, millet was planted on a 90 degree slope. The women digging there worked on their knees to keep their balance. In most cases, the small plots do not provide adequate subsistence for women's large families, let alone a cash crop.[24] If monetary needs are immediate, subsistence crops may be sold which may leave families in a position of "starvation"—having to buy food to eat during periods of scarcity.

Agricultural work is performed in short, labour-intensive bursts for perhaps four hours a day. Once the small fields are planted, they require little care beyond a bit of weeding and loosening of the soil. The growing is left to nature. Women and men observe the growth but generally do not engage in any kind of agricultural work again until it is time to harvest. Women perform other tasks and take time to entertain, visit with friends, or perhaps just sit around. After agricultural work, there remain still more hours of women's work. Along with general home tasks, it may be necessary to patch a wall or lay a floor with cow dung. It may even be necessary to build a new hut. Thatching grass must be collected nowadays from some distance away. During this research, December seemed to be the time when most of this type of work took place. People reported that they were readying their yards for Christmas. The activity appeared to share characteristics with the Western idea of spring house-cleaning.

If money is available and a permanent house is to be built, time away from digging tasks allows one to make the bricks to begin construction. Bricks are made in yards. The soil is dug from the yard and the gravel and cement must be purchased. For the most part, only women and children engage in brickmaking, although men may assist in digging the soil. Also, water must be collected to mix the ingredients. The mixture is shovelled into home-made wooden forms and left to harden in the sun. The entire process is expensive and time-consuming. Intense manual labour is required.

If garden work is in order, women will walk to their plots, carrying their hoes, and work there for most of the morning. Although digging is extremely hard physical labour, many women maintain that they enjoy it. During interviews with 51 women farmers, 41% said digging is their favourite activity; they said they like digging "very much", or that they "love digging." These were unsolicited responses, in the context of asking these women their occupations. Seven of the women (14%), all under 25 years old, wished for another occupation, such as teaching or nursing. One young woman said she preferred going for water over digging, while another said she would rather sing or visit with friends. Most yards have more than one woman living in them, so women usually have companion diggers. Since the garden plots are close together, women dig a bit, then lean on their hoes and have conversations with their neighbours and others passing on the paths. They talk, joke, flirt with passing men, and catch up on the neighbourhood news. Babies and younger children are in the gardens with their mothers, so women will frequently stop their digging and provide for their needs: nursing the babies, sympathising with scrapes and bruises, or joining in the play of older children.

WOMEN RESTING

Shortly after noon, women begin to leave the plots and make another trek for water to cook the midday meal of *ovukima* (a stiff porridge made from maize kernels ground into a flour) or bananas. Normally this is ready around two in the afternoon. Women will divide the food among the number of people present: visitors, workers if they can afford to hire them, the children, and lastly themselves. Following lunch, women will usually sit or recline on the grass for a few hours, gossiping with others or dozing in the mid-afternoon sun.

Around four or four-thirty in the afternoon, women will "go for water" again to bathe young children and themselves and to wash the utensils used at lunch. This trip normally takes a bit longer than the others, as women will stop and talk to those on the roads and paths who are also collecting water[25] or returning from the nearest market. When these tasks are accomplished, they will return for more water for the evening meal and look for firewood. School children will have returned home and they may assist in these chores or at least care for the younger children while the women are busy. It is usually between seven and eight in the evening and dark when women begin to cook the evening meal, and even then, only "If there is food." Food comes from a number of sources: from the gardens, if the harvest has not been depleted; from the market, if there is money to buy it; or from relatives in the cycle of giving or loaning.

The main portion of the meal is *ovukima*. Maize kernels are removed by hand from the cob (the cobs are given to the cows) and traditionally were ground into flour on stones. Grinding by hand is very time consuming. Grinding mills do a much more efficient job, but using them necessitates walking to the mills and having the cash to pay for the service. Robbai made the following statements in reference to grinding mills, traditional food, and political powers:

The British said modern is best, going from darkness into light, but [President] Moi says, go back to the traditional ways, use your hands to grind. We lost our traditional food. We planted the maize only, but now we have gone back, we are planting millet, sorghum, beans, vegetables. We were foolish to leave it.

Women or young girls must make a trip to a central grinding mill to have the kernels ground into flour for a shilling or two, depending upon quantity. From one village this is a distance of eight kilometres, or translated into walking time, an hour and a half to two hours in an already tiring day. Although many people buy or grind a two-day supply, there are those who do this on a daily basis, scraping up a few shillings here and there for the purchase. This is often regarded as a great inconvenience. For example, Ritah complained that once the harvest food was depleted, her father-in-law was making her look like a fool travelling the distance daily to the market, collecting the maize he had purchased from him, along with a shilling to grind it. "He should give enough for at least two days, if not a week. I look foolish," she said. The father-in-law's point was that having too much flour in the home at one time permitted misuse. "They will eat it all, or give too much away," he said.

This extra work for *ovukima* may seem excessive, but in a literal and symbolic sense, a meal without *ovukima* is not a meal. No matter what food people may consume, not taking *ovukima* means they have not eaten.[26] Ideally, the meal is prepared and consumed by nine in the evening. Once the meal is complete, younger children are bathed (if this was not done in the afternoon) prior to sleeping. On many occasions, children are given porridge, or perhaps roasted maize or tea if they are too young for the hard kernels. They may go without the bath if the time gets late and they simply fall asleep. The utensils from the evening meal are left aside. At this point in the day, women or children no longer have the necessary energy to fetch more water to clean cooking utensils. Travel to the river can be dangerous after dark, and thus the warnings of church groups against letting the *ovukima* pot "sleep overnight" are ignored. In spite of concerns about hygiene, the easiest way to wash this pot, with its caked-on *ovukima* and burnt bottom from the three stones, is to let it soak overnight, which is the common practice. Most yards only have the one large cooking pot. It is used for all cooking: tea, vegetables, bananas, and *ovukima*, along with heating bath water. Bedtime for women comes when all of the above chores are completed, usually sometime between ten and eleven at night.

Chores take precedence except when social demands interfere. This is a society of obligatory visits and presentations. Even during peak agricultural periods, the requirement to visit and receive guests interferes with the completion of "home work." A death or serious illness in one's extended kin group or a death in the village in which one resides results in a complete interruption of work. Logoli people do not dig if a relative has died. It would result in a very strong *olovo* (curse) being inflicted upon the living with still more illness or even death. Furthermore, it is believed that the land dug during this period would not produce. In the case of serious illness or death, depending upon the closeness of the relationship, women gather food, other resources, and transportation money to travel to the yard of the afflicted family. This also occurs when an individual dies within the village. Women put down their hoes and gather with men in the yard of the deceased. It would be an unusual week in Maragoli if work was not interrupted for illness or death. Women may also have to travel the kin network "visiting" in order to obtain food for their own yards, money that is urgently required for school fees, books, or transportation, and to call on other relatives to fulfil obligatory visits. Women may also refuse to dig as a result of problems they have in the yard: arguments with husbands or in-laws, or slights or criticisms they have detected. They may also refuse to dig if they are ill; malaria is the name usually given to the illness. Again, it would be an unusual week in Maragoli if digging or other chores were not interrupted to fulfil these needs or express these sentiments.[27]

Although the above tasks and responsibilities must be performed, on an individual basis the actual methods and success of their completion depend on individual contexts and circumstances. Consider the following two examples: Joyce manages with creative planning to conform to Maragoli norms. On the other hand, Ritah confronts the norms and questions their direct benefit to her.

Joyce

Joyce is 28 years old. She married in 1982 and has three children, two girls and a boy. Her husband works in wage labour in Kitale. She is the eldest in a family of four and her siblings are still at home. Joyce's mother is Avalogoli, her father Tiriki, so she is *umumenya* (an outsider), as "insiderness" is traced patrilineally. Joyce wanted to be a nurse, but there was no money for her training. She decided to marry as she did not have enough education to work. Since her husband's parents are dead, he calls himself an "orphan." His father died first and his mother refused the custom of levirate, preferring to remain working as a nurse in Nakuru, some distance from Maragoli, until she too died. Joyce's husband's "father" (actually his father's brother) gave him land when he decided to marry, one half acre. Joyce's husband maintains this "father" "grabbed the land" left to him by his own father, and the half acre is not an adequate replacement. This father also assisted with the *uvukwi* arrangements, discussion and payment. Joyce was already living with her husband when the arrangements took place.

Even as an *umumenya*, Joyce is typified as an "excellent wife" by the community. A usual criticism of daughters-in-law stems from the fact they are not Logoli women and therefore do not know the "proper ways." To call a woman an "excellent wife" means that she fulfils all the responsibilities of women's work cheerfully and quietly. She does not answer back, even when provoked or abused by her husband or other men. She stays in the yard and does not run to her father's yard when difficulties arise. And needless to say, she does not "run to men," that is, she is faithful to her husband, no matter how tested or tempted. Joyce's husband does not share an equally good reputation. He is known as a drunk, an abuser, a poor provider and not deserving of such a good wife. This is paradoxical, of course, because part of the criteria of her excellence depends upon her acceptance of his violence. Joyce describes her situation:

CHILDREN AT NEWLY CONSTRUCTED HOUSE

My husband was not satisfied with the land given him but I walked the land with him and insisted we accept. He would never give me land if we did not take that piece. I pushed him to build, but left to him nothing would even have begun, ever have been built. I built my house [men are supposed to build houses].[28] For a time I lived in one room and I could be seen from the outside [the mud had not been applied to close in the house]. In those days it was ten shillings to get someone to dig the mud and thirty shillings for someone to plaster. So I had someone dig for the building, enough so I only had to wet it for more, and I plastered it myself. My children were very small, so I got up early, fed them porridge and took them with me to dig. When they woke up, I gave them more porridge, put them back to sleep and dug some more.

Women have to have a mind of their own; women have to push husbands. Ritah has no wish to work, no plans, just sits and waits, no one knows for what. She needs to push her husband for land. I rise at six in the morning and fetch water two times. Next I sweep the house as I have chickens in there and make tea. I wash the utensils and the clothes. I go to the *shamba* [in Luragoli *mulimi*] to work until one and then I make lunch for the children. After that, I wash the utensils and the children and begin to prepare the food for the evening meal. I wash the utensils once more and go to bed around ten. I have a relative who helps me fetching water and minding the children while I dig. I give her food and clothing. Often, in the evening I will prepare the vegetables for the next day's cooking and I always have water and if possible firewood for the next day. Before February, I plant for the long rains, maize, beans and sweet potato. I watch to see if the rain begins to come. The sweet potato will be ready in April, the beans in May or June, depending on rain, and the maize will come in July, the end. From February until April I will have to buy maize as mine has gone; in April when sweet potato comes, I will buy less maize; one sack will last two months. If there is no money we will eat less and April will be the hardest month: we will eat bananas instead of *ovukima*. The most difficult month is April, but if people plan well they don't have it so hard. Not many people here plan, so they will have starvation.[29]

I like to dig; I do not like sitting and doing nothing. I would like more land to dig and lots of cattle. Then I could educate my children as I could sell more. Now I can only sell a few cabbages, sometimes tomatoes or a banana, but my land is poor, maize only grows so high [she gestures showing four feet, not the usual six or eight feet]. I would like to finish high school and train for nursing. My husband must decide if this is possible. Then I could buy more land and educate the children so they may do better than I have. My husband could help me with this if he would stop paying 30 shillings a bottle for *chang'aa* [local liquor distilled from maize].

Joyce performs "home work" willingly. Her view of marriage is active, but fundamentally traditional in context. Joyce believes that a wife must move her husband to live up to expectations and be disciplined enough to avoid temptations.

Ritah

Ritah is 22 years old. She lives in the yard belonging to her in-laws along with her husband and their children, an older daughter's teenage daughter and an unmarried son. The unmarried son lives in the kitchen hut where the animals also sleep. These sleeping arrangements cause dissention as frequently the young man refuses to open the door and allow Ritah access to the three stones and the cooking fire. On a number of occasions, this dissention took the form of physical abuse, either the young man beating her or her beating him. As the assaults were never witnessed, it was difficult to say who was beating whom; both parties always managed to produce marks on their bodies. What could be witnessed or overheard was his verbal attack: often he called her *mugenda gendi* (a woman having children here and there), and more recently, *umulaya*, a prostitute. Another unmarried son who has land nearby but no house also takes up residence occasionally, sharing the kitchen hut. Her husband's family in residence at the time of the marriage included her husband's parents, two married brothers, their wives and children, and two unmarried brothers. For some time after Ritah came to the yard, she and her husband shared another brother's house with the two married brothers, their wives and children, along with the two unmarried brothers. In August of 1987, the brother whose house they were living in and his family also took up residence there. The two other married brothers left the yard, and Ritah and her family moved into an unfinished cement block building that was being constructed for cattle. The building is without windows and water pours through the roof. Insects accumulate because the floor is unfinished. Some of these insects are dangerous to the crawling baby. Ritah's husband has been given a piece of land by his father, but the ownership of the land is disputed. Taking up residence, that is, constructing a house on it, would be "death," so they remain in her father-in-law's yard.

**JOYCE AND RITAH
WITH CHILDREN**

**JOYCE AND RITAH
FETCHING WATER**

Ritah's father-in-law has considerable land; however, little of it is planted. The two young men are considered lazy, the mother-in-law is old (and some say lazy), and Ritah, the one younger woman in the yard, refuses to dig. Two women and one man are hired on an almost continual basis, but much of the land "sits" and there is a heavy reliance on food purchased by the father-in-law. This is tenuous, as he frequently gets angry with his family and cuts off the supply of food. Not only are the members of the immediate family living in the yard affected, but the workers, who require tea and a meal along with their wage, stop working.

Ritah is not "liked" by either of her parents-in-law, and frequent arguments and criticisms are directed at her and about her to others. She is criticised for failing in her duties, for not cleaning the house and yard, not fetching water, not chopping firewood, not assisting with cooking, and above all, not digging. At one point, her father-in-law went so far as to ask the Assistant Chief to remove her from his yard. The Assistant Chief effectively sidestepped the request by suggesting he give his son an appropriate piece of land so he could move there with his wife. During the months of fieldwork, Ritah engaged in digging for only two days, after a bullock was sent by her father-in-law for her father's funeral. She frequently refused to assist her mother-in-law with the tasks at home, sitting in the yard with her children, seemingly ignoring the torrent of criticism directed toward her. On the surface, it appeared that the criticism might be justified.

Ritah was "married to the yard during the rainy season, April 29th at 8 p.m. of 1984." Her union was one of *kuvahira* (elopement) rather than *urukali* (marriage). Proper marriage arrangements had not been made by either of the families. More to the point, an agreement on the marriage and *uvukwi* discussion had not been made. Their first child, a girl, was born in December of 1984. The second, a boy, in November, 1986, and another boy was born in April of 1988. In December, 1988, Ritah "walked" with her three children, returning to her parents' yard. As *uvukwi* discussion had not taken place nor any token "payment" made, the children do not belong to their father's home. Until this is accomplished, they belong to their mother's natal home. Following is Ritah's description of her daily work and defence of what her in-laws consider to be "disrespectful, lazy and uncooperative" behaviour:

I did not want to marry. I wanted to be a nurse, but there was no money for training. I have five sisters and six brothers. Two sisters and one brother remain at home. There were no school fees for me. My brothers were not working and my father was sick. I went to Form Two. When I was seventeen, I left school. I liked school. If I had waited until my brothers got jobs I could have gone back to school. But I worked at home for a year, helping my mother, digging a small land. It is so small we were often hungry. Now for example they have finished the food ["now" is September, from the July harvest]. I thought I would just sit there, and it was time to go, so I decided to marry. I met him at school first. He was coming to the schools, looking for a wife. Nowadays Maragoli men fear to marry in Maragoli, there are too many people, they fear they will marry a relative, so he was looking in Bunyore, where I was schooling.[30] My parents did not know I was seeing him, but his parents did. I often visited his home, even staying for the night. So I came here, and my parents found out after I was here. When I first came here, I did *everything* there was to be done in the home, even the cows [boy's work]. I worked very hard to impress my in-laws, and now the father of the home respects me and the mother of the home respects me and I respect both of them very much. I just did everything there was to do.[31]

In the morning I was rising at six, and getting the water. I chopped the wood, made the fire and heated the water for washing bodies. Then I cleaned the cow dung and swept the kitchen and cooked the tea. Then I went for more water and washed the utensils and the clothes. I laid the bedding on the grass. If there was flour I made porridge for the children. Then I divided the rest of the water to [among] the cows. Then I would ask my in-law [mother], what work there is to do. Perhaps she would set me to plant or weed, maize or beans, or just dig. Then I would cook the noon meal and divide it among people. After eating I would rest a bit, then wash utensils, and fetch more water. If there was food, I would cook the evening meal, then wash the children and go to bed around ten or eleven. This is hard work, I would rather work out [do wage labour] and use the money to feed people at home, build a house, buy clothing and soap to keep it clean, remember parents and parents-in-law with something little. I like the home work, but I should have my own house, my own yard, my own land to dig.

But my father has written to my husband's father two times, suggesting that a little bit [*uvukwi*] should be sent. My father has said, "Even though I am too sick to eat, a small bit of food [euphemism for money] should be sent to place at the corner of my mouth." There has been no answer. *Uvukwi* for me should be five cows and 3000 shillings, my father has said even if my schooling is not high, I work hard, I am worth that much. My in-law must move first, he must give the first cow. But he is refusing. My in-laws refuse to send me nicely to visit my home, yet when I do, my parents send me nicely back here.[32] The last time I visited my home, there was hunger in this yard. My mother sent a very big container of flour, so much that some was given to my other fathers-in-law [husband's father's brothers]. Also I was sent with a chicken and two kilos of meat. Now when I want to visit my mother and my sick father, my in-law [mother] is saying there is nothing in this yard to be sent. I am to return my mother's container empty! My people will think I am coming from trees, not people. So I ask, what am I? Am I not fit to be here? If this is so, I was supposed to be told much earlier, rather than waiting, waiting for nothing.

The reason that Ritah does not willingly do "home work" is a direct response to the failure by her husband and his family to her natal family's demands that land and *uvukwi* be provided. Sons are supposed to get land from their father. Although a marriage is supposed to be a reciprocal arrangement, in this case, only Ritah is held accountable for not doing the "home work." The failure to observe tradition is ignored.

These two cases show that the responsibility for women to "provision" for the everyday survival of their families is overriding and enormous. Additionally, as is obvious from the information given, the results of "home work" are an inadequate source for family survival. An input of cash is also required to purchase supplementary market commodities. Cash for necessary commodities is only available to those who work in wage labour or to those who are able to access cash from those who work in wage labour.

Chapter Four

"OUTSIDE WORK"

"Outside work" is work for money. "Home work" is never rewarded with payment. Some women dig for others for a wage only during peak agricultural periods. A few do agricultural labour for others throughout the year, and more would like to. Most people, however, cannot afford to hire labourers and few have enough land to justify employing others. Private entrepreneurial work consists of selling cash crops at a market or petty trading in goods or foodstuffs from shops in their homes or along the roads and paths.[33] A few women are prostitutes and others make and sell *busaa* (millet beer) or *chang'aa*. Full-time wage labour by women is not common in Maragoli. The government is the main source of full-time employment. Women may work as civil servants, clerks, or secretaries in the few government offices, or as teachers or nurses. A half-dozen or so are employed to assist with Women Groups, which are organised and licensed by the government to assist with women's development. Other possible wage positions are teaching in *Harambee* schools where parents pay fees, or as barmaids. Domestic work as babysitters or as maids for women with salaried jobs are other possibilities, but for the most part, relatives usually perform these tasks in return for food, clothing, or school fees.

"Digging for Others"

A number of women have agricultural labour for others as their only source of cash employment. Of the 74 women who spoke to me in this regard, 27 or 36% dig for others on a regular (5; 7%) or a part time (22; 30%) basis. For 44% of the 27 women who do this work, digging was their only source of cash. Some women may use digging for others as a supplement to their limited cash resources from other areas, which might include support or gifts from husbands or other relatives. The 74 women gave the following people as sources for assistance, which came in the form of cash, clothes, or food: children, husbands, parents, brothers, sisters, brothers' or sisters' children, parents' brothers and sisters, parents-in-law, brothers or sisters-in-law, or neighbours.

The daily wage for digging was raised from seven shillings to ten for women, and from 12 shillings to 15 for men, on May 1, 1987. People say "the government" directed this wage increase. The responsibilities of field digging appear to be the same for both men and women, but women are nonetheless perceived by other women as being the harder workers and as working longer hours than men. Although women and some men feel the wage gap to be unfair, only one employer paid women and men equally.

Women and men say that they begin digging at seven o'clock a.m., have a tea break at ten o'clock a.m., and then continue. Men generally work until noon and women until two o'clock p.m. Upon completion of the day's work, a meal of *ovukima* and meat should be provided by the employer. Workers should also receive their daily wage at the end of each working day, although a few who are hired on a regular basis are paid monthly.

During the period of this study, 27 women diggers and four men diggers were observed throughout their actual working days. The results of these observations revealed a contradiction between what the workers say about their working days and what really takes place. First, digging for others is contingent upon the same conditions as digging one's own land. Furthermore, although those hired may say that they will be ready for work sometime between seven and eight in the morning, social convention demands that morning greetings and sociable conversations occur prior to anyone leaving for the field, and this delays the start of work. Generally, the hired workers leave the yard, hoes over their shoulders, somewhere between eight and eight-thirty. Actual digging is delayed to around nine. Between ten and eleven, men return to the yard and sit, waiting for their tea. The women remain digging in the field until their tea is brought to them. Taking tea usually consumes the better part of an hour, and except during peak agricultural periods, men usually do not return to the fields. If the rain holds off, women resume digging and continue until sometime between one and two in the afternoon. If the rain comes before that, digging is finished for the day. They return to their yards, receive water to wash their hands and feet (people dig barefooted in Maragoli), and wait for their meal. On many occasions, the "proper" meal of *ovukima* and meat is not available, so *ovukima* with green vegetables (which is almost "proper") or cooked bananas (not at all "proper") is substituted.

Only on a few occasions were workers paid immediately after the meal. They frequently sat in the yard waiting for anywhere from one to three hours to be paid. On several occasions, the employer negotiated a substitute for cash, like maize flour or firewood. Cash was preferred, so arguments frequently broke out. The consequences of such an argument are two-fold: diggers may refuse to work for the next few days and may also report any injustice to those they meet on their way home. To protect their own reputation in the community, employers prefer to settle the matter amicably prior to diggers leaving the yard. A number of employers who have the reputation of being "mean" are unable to hire diggers. From both the employees' and the employers' positions, digging for others is very much a wait-and-see process. Employers wait and see if the diggers report for work, while workers wait and see if the employer is able to supply the tea, meal, and the wage. Digging for others tends to be a very unreliable form of employment. The cases of Estella and Florence, who both dig for others, illustrate these conditions.

Estella

Estella is 49 years old and has given birth to thirteen children (five girls and eight boys, two of whom died). In addition to Estella's own children, her husband's first wife left three daughters for Estella to care for. Estella was a market seller for a number of years during the time her husband worked in wage labour in the Eldoret area. Her husband became "sick" and the family had to return to Maragoli, to a piece of land less than three quarters of an acre large, inherited from his father. This land was utilized by a relative for the 20

ESTELLA

years Estella and her husband lived away, but it was vacated when they returned to take up residence. Estella digs for others on a regular basis and maintains that this is the only source of income for her large family. When asked if she received any assistance, she replied, "No, there is no one to assist." Close observation over a period of time showed that Estella was very resourceful at generating support from the kin network in the form of cash, clothing and food. One brother-in-law was quite generous in providing additional land on which she cultivated crops for sale, and he also on occasion supplied food. Neighbourhood gossip said that he provided Estella's yard with more food than he did his own. This was a source of some dissension. Estella met her in-laws' anger by out-yelling them or with humour. She is an articulate and bright woman with a particularly assured manner in dealing with the difficulties of women's work in Maragoli society. The fields where Estella digs are "noisy fields," with much loud conversation and laughter. In spite of her resourcefulness, Estella is correct when she says she works very hard for very little. Despite her efforts, there is hunger in her yard:

My husband worked for a company in Eldoret. He was working with the trees, stripping bark, making sure they were not cut and growing properly. I bought things and was coming to sell them there at the market. I sold onions, potatoes, tomatoes and other vegetables, and sweet as well as English potatoes. We had money then. But my husband got sick; we had to come home. During those days I was very happy and I was able to earn money. My children were well-clothed and they were well-fed. Also, they were able to get education. The way things are now, by digging alone, we go hungry many times, the children are not well-dressed, things have changed. We go hungry...but this is life. Then my children were well-clothed, ate well, and school fees were paid.[34] I am paid ten shillings a day for digging. I dig every day. And that is too small to feed your family. On my land, it's small, you plant beans, you plant maize for the children to eat, you cook it, whatever is left you cook for the family, there is nothing to sell. If God wishes, and you have money, you can then buy some things and sell, or grow some things and sell, and then you know this is where sugar is going to come for my family, this is where salt is going to come from.

Eight children are at home. The oldest [daughter] who is married has five children but there has been no cow coming from there, no *uvukwi*, those are the things that help. During the days we were away from here my husband drank what he earned; he didn't know the home. Nowadays there is a change but he doesn't earn any money. I have nowhere else; I can only dig, here and on this small piece we have. If you have money and you are working that will make a change, then we can get land where we can say, "Muyesu [her son], you go to that land and we stay where we are." That's how it should be. The way it is now, if he marries he would build right on the three-quarter acre. We will have to divide for four sons. That's it; they will be there. Where can you send your child? You stay together; whatever you get, you eat. If my husband had a chance before, without drinking his money, and thought about where the children are going to be, it would be different. It's too late. After working so hard and you have not been paid, and you get home and there is nothing to eat, you sleep without eating food, where does enjoyment come from? There is not any. There is not. Sometimes, you get your ten shillings [from digging]. You go and buy two things, kerosene. You have to have kerosene, then you don't have sugar, you don't have salt and you have to go on what you bought. You have to buy what is necessary for that day and you may not buy food. If you sit, then you will be very poor. There will be nothing. You have to go on. You must have the heart to continue.

Estella works hard. She completes the necessary "home work" and digs for others. The reciprocity expected from her husband's family is minimal in her opinion. There is a shortage of land. No *uvukwi* is paid for her daughter. Moreover, she feels her work for wages is not adequately recognised.

Florence

Florence has eight living children; two have died. Her husband has one quarter of an acre of land, which was given to him by his father. The land is so small that she can "finish digging it in two days," so she digs for others on a regular basis. Her husband also digs for others, which—being "outside work"—is acceptable. He works in the Kitale area, some distance from Maragoli and he seldom comes home to visit. Florence is very quiet and shy. She works diligently, seldom engaging in the conversation or fun of digging with others. Five of her children are still at home. Her oldest son works in Nairobi and sometimes sends 50 or 100 shillings. Florence describes her situation:

> My husband used to drink; now he has stopped and he spreads the word of God. He gives 100 or 150 shillings a month to the home. I give the remainder. I care for a cow; I use the milk and I will get a calf for my trouble. Sometimes I sell green vegetables, but most times we eat [them]. Sometimes my sister or my son buy clothes, if they can. I used to be better; now I have a lot of difficulties. There is no proper care for my life nowadays. The government budget makes things too high [prices]. If I can buy sugar, some little tea, soap, it's all right. Sometimes I can manage fish, and once in a month, I like to have meat. Life is difficult. I like when my children feed properly, when they sleep without crying.

The cases of Estella and Florence show the precarious livelihood that can be wrung from a combination of small domestic farm plots and digging for others. Hard work and long hours in agriculture, however, are not usually enough to support a family.

Entrepreneurs

Women who are in business for themselves can be classified as entrepreneurs. Although it might be expected that women shopkeepers could be designated as entrepreneurs, this is not the case in Maragoli. For the most part, women who run shops selling goods must be excluded from this category, because it is men who both provide the money to build or rent the building and acquire the licence and the shop's inventory. At Mbale market the rate for renting a plot with a small shop ranges from 220 to 500 shillings monthly, depending upon its location. In the villages, the rent averages 100 shillings monthly. Annual market licence costs for a shop are roughly as follows: retail businesses (food, clothing, general merchandise sellers, etc.) pay 1200 shillings; wholesale business, for example, those who supply the retail shops with their goods, pay 3000 shillings and up. Bars also pay 3000 shillings and up. It appears that how much "and up" is paid is decided by the county council. A carpentry shop, for example, pays the following: 1200 shillings for an annual licence and 220 shillings per month rent (for the building and the plot it sits on). The owner of the plot and building gets the rent, the county council (regional government) gets 790 shillings of the licence fee, and the remainder is sent to the federal government offices at Kakamega. The penalty for not acquiring a licence is a jail sentence. Esinga, a carpenter, along with his wife and his mother, who were unlucky enough to be in the shop when the police came, spent time in jail because he was operating without a licence.

Husbands also "give permission" for wives to work in the shops. Wives recognise men's ownership when they express their desire for husbands to "set them up in business" (i.e., give funds and permission). Wives see themselves as benefitting from men's generosity, even if they provide the labour and give the husbands the profits from their labour. Working all day in a shop cannot even be classified as working for others, as women do not receive a regular wage as they would if they worked for a shop owner who was not their husband.

Women are considered entrepreneurs in Maragoli if they are able to support their own business endeavours without the aid of their husbands. Entrepreneurial activities thus include petty trading from women's own homes or large markets. This category also includes those women who sell homemade brews, engage in prostitution and provide services such as sewing.

A few women at the larger markets sell their wares on a daily basis but the majority sell at the more congested Saturday market. The licence fee for selling "outside" a shop ranges from two to five shillings a day. The fee is determined by location and tables which are supplied by the county council. Often women forgo the use of the tables and simply place their vegetables and goods on the roadway. However, the county council clerk is within his legal limits to charge them a fee if they are selling anywhere on the market, with or without a table. The sellers and the clerk frequently have disputes over the fee collection. In Nairobi, unlicensed women vendors avoid the *askari* (police); at Mbale, they avoid the clerk, who threatens to call the *askari*. Other costs include transportation money, so unless they know they will sell goods, women usually cannot afford to go to market on a daily basis. Women must also perform their home work and cannot often manage the time to "sit on the market all day." Fruit and vegetables sold may be bought from others and re-sold at a profit, or received from neighbours and relatives who provide a commission of ten to 15 percent, depending upon the distance women have to carry the goods.

The majority of the women say they make very little money. Yet a few appear to do quite well, as evidenced by their semi-permanent homes and their children's attendance in the fee-paying schools. Women who do not sell at the market maintain the belief that market sellers are able to make a good living, and during most discussions on development, women wished for more land to be able to sell cash crops at the market. They presume, of course, that they would be able to return home at the end of the day with money. Other women sell on the roadside and paths that lead to the major markets. Prices are a few cents more than at major markets, and women are perhaps able to sell to those who do not want to spend the time it takes to walk to the market proper. Others will purchase a little extra at the larger markets and sell for a slight profit from their homes to their neighbours, again benefitting from their desire to save time. More frequently, people purchase goods from women's homes when it is too late in the day to journey to the larger market. Jerida is one of these entrepreneurs, selling both cash crops at the market as well as market commodities from her home.

Jerida

Jerida is 42. Her husband works in wage labour in Nairobi. She gives her occupation as digger and market seller. She has seven children, all living and either in school or working. Jerida has approximately five acres of land, which is considerably more than most women have. It is her husband's share of a very large family land in Idakho Location. At the time of this interview, her daughter-in-law had delivered the first grandchild, so Jerida was extremely busy "feeding her properly" to ensure a good milk supply.

JERIDA

Jerida hires diggers and sometimes oxen to assist with the agricultural work. She prefers to hire the oxen at a rate of 100 shillings a day, since ploughing is faster and cheaper than feeding workers over several days. On two occasions, she hired the oxen and paid a deposit, but waited for almost three weeks for the work to be done. Her main cash crop, almost one acre, has been cabbages, with smaller amounts of maize, cowpeas and cowpea seeds.

She has recently availed herself of the government-assisted French bean crop.[35] Although her first French bean crop made very little money, she has decided to try them once more. Jerida is an extremely hard-working woman, spending long days in the garden in home work. She does not sell at the market herself, preferring to pay ten percent to a seller. This arrangement allows her to remain working at home. She keeps a supply of kerosene, dry fish, washing and bathing soap to sell from her yard. She estimates that she earns 800 shillings a month from this trade, which is a very good income. (Compare this to those who dig "daily" for others, who earn between 200 and 250 shillings a month.)

In spite of her hard work, Jerida's relationship with her husband is less than ideal:

My husband works in Nairobi. He has not forgotten his home, he comes [usually] once a month. He only brings 300 shillings with him. The children help; they send another 400 shillings [three are working, two in casual labour]. My husband may have a friend in Nairobi. You can say you are alone [only wife] but there may be another one. Here in the yard I'm the only one. I work all the time, from early morning until late at night. That's the only way one can progress. My children have learned this from me. They don't see their father working, but when he comes home we dig together. I have good land, cows, a goat, and chickens. We eat well. But life is difficult for women. Many men don't keep their wives. Instead they go get other women outside and don't maintain their home. So women have to maintain the home and children. Men have *itama* [excessive sexual desires]. For women, their reward is the good reputation from the community, that they are responsible wives in the home. Men prefer roaming about for drinks. They don't do any job in the home to promote their life. Progress is unity. Unity starts from husband and wife, then to children, then to neighbours. With that unity things in the home run smoothly. If there is no unity between the husband and wife the children will be the same; the home will be disrupted. Jealousy and gossip are a problem. Women and men drink. If wives don't get home earlier than the husband they get beaten. I do not drink; I am a farmer and a market seller. I work hard. Although I am tired, my life is a good one. My children are being educated. They have food and clothes to wear. I have been abused. Two times I have hired men to do a job. They promised they would come on a day, then on a day [they promised on two occasions]. I made the food. They did not come. When I went to ask why they had not come to plough when I had paid them 200 shillings, he told me I was a fool. Then he said he could choose any day to come or not, even though I had paid the money. This was my in-law [father-in-law's brother]. He is my father. This is not a normal way to act. But I persevere and we women assist one another, my co-wives [sisters-in-law] and the groups [Women Groups].

Jerida is a success, expanding "home work," petty trade, and sales of crops at the markets into a good living. The support of her husband and her status as a hard-working wife in the yard are important to her. Despite this success, she experiences the same lack of reciprocity from men that other women suffer.

Making and selling the local brews is an occupation of both women and men in Maragoli. Women usually assist their husbands in this enterprise; however, they do not usually receive the proceeds. Making and selling *chang'aa* is illegal, but *busaa* is permissible if a licence is purchased from the Assistant Chief. Most avoid obtaining a licence, as the cost is 20 shillings each time, and the licence limits the selling price. Without a licence, a 500 gram container of brew can be sold for three shillings; with a licence, the maximum legal price is one shilling 50 cents. Prior to the new regulatory law, the same container sold for 60 cents.

Distilling brew is mostly an underground activity. Sales are made on the regular days of meetings of the Assistant Chiefs, or on the occasion of a fundraising event or funeral which will be attended by all officials. The sellers even appear at the functions themselves for a short time before going off to sell while the officials are otherwise engaged.

Many of the men who sell brew also have a reputation for drunkenness and abusive behaviour. If women whose husbands are involved in distilling brew report their husbands' neglect or abuse, they leave themselves open for the "entire government to enter their yards." The illegality of the business means that a choice between any difficulties—such as neglect, hunger or abuse—and government intrusion must be made. Erika provides an example of the negative consequences experienced by women who are held completely accountable for men's behaviour and of the ideology which supports this behaviour.

Erika

Erika is 45 years old and has nine living children. She and her husband brew and sell *chang'aa*. When she married her husband in 1967, she "found another wife there." Her husband and the woman separated after she came. The woman left one child, a girl, with Erika. She gets income both from her land and from selling brew, but brew-making takes up most of their time, so they rent over half of their land to others. The money received from rent and from selling *chang'aa* "goes to drink." Erika says it is mostly her husband who drinks the money. Neighbours believe that both of them drink on a continuous basis, neglecting their home and children. Erika maintains that her husband constantly abuses her verbally and physically. She says she cannot leave him because she has too many children and there is no one to help her. In her words:

I have land. If there are crops, I can sell. But I spend time making *chang'aa*. There is money to be made, if my husband did not drink it all. He used to dig but now he only drinks and abuses. I sometimes get money if I dig for someone,[36] but usually I don't have money. The school people are threatening to take my house. They have already taken some of my things to pay for school fees. What right do they have to come to my yard and take my possessions? Now, there is nothing for them to take, only the cow, which is not mine. Myself, I do nothing. It is for my husband, because he is the one to know what is going on and the one to look after his home. I'm the one looking after cattle, chickens,[37] children, and yard. My husband just goes drinking. Responsibility comes from me. Other women are not being beaten like myself who is always beaten. Even during the first year of marriage. I went to a funeral. He got very angry and went after me. I came home and I was changing clothes. He chased me to the neighbours. I was in my undergarments. He ran there and with a tree branch and beat me very badly. I thought, the kidneys will be totally finished. Without me, he would not have the land. He tells me I am nothing in this yard, but I brought two chickens to be slaughtered during the demarcation of the land. Without those two chickens he would have no land. [Marriage to her allowed him to be given land from his father, and permitted the demarcation to take place.] He accepts this, if he is not drinking, but he is always drinking. He beats me with his walking stick, on my back. I am always feeling pain in my back. To be beaten on the back is very bad. It will cause the bleeding to be inside the body. It's better if the wound bleeds out, the blood comes out. I have complained to the Assistant Chief, to the neighbours and to my brother. But nothing changes, a drunk is a drunk, they only tell me to go back to my house. They say, you are married, you drink alcohol and you do not go to church. But I do not drink, I tell them, and I am Catholic. Even death will not make them intervene. My father-in-law had three wives. My husband says, "I will one day kill you because my father killed his wife and a child." My son [aged eighteen], who hears this, says, "Go ahead and kill me if you want to kill me." It is good to love your neighbours, and for them to love you. But no one cares for me, not my neighbours, not my relatives. I make, I drink, I sell a little, but it is never enough.

Erika's reputation in the community has deteriorated to the point that she cannot get any assistance from kin, affines or officials. Her statement, "no one cares for me," is a realistic assessment of her situation.

An even more unsatisfactory occupation in Maragoli is prostitution. Prostitution appears to be a losing financial arrangement as well as a culturally unacceptable activity. Prostitution is often associated with working in the bars. However, the barmaids with whom I talked denied having anything to do with prostitution, and the one verified prostitute I knew of had married, and refused to admit to any activity but serving drinks and food. The information from the community was that barmaids were paid a few shillings and drinks if they also provided sexual services. Certainly it appeared that working in bars or engaging in prostitution was a last-ditch endeavour, and not anything "good" women would resort to. Those few who are actively engaged in prostitution not only suffer community disapproval (which interferes with their claims for support), but seem to profit very little, making a few shillings here and there, and perhaps a small supply of brew or *bhang* (marijuana), or some sugar or tea. The few neighbourhood prostitutes were "known" to have venereal diseases and also to "run" with fathers and their sons, which creates the potential for a strong *olovo*, as fathers and sons may not have sexual intercourse with the same woman. This *olovo* manifests itself by swollen testicles. One woman engaged in prostitution is Hawa.

Hawa

Hawa was invited for an interview at ten o'clock a.m.; I sent a male assistant as an escort for her. (My reputation would suffer if I visited her yard.) When they arrived, they were followed by a group of children from the primary school. The children had noticed Hawa and a man walking together on the road and pursued them, assuming they would be able to observe the two involved in sexual intercourse; her regular trysting place is a nearby forest. It was a considerable disappointment to the children to observe only the *Musungu* (European) asking yet more questions and busily writing answers.

Hawa is 45 years old, an *umumenya* from Kikuyuland. Her mother is Kikuyu and her father is Somali. Logoli people (both men and women) see marrying Kikuyu women as "dangerous." Kikuyu women are known "walkers;" that is, they leave their husbands, and more important, they tend to take their children when they "walk," even if *uvukwi* has been "paid." Hawa married in the area sometime around Independence (1963) and has had a total of ten children, of whom two have died. She receives no support from her husband and there are family conflicts. In fact, her husband lives and works in Nairobi and has had a family there for some years. He does not come at all to Maragoli. She estimates that it has been seven years since he has come home, although she remains on his quarter acre of land with its tumble-down mud hut without a "proper roof." A number of her children are the result of other unions, and she maintains she will send them to their fathers when it is time, demanding to share their *uvukwi*. Only three children, the youngest, remain with her; the others have "run away." She discussed her situation with me:

> I was raised drinking. I drink every alcohol possible. I was raised not knowing my father. My mother always rents land. Once when I went to Nairobi I met my husband. I like digging. I grow cabbages, beans, and maize. But here you cannot have much land. I would like to work for others, digging, fetching their water, but the women here are bad. They always bite backs. The women are afraid I will take their husbands. I used to have long hair; I was very pretty. If I sleep with men, I will be like a dog to them. If I work for someone digging, the women bite my back. They say I am everyone's wife. Every time they see me coming from a place they think I have sex there. If I had been everyone's wife, I would have twenty children now. I sell *bhang*, some *inasoli* [opium] to get money to drink. Men are all right if you understand each other. There is no Maragoli neighbour who will help me. I did not leave. When my children marry I will get their cows. I am waiting for that. My husband beat me very badly. He has not returned here since that time. See the marks remaining on my head. It was split from the firewood he hit me with. I drink with men. Then I date them.

Hawa's difficult life as a prostitute exists alongside her responsibilities for home work. She is unable to work for others because women refuse to have her in their yards. She cannot depend on others because of her established reputation. She looks forward to the time when her children are grown and she can return to her mother's home.

Full-Time Wage Labour

Full-time wage labour differs from other wage labour in that it is more structured. Working in full-time wage labour requires daily attendance and provides a reliable monthly wage. Time off for any reason must be arranged and taken without pay. Time off for certain reasons, such as a funeral or illness, must be legitimized by an official document. A telegram from a family member or a letter from the assistant chief of your district are considered official documents. The employer decides the amount of time off necessary. In the case of death it is usually one week for Logoli people. The employees may be advanced some salary, which is deducted when they return to work. On occasion, the employees may be permitted to deduct the unpaid leave from regular leave time. Other obligations must be fulfilled during holiday periods. Most workers in full-time wage labour in Kenya receive a thirty day holiday annually with pay.

Full-time wage labour opportunities in Maragoli are scant. Out of the 410 women interviewed, only 16 or four percent worked in full-time wage labour. Access to these opportunities depends on a number of factors. The first is education. Few women or men are able to obtain wage employment from the largest such employer, the government, either without passing at least their Form Four exams in the first division or without some type of specialized training, which is dependent upon the completion of upper-level Secondary school, at least a pass in Division Three. However, attending school depends on the availability of educational fees, and although people say that nowadays more emphasis is placed on educating girls, as girls "never forget their parents," the truth of these statements is not supported by statistics. Educational levels and general literacy levels of women are very low.

Joseph Kisia, a Maragoli historian, says that Avalogoli did not traditionally believe women should be educated. It was not until the 1950s that they were encouraged to attend school. It is his opinion that this lack of formal education has "retarded" their development on the farm and in wage labour. According to him, it was the Friend's Church's (Quakers') insistence that women be educated in schools along with men that has changed the situation. Originally, missionary education emphasized "home economics"—cooking, hygiene, and crafts for girls. He contends that education is now equal for boys and girls in Maragoli. Although statistics for Maragoli were unavailable, the provincial statistics for Kakamega District, where Maragoli is located, still show a higher male enrolment in primary school. This gap increases through secondary school and university. For example, the Provincial Statistical Abstract for Western Province in 1975-1980 states that in 1980, 162,725 boys and 158,136 girls were enrolled in primary schools; 17,767 boys and 12,784 girls were enrolled in secondary school (Original source, Central Bureau of Statistics). However, these statistics are skewed, as more males than females repeat schooling in order to upgrade.

Another variable in obtaining a job is patronage or kin "fixing." Who you are connected with and know is a criterion; that is, individuals find it impossible to obtain employment simply by virtue of their performance. Possibilities of employment come from those among a person's kin who already have a position or know someone in a position: "These are the people who assist others in obtaining employment."

A further variable pertains to husbands giving wives permission to work in wage labour. First, the husband must allow the wife to leave the yard on a daily basis: "It is for him to give his permission; she has married to his yard." Many women say husbands give permission to allow wives to seek work. A few said husbands refused because they were afraid other men would "take them." Some working women said their husbands "gave permission;" others said their husbands "agreed." Those who said they could not get permission or agreement were not working; however some felt that *if* they could obtain a job, husbands might change their minds. A small number (ten out of 410 or two percent) said their husbands would never give them permission to work outside the yard.

If a woman is to work outside the yard on a full-time basis, other women in the home yard must be willing to perform the necessary daily tasks. Women say it does not really matter who performs them, as long as they are accomplished. Men say that home work is the responsibility of the wife, and that if she does not do it, she must find someone else to; he must also be satisfied with the results. Some women agree to assist and they benefit from the wage earner's generosity. If there are no other women in the yard, a "maid" must be hired. The salary for this service ranges from 100 to 200 shillings monthly plus food, and comes from the woman's salary. Women wage earners in urban areas are also held responsible for paying for these services. Diverse types of women hire helpers: among those I encountered were a young woman with little land and few children, and an older woman with more land (who also hired a "*shamba* boy") and children. Both drew enough salary to provide either some cash or living accommodation to a hired caretaker or relative to assist in the home. Even then, part of the work remains for the woman wage earner, engaging her in a "double day:" it is the wife's responsibility to obtain and cook the meals for the family, whether she works outside the yard or not. Poisoning and witchcraft through herbs is often spoken of in Maragoli; thus people are very careful about who provides food and cooks. Husbands say they prefer wives to cook their food rather than other relatives or hired help, although they will eat food prepared by older daughters and daughters-in-law.

An interesting paradox comes up in conversations with Logoli women. Those few who have a full-time job say they will be happy when they can retire from it and rest at home. Those who are at home engaging in "home work," however, wish for a job in wage labour, not only to get more money, but also to avoid the difficult "home work."

The Vihiga town council in Mbale Town hires a number of women, one for secretarial duties, another whose title is Community Development Assistant, two Location Women Leaders who assist with Women Groups, and one Nursery (School) Supervisor. The Community Development Assistant, Florence, is 27 years old with two children.[38] She has a relative staying with her who "baby-sits" the children during work hours. Her husband is currently unemployed. Her salary is 1500 shillings a month, with an annual increase of 60 shillings. She has a Form Four education and one year training at a Social Training Centre. The courses at this centre were in nutrition, community development, group work, physical education, casework, agriculture, child development, civics, English, and daycare training. She feels her training is adequate for the job in which she is involved.

Beatrice is a Location Women Leader who is paid 1200 shillings monthly with a 50 shilling annual increase. She was pregnant in 1988 with her second child, and her husband is unemployed. Her mother-in-law cares for her child at home. She achieved Form Four and has one year further training at a Training Institution. Her courses were in pre-primary teacher training, community development and relations, nutrition, home management, and daycare centre management. She was trained to be a nursery teacher or daycare supervisor, so she strongly feels that she is not trained adequately for the job she is expected to do, although she is very grateful to have a position. Maragoli does not have a daycare centre. The women spend two days in their office at Mbale and three visiting Women Groups. Despite the requirement to travel, these positions are not supported with a travel allowance. The women "foot it" or take matatus (buses or taxis), which they pay for themselves. The areas they are responsible for are large.

The Nursery Supervisor, Paulin, is paid 1480 shillings monthly, with a 60 shilling annual increase. She supervises 32 schools in Central Maragoli. She is an older woman with grown children. She hires labour to dig. The nursery school teachers she supervises are paid 1200 shillings monthly. The teachers' salaries come from fees, which are 30 shillings per month per child. If the parents do not pay, the teachers do not get paid. One nursery teacher, Mideva, said she is fortunate to earn 200 or 300 shillings a month. Florence, Beatrice and Paulin say they are able to benefit "a little" from their positions in wage labour. However, they also say that if you are working, all the relatives expect that you will give them some of your earnings. The expectations placed upon them have increased with their responsibilities, and they still remain accountable for tasks at home. The women say it is better to hire a non-relative if you can afford help. Once non-relatives are paid, the obligation is finished. With relatives, it "just goes on and on" and they do "little for the assistance they give."

Teaching is another wage-paying job that women can hold. Kenyan teachers in government schools or in government-assisted schools are employed by one governing sector, the Teachers' Service Commission (TSC). The development of this organization is said to have improved the benefits of the teaching profession. As one group, they are better able to argue for themselves in regard to salary and the conditions of service.[39] In addition, the Kenya National Union of Teachers (KNUT), both a trade union and a professional body registered under the Trade Unions Act, gives further protection to teachers' benefits and rights, and regulates professional activities, such as curriculum development. In addition to their salaries, teachers in government-supported schools receive a house allowance,[40] free medical services, maternity leave with salary, and the "Union looks after any problems they may have." Trained teachers also do not have to search for jobs because there is a shortage of teachers in Kenya at all levels. Women and men are chosen to enter teacher-training based on their performances in Form Four or Form Six, although thousands apply and there are not enough spaces to accommodate them all. Ideally, there is little or no gender discrimination in the teaching profession. TSC and KNUT are aware of how many women and how many men are taken for training, and have attempted to even out any gender gap. In one class in the area, 22 of the 36 trainees were women: "The best student in the class was a woman." Women are said to be given the "best" areas, that is areas where less hardship will be experienced. Men are sent to the more difficult areas.[41] Pregnant women trainees are given an eight-month leave, so as not to waste the training they have received.

The idea that boys are more deserving of education is said to be "no longer there." Indeed, one parent said: "My *daughter* bought me this shirt; my son in Mombasa works and gives me nothing." Both men and women who manage to survive the long and expensive process of teacher-training will be securely employed until retirement at age 55, if they manage to get a job in government or government-assisted schools. If not, they are dependent upon fee-paying parents.[42] Alice and Florah are in professional positions, Alice as a teacher and Florah as a nurse. They manage with great difficulty to maintain their reputations and advance themselves in the "public" domain.

Alice

Alice is 24 years old and a Secondary School teacher in the area. She is third-born in a family of ten children. She says that there was little opposition to her going on for higher education, except from her maternal grandmother, who wanted her to leave school while she was in Form One and get married. The family had the usual problems with fees, but they managed.

Alice's father is relatively affluent, as all his children are in school or working, his land is well-kept and fully utilized and the yard has cows, chickens, and goats. Alice's motivation to get a job was that she wanted to assist her family. She said that everyone in the family depends upon her for money, a burden that she finds to be "overwhelming." Alice has been living with her husband, who is also a teacher, since January, 1987. They have seven-month old twins, a boy and a girl. *Uvukwi* discussion has taken place and her in-laws and her relatives have agreed on 23,000 shillings and five cows. A 3,000 shilling "down payment" has been

ALICE AND FAMILY

given, and her marriage occurred in January, 1988. Alice discusses her situation in English:

> We live in a house supplied by the school. We have electricity and water and a gas cooker. We have a small house plot in my husband's yard at Bunyore, and six acres in the scheme in Kitale. We hire people to dig there, as we are teaching. So far, we have not sold cash crops. We are only beginning. On the schemes, workers are paid between five and six hundred shillings a month to dig, so it is expensive. There is no need of paying *uvukwi*. Am I a farm to be bought? It is unfortunate the parents are poor. Parents ought to contribute to the newly married to start them off. But there is nothing we can do; it's a custom. Also *uvukwi* is not the end of assistance to parents. Some men mistreat after buying, that is paying *uvukwi*. Some men refuse to help parents any more after *uvukwi*, think that's enough. On the other hand, if you don't pay *uvukwi*, the husbands think you are not valued by parents. You are cheap. It's a tug of war.
>
> People who get jobs in Kenya have been to school, these are the elite. They are able to integrate various situations. They are analytical and choosing courses of action. They have developed decision-making skills; this gives access to wage labour. Most women are not this; many men are not. Things have changed for women, but still it is very difficult; they must work very hard. In the old days, customs did not allow men in the kitchen; now they do. It's absurd to see milk boiling over in the kitchen while I'm taking care of the baby and he is reading. A more even distribu-

tion of labour is needed. Women need a word of appreciation for their hard work, in the home and caring for children. Here in Maragoli we cannot develop: the population is too high. The government is suggesting that maternity leave will not be given after the fourth child.[43] This is a good thing but it has not been passed yet. I will not be abused in my marriage. I will leave. My job is difficult. Children are beaten, sent from school for fees, for *harambee* this, *harambee* that. Seldom do I have my entire class to teach. Some are always missing. I have had to chase them for fees. This is not my role; my job is to teach them, so they may better their lives. I refuse to beat them. I try not to upset them. I want them to learn. But many do not want to. Girls only want to chase boys, and boys the girls. But a few learn. Teaching is difficult.

Alice takes a different position from most Logoli women. She complains of having to follow traditional ways in these difficult economic times, even as she adheres to them. Although many people complained about the "high cost" of *uvukwi*, on no other occasion did women suggest that parents should assist a newly married couple and not follow the custom of *uvukwi*. Alice's feeling is not typical of Logoli people. It comes about at least in part because Alice's *uvukwi* is quite high and both she and her husband will have to contribute to its payment, as she says, "at the expense of our own development." She sees that she is caught in a bind. Not following the traditions will place her in a position of being without a good reputation and thus at risk in the community.

Florah

FLORAH

Another professional woman, Florah, manages to work within as well as outside the traditions. Florah's occupation is nursing. The same criteria are required for nursing as for teaching, except that one must have completed secondary schooling in order to be admitted to train as a nurse. A category allowing "untrained" to work as nurses does not exist as it does in teaching. Nursing is seen as a secure profession because there is a shortage of nurses in the new health centres which are being opened in Kenya. A disadvantage of nursing is that it's very difficult for a nurse to get a posting close to her rural home. Although a teacher's placement in his or her "home" area is not guaranteed, it appears to happen more in that profession than in nursing, where "home" placement is seen as a matter of "great luck." Home placements are far more economical, as one has the production from one's land as an added resource.

Although Florah worked in her occupation for some years in Nairobi, in 1984 she moved back to her home area, taking up residence on her husband's land and working at the Maragoli Rural Health Centre. Florah is 41 years old, and has eight children— three boys (two are twins) and five girls. Her oldest daughter is married and working in Nairobi. The second-oldest daughter works in Mombasa, and the third is in university. The remainder, except for the two youngest, are in school. Florah sees herself and is seen by others as a progressive, forward-looking person, although she is criticised for being "too independent." Along with working in wage labour, she maintains ten acres of land in Idakho with the assistance of her children, a babysitter and a hired "*shamba* boy." Part of her land is planted with tea, which produced for the first time in 1988. Currently, she is building a very large, permanent house. Florah spent her growing years as an "outside" child, because her mother did not live in her father's yard. In fact, she was married to another man: she "married elsewhere." Florah was acknowledged by her biological father and, from the time she was very young, visited his yard on a regular basis. She describes herself during the formative years as a "temporary person," never knowing quite where and to whom she belonged. Her current marriage is her second; the oldest daughter is from a brief liaison when she was still attending school. Although she lived with the child for a brief time at the father's home, his parents "chased" her and she went to live in Nairobi with her mother. It was while she was living and working in a factory in Nairobi in 1965 that female relatives encouraged her to marry a man working and living in Nairobi. She credits this husband with "moving" her to complete her secondary schooling and engage in training for the nursing profession. Florah provides the detail in English:

Then immediately after I joined with him he decided to take me for further education. He could come, pick me from my job, take me to the evening class at the college. I did my O Level there. For two years he was doing that. So after the exam I managed to get my certificate and it is with this certificate that made me to join nursing. So he also motivated me to try that expectation. Then I applied; I joined nursing and then did that for three years. I needed teaching a lot. I really loved teaching. I went for the interview. When they brought the reply I was one month old in the nursing training, so I thought it was not fair for me to abandon after the one month's training and settling...I continued for three years training and qualified. He also asked me to continue with the evening classes...looking for A Level...but then as I was continuing I became pregnant and I became too lazy to continue. But after, I managed to do my Midwifery also.

Florah was able to gain an education and further her possibilities for structured wage labour and its security, but her second husband did not remain with her. Despite the help and advice of female relatives and her second husband, she eventually became totally responsible for the support of their children:

I came here to acquire his land, then at least to do some cultivation and to harvest some food for the kids. Because I sensed that with high school fees and my small salary I could not afford to pay the fees, bring the rent, electricity and water, transport to and from various schools and then feed the kids [in Nairobi]. 'Twas too much for me, I decided to come home and work in the clinic and start a little farming. Nothing was cultivated, it was a forest, the mother [mother-in-law] was living in the middle of a forest. I could not believe it!...In the process of coming home I found that he was not assisting me at all. I sat and thought what could I do? Then I thought of at least getting something from him through the court...through the Children's Department. To assist with the school fees. He thought I was joking, because [if] I was staying in his yard I could not take him to court. Because according to tradition you can only take your husband to court, or to the elders if you are staying apart and if you are staying at your parent's home. If not the others [husband's other wives and their children] would get all, the [husband's] salary, the land. Especially the barmaid. The [his] whole family were defending me. Then I managed through the Children's Department. I managed to get his salary attached. That's how the house is being built. [Using money from the husband's salary for school fees allows Florah to use some of her wages to build the house.] I'm getting one-third of his salary. His employer slashes it, the computer has to computerize it off from his salary and then they put it in cheque form and bring it to Kakamega court. The court informs me to go and collect the cheque and then cash it at the District Commission. It is now a year since I have got that. He was really very angry in the beginning, but now, after finding that I don't use the money for myself, it is only for the school fees for his children...I showed him. He had to see that the expenditure is not for me but it's all for his kids. Not shopping, because I have to do the shopping myself. I feed them when they are at home; I buy them shoes and all this. I pay for the people who help. So he found that I was not misusing his money. He does not see where the two-thirds goes, he only drinks, he doesn't know, but this one-third now, he is seeing what it is doing, what good it is doing.

Florah relied on tradition in order to receive her land. However, utilising her knowledge of law and taking her husband to court for child support while residing on that land created some difficulty for her in regard to her reputation in the community. Her husband was summoned but failed to appear in court a total of 24 times. The final summons was issued to the employer, asking "whether this man was existing or not," so he was given a compulsory leave of one month to come and appear in court. "That's how I managed. He was not caring for the Children's Court, vice-president's Office, he could not even come. I have a big file with letters...." In 1989, Florah's husband was interdicted (fired) for drunkenness and the support ended. He returned "home," that is, to live in the yard. Correspondence provided the information that he had a stroke in 1990 and was a "dependent," although he "remains drinking." He died in 1993. Immediately after his funeral, his brothers attempted to confiscate his land and the house Florah built. They accused Florah of "only supporting the other side," meaning her Logoli relatives. She has remained "firm," refusing them anything: "I fed all of the relatives for two months during the funeral; they will not get my house and land."

For women in all aspects of any wage labour, the costs are high. Digging for others, entrepreneurship, and structured wage labour positions are difficult to get and usually do not offer a dependable income. A regular, wage-paying position allows these women some purchasing power and generates some value: most of those interviewed appeared to have, in Maragoli and Kenyan terms, a better quality of life, as evidenced by availability of food, clothing, better housing, and the means to educate their children.

Conclusion to Part II

Today, "home work"—the cultural designation of women's production of food and staples from plots of land—is an inadequate source for providing family needs. Survival—and if possible, "progress"—requires women's involvement in "outside work." Shortages of land, the necessity for market commodities, and changes in the relations of production demand women's activity in both private and public domains. Indeed, the theoretical division of domains into public and private is not necessarily appropriate to Maragoli life, as it disregards women's actual economic activity. Both women and men agree that women are responsible for "home work." Notwithstanding the non-participation by men in providing land, *uvukwi*, or other sources of traditional support, women are still considered the caretakers of values surrounding male elder rule. Women are held accountable for traditional values by both men and women, while men are not. The non-compliance by men with culturally-defined values is problematic for women. It exacerbates the economic inequality already caused by gender roles. Women are aware of this inequality. They recognise that their "commanders" are not acting in their best interests. Their direct experience of the social and economic consequences of this situation begets the question: "In whose interest are they acting?" Their awareness of the articulating dynamic between a collective and capitalist ideology is most clearly demonstrated in women's action and political decision-making as portrayed in Part III.

Part III

BACK DOOR DECISIONS

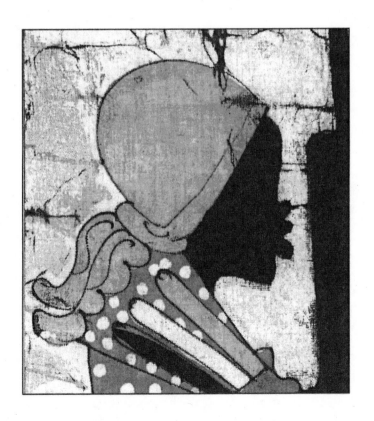

Introduction to Part III

From the time of the ancients, we have always done so. It is rooted in the past with Imungu *(God) and in the cave at Muwg'oma that the man will be the commander.* (Kagonga)[44]

Last evening Mudasia came back drunk with two of his brothers. He yelled and told all the children to leave the house. He came after me with a ubanga. *One of his brothers stayed at the back door of the house and one stayed at the front. This was to stop me from leaving and to hear how he would teach his wife a lesson as they are saying I am too independent. I took the* ubanga *away from him. I said, "If you want to fight with* ubangas *I have the sharpest one in the house."* (Florah)

It is believed in Maragoli that men are the decision-makers. This is "the Avalogoli way." But even within this society in which patriarchal senti-ments dominate, women act to produce value for themselves that goes be-yond these expectations. The dominant ideology in Maragoli supports the authority and power of men over women, the rights of men to treat women as they wish (including physical abuse) and to benefit from their labour, support, and incomes. Central to this sentiment is the right of men to make decisions and the obligation of women to obey. However, as we shall see in this section, the very physical form of the house presents an alternative and more equal structure of relationships.

Front doors of houses belong to men, back doors to women. Wherever women gather and whatever women do is considered the *chandangu* (back door). The importance of solidarity, of women supporting women, is indis-pensable in a society where women have a history of productive results from uniting, as they say, *"kuvumba ha chandangu"* (gathering at the back door). Acceptance of *vivuni vye chandangu*, the power constituted through the back door, implies acceptance of the power of women. Men are criti-cised if they accept the decisions of women, as they are thought to be listen-ing too much to women's opinions, or even taking direction from them, "listening to the back door." In this criticism lies an implicit recognition that there is power at the back door.

When we examine the ideological and institutional conditions affecting women's decisions in the cultural contexts of reciprocal obligations and benefits, and even in politics, we discover that women gather information and gain influence that enables them to act in spheres of life that extend beyond the "back door." Indeed, the spheres in which women use their power go from the very literal back door of the house through to the state level of Kenya. Their attempts to influence conditions take several forms. These forms tend to avoid confronting patriarchal sentiments directly, and are therefore usually oblique.

Chapter Five

THE HOUSE AND THE YARD

Women are responsible for "care of the entire house and yard." This is "home work," and therefore women's work. How it is performed impacts on women's reputations in the community. Digging the land, assuring a source of water and firewood, acquiring, preparing and cooking the daily food, caring for children, doing laundry, and cleaning the house and yard is women's work and entirely within their spheres of control. In actuality, a "man's yard" is under the control of his wife, since she assumes the obligation for care and utilises her power as elder woman to designate the necessary tasks to younger women and younger men. Patriarchal sentiment is implicit in these designations, however negligible it is in practice. Male authority is usually only called upon by women in the event that they need further support in getting tasks done, or by men if they are in the yard and notice the omission of tasks. Daughters, daughters-in-law, and women outside the yard label the yard "Mama [name of eldest child's] yard." It is men who name the yard after the man who owns it.

YARD SCENE

The tasks performed by an individual woman in a yard are dependent upon who else is in the yard, and her age or her other responsibilities, which may take her away from home. Early morning is the time for designating responsibilities. For the most part, they are delegated on a daily basis. A woman moves from one person to another in the yard, directing this young daughter to fetch the first water of the day for bathing, this son to chop firewood, that son to remove the animals and tie the cows, this daughter and daughter-in-law to fetch more water, another daughter-in-law to get the fire going and prepare the tea, while yet another is directed to remove the night's accumulation of animal dung. If she is still a "working woman," she will perform some of the tasks herself, usually providing bathing water and making tea for her husband if he is there. She then sets the tasks for the day for individual members of the yard. Young daughters and sons are encouraged to hurry to school if fees are paid, and daughters-in-law are sent to get water for washing clothes. If she is able to work at all, this elder woman will usually take on the task of sweeping the yard herself. If not, another woman is directed to do so.

When early morning tasks are completed, the elder woman sends her daughters-in-law to the field she has decided needs attention. She might join them herself, breaking up the ground, planting, hoeing, or harvesting, depending upon the time of year. If workers are hired in the yard, she provides them with orders for their daily work, their tea and food, and if she has the money, she pays them when they have finished. If she is leaving the yard for the day, she will provide direction to the members who remain behind before she goes. It is her responsibility to see that tea and food are in the yard for workers as well as other yard members. This may entail her walking or sending someone to a shop to make purchases and to the grinding mill to have the maize made into flour. She will either go for more water to make mid-morning tea and the mid-day meal, or direct another to perform these tasks. At the end of the day, she directs yard members to get more water, bring in animals, and begins the preparation for the evening meal. If the elder woman is away from the yard, the daughter-in-law longest in residence—usually the wife of the oldest son—assumes the authority.

Daughters-in-law recognise the power of the mother-in-law in the yard, even as they complain of it. They also have their own "home work" tasks to engage in, and are sometimes hard-pressed to accomplish everything in a day. On occasion, this pressure will result in a strike, during which a daughter-in-law will refuse to provide the assistance her mother-in-law expects. The mother-in-law then complains to her sons, expecting them to invoke patriarchal sentiment and get their wives to cooperate.

A daughter-in-law prefers to have a congenial relationship with her mother-in-law. A congenial relationship will aid in gaining the mother-in-law's support for *uvukwi* discussion and payment. It will also allow the daughter-in-law to assume more authority over her own house. If the relationship is not congenial, an elder woman can create difficulties inside and outside the yard, as she complains to others in the community that her daughter-in-law is not working as she should. Thus, this relationship has influence on the reputation as well as on the *uvukwi* of the daughter-in-law. In turn, a well-functioning yard provides the elder woman with status, as she is recognised as a good manager.

The relationship between the elder woman and her first born son's wife is different from her relationship with other daughters-in-law. Although women assume that all their children will care for them in their old age, there is an expectation that a mother will end her days in her eldest son's yard. This provides this daughter-in-law with special status: her mother-in-law may consult with her or may support her in times of difficulty with her husband or his other relatives. An elder woman usually believes it to be in her best interest to acknowledge the circumstance of her oldest son's wife, since it may influence her own care when she is an old woman. Kagonga, for example, lived in a situation of neglect. When I first visited with her, I found her eating the mud from her house. When I asked her daughter-in-law why this old mother was starving, she first denied that was the case, telling me, "we all have little." Later she explained how Kagonga had been "fierce" and "cruel" to her for many years. Febe, on the other hand, tells how well her daughter-in-law treats her: "In this yard, I am the first to eat."

Daughters-in-law also believe it is in their best interests to have a congenial relationship with their sisters-in-law. Married daughters living elsewhere maintain a close relationship with their mothers, fathers and especially their brothers, who they often call upon for support. They have influence in their natal family; they bring cows and gifts. Daughters-in-law in a yard will often turn to these sisters-in-law, who after all face the same situations in the yards where they are married.

Unmarried sons who are past puberty may also create difficulty for daughters-in-law. Instead of following their sisters-in-law's direction, they may attempt to impose a patriarchal rule more appropriate to husbands, husband's elder brothers, or fathers-in-law. In this situation, a husband will usually recognise the viewpoint of his wife and call on the young man to change his behaviour: "People will be asking if you want to be married to your brother's wife!"

A woman's power in a yard is relative to her position in that yard, to whether she is elder woman, daughter, or daughter-in-law. As can be discerned by the activities of "home work," one woman alone in a yard faces tremendous obstacles, not only in terms of work itself, but in the absence of the support of other women. In such a yard, a woman will invite a young female relative to live with her to assist and also to "keep her company." Women will also encourage their female relatives to marry into the yard or close by. Men frequently approach female in-laws for assistance in getting wives.

Women will usually support women if they are confronted by men. On a day-to-day basis, men have little to do with what happens in the house and yard. Men are seldom in yards. Some are "tarmacking" (looking for work) or "losing the day" at the market or on the roads. For the most part, women will put aside their differences if it means avoiding men's power, or if dissension impacts on their reputation in the community. Women may call on men's power as a threat; men may exercise their authority if "home work" is not done, but more likely they will act only in regard to those aspects of it that directly affect them. Although the relationships within the house and yard are essentially hierarchical, the responsibilities all belong to women. A house or yard that runs inefficiently impacts on a woman's reputation. It disallows her categorisation as "good wife," and interferes with her claim for help from the collectivity.

For women's responsibilities in the home to be complete, they must purchase, receive as gifts, or borrow certain items from the commodity market. "Tea and sugar" is an idiomatic expression for anything bought at the market. Necessary items other than food are water containers, clothes, shoes, blankets, utensils, seeds, and fertiliser. Other items include batteries, newspapers, supplies for repairing and building, furniture, lamps, animals, and more land. The majority of people call themselves *avadaka* (poor people), as they have restricted access to these market commodities. What is accessible comes primarily from women's work and gifts. If women have access to cash, men expect them to use it to provide food or food-related goods for the home. Although women's access to cash is usually minimal, and their earnings go mostly toward "home work," it nonetheless provides women with a further resource beyond men's control. Only a few men have full-time jobs. Most of these men work outside Maragoli, and by the time they pay their own living expenses, they have little left to contribute to the home.

Of 34 husbands working full-time (out of a total of 78), only four work in Maragoli. Maintaining living accommodation elsewhere is expensive. For example, a 1988 budget kept by a man working in Nairobi gives the following as shilling expenditures for one month: rent, 500 shillings; area watchman, 50; transportation and food, 1020; laundry, 38; donations (funeral), 90; medical, 769 (an unusual expense as one is not sick every month, yet something necessary, as obtaining medical care in Nairobi is seldom free); repayment of debt, 200 (borrowed the previous month); transportation to Maragoli, 250; for a total of 2917 shillings. His monthly salary is 2100 shillings, so he was not able to take money home, and he remained 817 shillings in debt. Even without the medical treatment, he would not have been able to contribute to the home in Maragoli. Some men also engage in budget strategies: for example, many do not come home on a regular monthly basis so that they can save on transport and instead they attempt to accumulate cash to provide home assistance three or four times a year. This is tenuous however, as they may end up spending it on relatives, emergencies, or women and liquor. The strategy used by the man above was to draw upon wage labour and the kin group. He received a 650 shilling salary advance, borrowed 200 from a friend (to be repaid the next month), his "sister" (cousin) gave him 100, and his mother-in-law gave him 250 to cover his transportation cost to Maragoli. The last sum was given so that he could attend to a family responsibility at home, that of negotiating with his father for a piece of land for his wife to work.

Land

Men own land by inheritance or—less commonly—by purchase. As people see it, women are only given access to the land by marriage: "Men are the ones to give land to their wives." Although the proper "Avalogoli way" is that fathers give land to their sons, they do not always do so. Land is scarce now, and therefore expensive: a one-half acre plot in South Maragoli averages 50,000 shillings, with land in North Maragoli only slightly lower. The purchase price for land inside or outside Maragoli requires considerable wealth, and many fathers and sons simply do not have and likely will never have the means.

Out of 410 women, only two women spoke of "my land" (they had title deeds in their names). The remainder characterised the land as "our land," or "our family's land." All sons on the other hand, married and unmarried, were considered to be "living at home;" that is, even if they were away, they had a place at home where they were entitled to a piece of land for their wives to dig. The wives of the 78 married men I spoke to were living in the men's home yards, even if the men were working and living elsewhere. Thirty-four (44%) of these men worked in wage labour (only four in Maragoli); four worked at temporary jobs in wage labour, and one was in jail. For the most part these, married sons did not have a title deed or numbers for "their" land. Title deeds or land numbers were held by fathers in 49 cases; fathers' brothers in three; grandfathers in five; a grandfather's brother in one; in two cases where fathers were deceased, mothers had the land numbers; one son of the oldest house and one oldest son had a title deed; in one case, the title deed was in both the mother and the father's name; in six cases, no one had a title deed or number; in two cases, information about the title deed was unknown; and in one case the individual had no land. The remaining six sons (for a total of eight or 10%) had the title deeds to their pieces of land.

Within the cultural mandate, mothers, fathers, and brothers advise women of the disadvantages of "marrying land" which has many sons. Miriam provides an explanation:

The reasons why we had bigger land before is like this: in one household you had one son, so he got all the land, but when the sons increase so you have four, you have to divide that land into quarters. Look, I was married to the only son; I have big land, that was my luck. When I got married to that home, I had three sons. The first one had land, the second one had land, the third one had land. No serious problems because there was only one son where I married. With Abigail, there are three sons where she is married, they have sons, and she has eight sons; Freda, seven sons where she is married, they have sons and she has one son. And there it goes; the land is gone!

Marrying where there are too many sons is a point on which women can be criticised. Voilet's mother asks her, "Why did you marry there? They do not have enough land for you. There, they have too many sons." Criticism such as this would be applied where elopements have taken place. When elders (both women and men) are involved in marriage decisions, one of their responsibilities is to assure that enough land is available for their "daughter's" future use. Once women begin to overproduce children and underproduce subsistence, it is these elders who will be held responsible for not properly assessing the situation initially, and therefore they try to control the situation before a bad decision is made.

Women can own land. For example, a woman with a "good" reputation can maintain "ownership" of land.

Finasi

With the approval of the community and information received at the church, where women gather, Finasi, a woman with "no sons,"[45] was encouraged to counter the cultural prescription that land must only belong to men:

The reason for the conflict was clear. That was because I had not had any sons. They wanted to divide the children so the children would stay with their aunts [father's sisters], and one to stay with and care for their grandmother [father's mother]. I was to leave, and the land was to go to my brother-in-law.[46] That was the major reason for conflict. I refused to leave for two reasons. One is that my children would experience serious difficulties. Two, was the fact that if I leave, since my brother has built me a house, I will leave embarrassment to my brother.[47] Now I take care of the old mother; it has changed. She is not the way she was before. Because before it was her daughters and son who put [the] idea into her that I should leave. The land was to be given to my brother-in-law...he wanted it for his own son. Her [the mother-in-law's] own daughters and son persuaded her to get rid of me. This was after the death of my husband. And the public refused to accept what the family was saying. And also, the government of Kenya, following the government of Kenya from Moi, that if you only have even one child and the child is a daughter and the father dies, the daughter has a right to that land. It is the law. I could keep the land and I could leave it for my daughters when I die. The matter was discussed in all the churches. And it was also spelled out clearly at the funeral that I would not leave. The public around, and all the neighbours and all the people concerned, told to me very clearly, you cannot leave. For you don't know when your children grow up and get married, whether they will ever have peace there. They have to have a place to return. They are entitled to that. We go to church and somebody is sent from Nairobi who knows the government law, and he tells people in the church. These government people told me you need to get a title deed because you don't know about changes; you think you have land and then you don't. But the problem with that is there is no money to go to the offices to change the title deed. My husband had the number to the land; I have it, it is eleven. What it means is that if I have money, then I go to ask the Registrar's Office and then the number will be transferred to me. A long time ago, the cost was 100 shillings, but they say it is added every year. I have been defeated [unable to afford the cost]. According to the changes it would be better to do that [acquire the title deed], although I am secure with this law because everyone is agreed. What I would like to have is the number and the land transferred to me. That's the most important thing, although nothing is said [by the husband's family], but you never know.

What stopped Finasi from actually obtaining the title deed to her deceased husband's land was lack of money, not the restrictions of patriliny ownership:

Kenyan women have equal rights with men in matters of succession to property...the Law of Succession Act, Chapter 160 which came into operation in 1981 after being enacted in 1972, gave a widow and her daughters equal footing with male relatives in property succession (Attorney-General Mr. Justice Mathew Muli opening a four-day regional conference of the International Federation of Women Lawyers in Nairobi, December, 1987).

The meaning of "equal footing" appears to be contextual. For example, in Kisumu, a 70 year old (Luo) woman won a legal suit over the inheritance of her father's land against her father's brothers and male cousins. The male relatives' application stated that the man's daughter had no right as a married woman to inherit her father's land: "Luo tradition [does] not allow a daughter married elsewhere to go back to her father's home and inherit his property." These male relatives were supported in court by elders and an Assistant Chief of the area. However, the judge said, "The law of Kenya allows a man to bequeath land to his married daughter or any other daughter" (Daily Nation, January 28, 1988). A current case in Maragoli has three daughters selling a piece of land. Their father had no son. This deceased father has living brothers who are seeking a settlement, either in the form of the land itself, or at least in a part of the cash proceeds from selling. All daughters do have a right to a home, as Finasi is saying; therefore, even if another member of the family inherits the land, a deceased man's daughter may always find a home on that land. It is "her home land;" she belongs to the patriliny. Contexts will determine whether or not she will utilize that right.

In interviews, 41% of 94 women who spoke on the subject believed women should not own land. They said, "Men are the ones to give land to their wives;" "Men own land, women do not;" and that women owning land signifies "trouble in a marriage." These comments are in keeping with the patriarchal sentiment. Barnard, a teacher in his fifties, provides a synopsis of customary responsibilities:

The land should always be owned by the husband; he should be the owner; he should be in charge. You cannot have two decision-makers: it just creates arguments. One person must take the lead and it should be the man. He is the one who knows more, even when women are educated. Those families who have problems, it is because this is not followed. Although we all have a higher authority who makes the ultimate decisions [God], it is a man's duty to be in charge of his yard, his wife and children.

Many Avalogoli believe that "God created man to be the pillar of the house." Achura provided this reasoning when asked who makes the decisions in his home. When his wife laughed at his response, he amended his answer to say that they "discuss." Febe believes that it "depends upon who you marry. If you agree to work on things together, that works out well. It takes both husband and wife to make the decisions that bind everyone."

In the same interviews as above, 47% of women believed that women should own their own land, and a further 10% gave qualified responses: "Women should own their own land if they have their own money to buy," or "No, women should not own their own land, but if they have money [to buy], they may." Two women had a legal ownership of land through title deed. Both of these women work in wage labour and utilised money from their wages, and one of them borrowed (from a male employer) to purchase the land. Both women were married; however, they described their marriages as "not steady," and both had difficulty in registering the title deeds in their names. They had to "fight" for the deed. One of the women received assistance from the area M.P. in procuring the title. Even though men and a lesser percentage of women believed that women should not own their own land, 57% of the women believed women should or could own land. Although men own land by inheritance and make decisions about that land, women today have access to resources and added power to sway these decisions.

One of the more recently available resources for women is information. For women, many of whom do not read, legal information comes mainly from churches (which most women attend), the radio, or *barazzas* (meetings) which they attend. Government representatives provide information at church gatherings on wages for digging, prices for commodities, laws, and aspects of subsistence. As Edelia says, "government emphasis is on women and *maendeleo*; the women have become productive."

The degree to which women manage cultural edicts about what is proper affixes to other aspects of male "rule" as well. Men generally own the land and are said to make the decisions about crops grown on that land: what to dig and plant, when to harvest, when to sell, and when to give to relatives and friends. These men are described as "walking the land," and saying to their wives "now is the time to dig, to plant, to weed, to harvest." When 94 women were interviewed, it was assessed that in 51 cases, men made these decisions. In two cases, men made most of the decisions about the land, but the women were "free" to sell surplus crops if any were available. However, in 22 cases, women said their husbands discussed the above aspects with them and they reached mutual agreement, and in 19 cases, women made the decisions on their own. Thus in 46% of the total cases, women either made or contributed significantly to decisions about crops produced on men's land. Some men occasionally recognised and valued women's contributions. In his sober moments, Mudasia maintained that he was appreciative of his wife's ingenuity and management. He said, however, that "people are jealous of our development, and when I am drunk they convince me to apply a firm hand." Women also recognise their own value: Amy says, "If I care for the land, dig, plant and harvest, then I make the decisions about the land." Although generally men make the decisions about subsistence economics, women can gain influence in this process. In a context where many yards have an absent commander leaving the women "in charge," statements like Amy's are becoming more frequent. Some men "forget the home" completely, neglecting the *vika* appropriate to the "Avalogoli way."

Vika

Women kin, affines and even friends act within inter-household exchange networks as they follow *vika*. Food gifts take place on a daily basis; relatives and friends visit one another with covered baskets which may contain beans, eggs, bananas or maize flour. Baskets containing goods are always covered. As Ritah and Joyce explain,

> People have jealous eyes, they want to know if my gift from you is more than they have received. People may demand the same gift and perhaps you don't have. This will create difficulty among people. They can never be seen.

The basket is handed to the hostess upon the visitor's arrival, and when the visitor is ready to leave, it is passed back to her containing a different food gift. Baskets may "never" be returned empty.

Women believe that men attempt to curtail women's aspirations to gain status through *vika*. If men attempt to control women's production, women see men as preventing them from gaining a reputation for "treating visitors nicely." Women complain of this interference, as well as of men's neglect of the hierarchy that exists in *vika*. "Closer" relatives should give and be given more than those who are considered "distant." For example, when wives' brothers visit, bearing gifts such as meat, tea, sugar, and when possible, cash, the proper response is to feed them well with at least a chicken, if not a goat. The husband who does not provide this reciprocal gift leaves a blight on the wife's reputation and status within both kin networks. Brothers visiting the yards where their sisters are married must be "treated *very* nicely," and "fed *very* well," with food provided by brothers-in-law. This has to do with *vika*, particularly if the brother visiting is connected to his wife's husband through *uvukwi*. It becomes even more important to provide appropriately if *uvukwi* has not been discussed or paid in its entirety. A question remains as to the sister's "worth;" thus, if her brother is "treated very nicely," a respect in that yard for his sister is conveyed. Where it has been paid in full, the situation becomes less stressful. The brother "knows" his sister is well thought of in the yard. Frequently the provision follows a pattern: first tea, groundnuts or bananas (sometimes both) are provided. Following that, a main meal consisting of chicken or beef and *ovukima* is served, followed by yet more tea with bread and butter or margarine. The brother will be sent off with a chicken, perhaps bananas, sugar cane, or even maize to take to his own yard. Should the brother's family accompany him, the first visit of every one of his children will be acknowledged by a gift of individual chickens. It is seldom that women are able to fulfil this obligation on their own, and therefore they believe their husbands ought to assist to convey respect both for their wife and for her family. Joyce was extremely upset when her brother visited and her husband Vihima did not provide her with the ingredients for a "proper meal" to welcome him. Joyce describes her husband's lack of respect for her and her family:

My brother came to visit this morning. My husband has gone to drink. He only greeted my brother and then left him with me. He did not stay to entertain him. I believed he had gone to buy a chicken so that I may cook for my brother. Instead I find he has gone just there [a close by yard], to drink. He has not directed me to cook my brother very good food. I have been shamed. You know, brother [brother-in-law], the *uvukwi* is only part paid. I have been shamed. *Muharikwa* [sister-in-law], when you visited with your husband his sister, he was treated so nicely, very nicely indeed. You were given pork, chicken, rice, potatoes, vegetables, with drinks. He was to have been given a goat, but that will come another time. For me, I am left only shamed.

Joyce's reputation is good; she was given a chicken by a relative, but still, the "joy of the visit" was reduced because her husband did not join her brother for the meal.

Vika to appropriate gift-giving and receiving take place throughout every individual's life. This is clarified by examining some aspects of women's involvement and power in reciprocal obligations and benefits; these are in evidence throughout all aspects of life.

Reciprocal Obligations and Benefits

Reciprocity pervades the economic, political and social spheres of Avalogoli life. Exchanges take place during both informal and formal visits, and during shortages. Reciprocal exchanges extend outward from members in a yard to all who may be connected to that yard as relatives, in-laws, and friends. For the most part, it is women who activate the social networks.

Avalogoli say, *"Mwana wovo ni mugingi vo mgongo"* (Your child is the supporting stick of your back). Additionally, children are responsible for *"Mugingi vo mgongo"* ("My name to go up"), in that children should "buy this for me" or "build this for me." "Logoli sons are to know again their father;" Logoli daughters "think of and care for parents in their old age."

Forty women (out of 94) characterised their and others' children as "good." "Good" is generally defined as working hard to achieve an education, assisting with the work at home, or offering some financial support to the parents. Forty-seven women characterised their and others' children as "bad." "Bad" is defined as the opposite of good. Seven women said children can be both bad and good, depending upon the individuals and contexts.

Relations between parents and children are extended reciprocally throughout the community. All those in an ascending generation are parents and the young are their children. Kinship relations provide a framework for the process of distribution as well as production. All parents and children must give and receive, most particularly those from *umuliango gwitu* (from our door), from the same *inyumba* or lineage. Relationships within *tsinyumba* (*inyumba* singular) give members a sense of affiliation and continuity, providing the basis for individual security. This bond between the individual and the group provides the "good life:" children, land, and cattle. Fulfilling this bond necessitates giving and receiving within the collectivity. Under the state system of *Nyayo*, following "footsteps of ancestors" via peace, love, unity and sharing, this is reinforced. It is thus not only part of Avalogoli history, but also the history of all Kenyans and the proper way, by state edict, to interact in daily life. As Sarah says, "It is the same as you people call banking.[48] When I face problems, I will send one of my children to the one I have given to and they will give to that child. It takes away my pain."

In amounts ranging from ten to 500 shillings (most at the lower end of the scale), 61% of women interviewed (out of 70) were able to generate cash for commodity purchase and redistribution fairly regularly through gifts. Cash came from husbands (who remembered the home), older children, parents, in-laws (parental and sibling), aunts ("mothers"), uncles ("fathers"), sisters and brothers (including cousins), and neighbours. Additionally, commodities were loaned and given by other relatives, friends, and neighbours. This support comes from and goes to those with reputation in the community. Avalogoli are truly offended by begging and beggars. They prefer to ask (*koteva*) or they say *"Ngonya"* ("Help me"). With *koteva* or *ngonya* there is always a relationship of interdependence. Those who ask and are asked are usually *umuliango gwitu* (from our door).

Women do not automatically hand cash gained through exchange to their husbands, although the demand is usually made. More commonly, they avoid these demands by spending available cash purchasing commodities like tea, sugar and kerosene. As people are now dealing in cash, it is difficult to ascertain who is able to assist. It is easy to establish who has a full granary if the request is for maize; it is not easy to detect cash, because it is easily hidden. There is an assumption among Maragoli people that women "always" have cash, but that women choose when to give money. Some husbands ask, demand, search and beat for the money they are sure wives have hidden away. However, women's ability to extend their reputation through the commodity market and the decisions they make about sharing add to their reputation and subsequent influence with men.

Women's self-image and community reputation is enhanced as their cash and commodity flow circulates the network of reciprocal relations. Their ability to provide an advantage to their children is also increased. Money for school fees comes from both mothers and fathers, and is given to both daughters and sons. Ideally, sons and daughters become more economically self-sufficient, and thus more marriageable. In return, they will contribute to the exchange network that which has been offered to them, and sometimes even more. Sons may be better enabled to come up with the increased *uvukwi* that families of educated daughters demand. Long-term advantages for daughters on the employment market are questionable, but there is a return to the family when a good marriage is made for their daughter: *uvukwi* is "higher." Goods circulate in the network of obligations and benefits, and heighten women's influence in their families and communities.

Chapter Six

EXPANDING THE BACK DOOR

Marriage

The first step to a legitimate marriage is *uvukwi* discussion. This discussion is initiated by men, followed by "payment" made to men, with appropriate "small" gifts made to women (mothers-in law). Women—mothers, daughters and female in-laws—are very influential in *uvukwi* processes. *Uvukwi* presentations begin the cycle of affinal reciprocity (they "open the way").

It is said that originally, the amount of *uvukwi* was the same for everyone. Jayi-Nora (who rebutted my question as to her age with, "How do I know?") was married during the Olololo-Lubwoni Circumcision, which is dated at 1900. During those days, when people were "still naked before God came," she tells how *uvukwi* was three cows and ten to twelve *tsimbago* (traditional hoes). The number of hoes was determined by a woman's "strength." That strength was measured in terms of the assistance she would provide her mother-in-law and her husband's lineage. It was thought that all "good" wives ought to receive twelve *tsimbago*.

Prior to *tsimbago*, *uvukwi* payments were in the form of fighting weapons. The elder Kagonga says,

Women who came before me got fighting knives. Usually they were those fighting knives, twelve of them. There were, in those days [prior to 1910], two divisions of war. The men from near Maragoli Hills were Avam'mavi from M'mavi and the ones over this way were called Avakizungu. So those from the Maragoli Hills came over here to fight. And so the men here had to get ready for war. They depended on women for that. That is why *uvukwi* was in the form of fighting weapons.

Another elder, Febe (who also countered the age question with "How do I know the years?"), married at age 30. She says, "Girls marry too young nowadays. They do not know anything!" She speaks of how in 1939 *uvukwi* began to change: it increased to four goats, three cows, and forty shillings. While it continued to escalate generally, payment began to vary more widely for different people. It remains unclear when material gifts to mothers-in-law entered the transaction—that is, when labour, symbolised by the *tsimbago* (traditional hoes), was replaced by market commodities and cash. Those who were asked said the change came with the introduction of cash. Originally, total payment of *uvukwi* was required before marriage. People believe that the present system of down payments and the continuing system of outstanding debits and credits occurred as a result of women's increasingly hard work and their education. Charles paid the last cow in 1975 from a 1955 marriage. It is not unusual for *uvukwi* payments to be spread out over decades; in fact, it seems to be the norm. For example, in Febe's case, the payment took 20 years. When Estella married in 1959, her *uvukwi* was seven cows and 700 shillings. Four cows and 100 shillings have been paid. Although *uvukwi* has escalated, many women see this as positive: members of a Women Group from the Friend's Church say, "That's the reward for parents: before and after birth they give [daughters] care and education." Since *uvukwi* may now be as much as ten cows and 46,000 shillings,[49] any hope of a complete payment prior to marriage has long since disappeared.

Currently, *uvukwi* presentations take the form of cash and cattle to daughters' fathers, and tea, sugar, cloth, head scarves, and smaller amounts of cash to daughters' mothers. One amount of money given is the *ambihu*, literally the gift for the one on whom the child first excreted, assumed to be the mother. This amount should come from the *uvukwi* cash given to daughter's fathers. The other cash and items given to daughters' mothers are not "counted" in the total tabulation. If a prospective son-in-law shows proper attention to a mother-in-law's gifts, he and his relatives gain her support in *uvukwi* discussion.

As a result of the difficulties involved in *uvukwi* discussion and payment, couples often elope now. They might simply decide, perhaps as a result of prior meetings, that they will stay together. Letters requesting *uvukwi* discussion end up coming afterward from the girl's parents. A number of situations were witnessed in which the young couple had not met prior to the elopement, or only met for a brief time to "examine" one another. The arrangements for the elopement were made by their relatives or friends (usually of the same age group). Aggrey tells how this may come about:

> Nathan, the oldest son of Samuel Egatwa, approached me for assistance in finding a wife as he was not experienced in seducing. He showed his good intention [buying iron sheets to build a house]. I discussed with my wife which of her relatives may make a good wife for Nathan. The characteristics of Nathan were put against the characteristics of my wife's relatives. We decided Anita, my wife's sister, was the one, the two would suit one another: a polite man must be matched with a polite lady. We wrote to this girl and asked her to visit; she agreed to try.

The young man's father and mother should be given an opportunity to observe the girl prior to writing a letter to her parents. Usually, she is taken to the home and "given" to other daughters-in-law, who will spend a night with her providing her with information on the yard she is considering joining, so "she may know how things are in that home." They will also ask her questions. The mother-in-law will question the daughters-in-law in the morning and "report" to the young man's father. In a number of cases, it was after the parents' approval that the young couple met, so that they "might lay eyes on one another for mutual approval."

Even when *uvukwi* discussion and payment are precluded as a preliminary step to a proper marriage, "appropriate *vika*" should still be followed after an elopement. Letters are supposed to be sent to inform the parents that the woman has not been in an "accident" or "stolen," as she has probably kept her liaison with the man secret. Ideally, the letters should contain an invitation to meet for *uvukwi* discussion. If the woman "stays nicely" for "two weeks," she will expect to be provided with a gift from her prospective husband and his relatives to carry to her parents and relatives in her natal yard. This suggests that there is choice on the young woman's part, to stay in the new yard or to leave it; however, it works both ways. The young man may decide he is not "satisfied," and set up the situation such that she is unable to stay nicely. For one thing, he must give the gifts for her first visit. Not providing these sends a strong message that he is not pleased with the relationship. If a woman is making the "short visit" to her parents (meaning she does not spend the night at their home), she should take along sugar, tea leaves, milk, bread and perhaps some money, "up to 200 shillings." The man may even cover the container with a new cloth for his prospective mother-in-law. The passage of time is noted by the woman and her waiting relatives. If time goes on and the gifts for the "short visit" are not produced, a message may come from the woman's relatives that they are "waiting to greet her." At this point, she may decide to return home, cancelling the marriage. If she goes with gifts, it is expected that she will return to her prospective husband's yard with gifts. Salome describes what gifts are appropriate:

She should carry ground [maize] flour, at least 10 kilos, a cock, and two kilos of meat. These will be covered with a cloth she may use in her new home. This will identify to the parents of the boy that she is loved. If her parents are Christian, they will take the first letter showing the *uvukwi* offer to the church. The elders will pray over that letter that she will make a good wife and the boy a good husband.

Any refusal of discussion or payment creates tremendous dissension both within and between families. The responsibility for initiating discussion and making payment lies with the yard within which the daughter chooses to marry. If this does not take place, women or men from the daughter's home yard will make visits and suggest the procedure begin. As a close relationship exists between daughters and their parents and brothers, usually the amount to be negotiated has already been agreed upon by the daughter and members of her yard.

Once arrangements for discussion are made, the bride and the women from the yard where she has married will rise very early and work very hard to accumulate the water and firewood and cook the food. Men from that yard should supply extra food for this purpose. Neglect of this duty is an interference with wedding ceremonies, both customary and more modern. For example, Zablon asked how it was possible to provide a wedding for his daughter when there had been no *uvukwi* discussion. His daughter and his wife maintained that the discussion would take place after the wedding, but Zablon's perspective was different:

> The young man and his parents, who are also Abaluhya, maintain the discussion will take place after the wedding. But how to pay for a wedding without some *uvukwi* payment? The payment comes from the discussion. I was very angry, both of them [mother and daughter] pressured me so much that I would just leave the house and go to Daniel's home. The women won, and the wedding took place. My friends and relatives contributed chickens and maize and the guests were fed at my home and the homes of those around me. There was no money coming from those people [the affines] to assist. To this point we have not seen the home where my daughter is married. We left her at the place where they register the marriage. The best man I appointed to fulfil that responsibility [taking his daughter to her husband's home] could not fulfil that responsibility. Now my wife and other ladies are discussing going there [to release the daughter]. They have already one child. We have not yet seen that child.

Obligations and benefits surrounding *uvukwi* are problematic for both men and women. As Joyce relates, even when *uvukwi* discussion has taken place and a "down-payment" has been provided, conflicts continue:

> I wanted to be a nurse, but there was no money for my training. I decided to get married, as I had not the education to work. If money is there, you get educated, then work, then marry later, not so soon. If you can't work, you just stay with parents, so you must leave and the only way to leave is to get married. My husband asked for me; the table was opened.[50] I was to pay some of the opening money, but I did not have any so I left the matter to my parents.[51] My husband paid 150 shillings to open the table, 100 was from him, 50 was from me. He paid for me. Two men came, the in-laws [father's brother and father's brother's son], and Helen, a woman from this side [from the husband's area] who was still giving birth [meaning she was a younger woman, not an elder]. She said nothing. *Uvukwi* was set at 6000 shillings and seven cows. They [Joyce's father and male rela-

tives] took 3000 shillings. It remains 3000 shillings and seven cows. I was satisfied. Since then, he has not paid, not even a little, or a cow. My parents are taking him to the court. One cow, one piece of cloth to my mother would have stopped this court.

The woman from the husband's area was sent to represent Joyce, who is not permitted to be present during *uvukwi* discussion. A woman in attendance is also said to represent the bride's point of view and/or the mother of the husband-to-be. However, I am told she seldom contributes to the discussion. Her role seems to be one of reporting the decisions to other women in both of the concerned yards, since men "never tell" what has gone on or what has been decided: they only "smile" or "frown." Mothers who have already contributed their opinion as to what amount should be set prior to discussion must be made aware of the final amount decided upon. It permits them to negotiate what they should receive. Because women serve the discussants food, and areas for private discussions are almost non-existent in this open society, in reality all are aware of events during the discussion.

In Joyce's case, the money for "down-payment" of *uvukwi* was supplied by her husband, Vihima. Vihima strongly feels that nothing more should be sent until his "father" (his father's brother) sends a cow, the "first cow," for *uvukwi*. "I am an orphan, and even if I were not the father *must* supply a cow" (*vika*). Vihima maintains he will "pay no more" until this has taken place. Late in 1988, Vihima's sister "convinced" her husband to discuss and worked to provide a "down-payment" for her *uvukwi*. Vihima attempted to maintain control over this down payment rather than allowing his father's brother this control. *Vika* dictates that his father's brother ought to receive *uvukwi* in place of his deceased brother and then pass it to Vihima to allow him to "finish" his own *uvukwi* payment. Vihima maintained that "father" could not be trusted because he had not provided the "first cow." Conflict has ensued, resulting in a hold-up of the sister's *uvukwi* payment, which she has worked "very hard" to provide and which will give her a "proper place" in her husband's yard. Her husband says he is "unsure" where to send it. *Vika* dictates that he may not send it to a son's yard when there is a living father.

Women's reputations depend on a successful and continuing *uvukwi* process, but many women do not enjoy even minimal *uvukwi* benefits and describe themselves as "stuck," "just there," or "just a slave" after eloping, if discussion and payment do not take place at all. In 79% of 94 cases, women reported that discussion and payment had not been completed. Discussion had taken place in 20 cases; discussion and part payment in 43 cases; and no discussion or payment in 31 cases. Many different reasons are given for non-discussion and non-payment: there are not enough children produced; there are too many children to be able to pay; there is not enough money to provide for affine responsibilities. Often, when asked, women were not able—or perhaps not willing—to suggest causes. In most cases, men put it to a general lack of finances. However, all women were adamant that *uvukwi* should be paid, and men agreed. Most people recognise that adherence to the institution of *uvukwi* is difficult given the lack of finances.

Uvukwi is an impossibility for most ordinary people. Many men and most women in rural areas do not have access to wage labour, and even if they do, wages do not allow for this kind of expenditure. In areas like these, the saying that "Elders have big pockets that never get filled" seems to apply. During another conversation among women who were waiting for a discussion to end, women complained that raising *uvukwi* "too high" will "make bad feelings:"

> The girl may get kicked from the home and the mother will then have to care for her daughter and grandchildren while the father will go consuming [whatever payment has been made]. These men are ruining children's marriage lives. They should set it at four cows and 2000 shillings as the girl has no education to speak of, she has not done anything, only goes to the river with us. The rest of the money can be used by the bridegroom, bride and their children to build a good life. If it is too high, they start life on nothing and eventually she will be thrown from that yard.

This criticism is not to say that *uvukwi* payments should not be made at all. Women acknowledge that *uvukwi* payments provide reason for the continuance of reciprocity, of the gift giving and receiving that allows some institutions to continue to function smoothly. As the women from Friend's Church say:

> it is the reward for parents and the young man feels very proud for having given *uvukwi*. It is another system of saying, "this is my wife." If not, the wife can say, these are not your children. In death, the parents would demand the body and children, even if there were ten children. Even if one cow is given, it makes the difference. If a mother is buried away from where she bore children it is a very serious *olovo*. This *olovo* says the children themselves would not get *uvukwi*.

If *uvukwi* is not forthcoming, it is in women's best interest to demand the return of their daughters and their children. Mothers and daughters recognise that *uvukwi* is an important means of enhancing their lives. Members of the Digoi Women Group say,

> Now girls are educated; the child helps at home; when she leaves to marry, the *uvukwi* will assist those at the home she is leaving. It gives strength to the married girl. She is someone with power, she is not just someone picked from the market.

These women continue: "*uvukwi must* be paid. Women must see it is paid, they must work hard to see that happen."

Women attempt to influence their own *uvukwi* process. They "work hard" either to accumulate cash and cows or to prove their worth so cash and cows may be sent. They "push" or otherwise "convince" their husbands.[52] If that is not successful, women may threaten to "walk with their children;" to effectively cut the husbands' sons and daughters from the patriliny. Although sons cut off from their fathers may be told to get their land elsewhere ("Your mother is not here; go there [where she is] to get your land"), mothers choose whether or not to pursue this choice, weighing the son's loss according to their own best interests. Daughters raised in their mother's natal home will bring their *uvukwi* presentations to that home, not to the father who neglected them. Fathers will ultimately say, "You can lose a cow from the home but not a child." When *uvukwi* discussion and payment is completely absent, women find the situation intolerable and call on their kin for support. Consider Ritah's experience.

Ritah

When Ritah and Aggrey eloped in 1984, *uvukwi* discussion was not initiated by Aggrey's father. It was expected that Aggrey's father must "make the first move," to send the "first cow." Ritah complained that Aggrey had not "pushed" his father to do so, even though when she first came to Aggrey's father's yard, she did everything that was to be done in the home: cooking, washing, fetching water, chopping firewood—even caring for cows, traditionally a boy's task. Her relatives had approached Aggrey's father on three occasions, asking for *uvukwi* discussion. When Ritah wanted to visit her natal home, her parents-in-law did not wish to provide her with gifts. After a long argument on the morning of the visit, the father-in-law finally relented, saying he would put sugar in the container, a traditionally appropriate gift for Ritah to take along. The father-in-law instructed Ritah and her sister-in-law (who would travel with her) to wait and walk with him to market, and to carry his bag. He walked ahead on the road and the two followed. "I will see what can be sent. Maize you bring back if they have it, also a chicken and some meat, if they have it. You take tea, milk and sugar."

After the three left the yard, neighbours, who were alerted by the loud voices, discussed the matter and provided an explanation. Their opinion is that these types of interactions are actually demonstrations of power, in this case the power of fathers and fathers-in-law, and mothers and mothers-in-law, over sons and daughters-in-law. These neighbours, both men and women, were all of the opinion that ultimately Ritah or any daughter-in-law would be able to visit, and that no Logoli man or woman would ever send a daughter-in-law to her home with "empty hands." This was unheard of. "It [the discussion] is only to show them their place [as children under the control of parents]," the neighbours said. However, at the time of the angry discussion there appeared to be no underlying understanding that everything would work out: the individuals directly concerned did not appear to be confident that the expectations of the normative social structure would come about in the end.

In this particular case, there was a further complication: it was inappropriate for Ritah to have visited her parents at all, because *uvukwi* discussion had not taken place. She therefore returned "without gifts," but with two letters from her brother: one to her husband and one to her father-in-law. In fact, Ritah did receive gifts from her natal home: a few shillings, some articles of clothing and sweet potatoes. However, these gifts were hidden from the parents-in-law. Ritah's mother-in-law approached her upon her return. She had been sent by her husband to question how the "visiting had taken place." This was her attempt to find out what gifts were received, and to obtain an appropriate share for the parents-in-law. Instead, Ritah only presented her mother-in-law with the letter for her father-in-law. Both in-laws were angry, and the father-in-law "only put the letter away, he did not even read it." Ritah's husband was aware of the gifts, but he too did not reveal them to his parents.

Ritah was not permitted to know the content of the letters, but her husband shared the information from his. In the letter, Ritah's brother reminded Aggrey's family that Ritah's father was very ill, and that without a discussion and some payment, Ritah would not be permitted to attend his funeral. As a "gone soul," he would haunt all the living who did not attend his funeral. Most particularly, he would haunt the affines who did not follow the *vika*. When Ritah's father finally died, Ritah returned to her mother's yard. Ritah's mother demanded that a mourning bull be sent from Aggrey's father's yard. Although Aggrey's father considered that the bull would also be *uvukwi* payment, Ritah's mother said that the animal he sent was "below the expected standard," both as a mourning bull and as *uvukwi* payment. Ritah's mother further demanded money if Aggrey's father expected Ritah and the children to return to his yard. Aggrey's father's comment was, "Does this woman think she can discuss *uvukwi*?" Eventually Ritah and the children returned to Aggrey's father's yard. But in December of 1988, Ritah "walked" with her children. Within a month of her action, her father-in-law began arrangements for the *uvukwi* discussion. Later I received a letter from Ritah, providing the details:

Father [her father-in-law] has come to the original point. He invited my parents for a negotiation of dowery [sic], three cows has [sic] to go and two cows, 10,000 Shillings has remained. These is [sic] the residual quantity.

Her husband wrote, "The dowary [sic] has been discussed. Five cows— 10,000 Shillings. Three cows are going soon."

Of all the people I spoke to in Maragoli (men, women and teenage boys and girls), only two suggested that *uvukwi* be done away with. One was a husband who described himself as "middle class" and lived and worked in Nairobi, although he maintained close ties "at home" in the rural area. His wife, however, who also lived and worked in Nairobi and described herself as "middle class," said, "My father must receive his cows!" The other dissenter was Alice, the secondary school teacher, discussed in Chapter Five above. She was of the opinion that *uvukwi* payments created a hardship for the young couple beginning their lives together: "It interferes with the progress of the young people. The parents should be assisting them to progress, not taking it [the opportunity for accumulation of wealth] away." However, in both these cases, discussions had taken place and contributions to *uvukwi* were made.

It is not in men's best interest to completely neglect *uvukwi*. Younger men who complain of having to pay ("Am I buying your body?") grow into older men who collect. They then insist that the system ought to continue.

Birth

A woman will not usually visit the yard where her daughter has married until the daughter gives birth. After each child is born, the daughter must stay in the yard and she is cut off from the exchange of gifts with her natal family until *kutulitsa mukana* takes place; that is, until she has been "released" by her mother. This is a literal "release," as without this visit from her mother and other women from her home to inspect her child and to give gifts, a daughter may not visit her natal home to see her kin, give or receive gifts, and none of her children may receive their first chicken from the home yard. Indeed, she is prohibited from visiting anywhere, although I did observe that this rule was not followed on a number of occasions. Considering the expense involved, it becomes more and more difficult to practice *kutulitsa mukana*. Some women wait a very long time for the visit from their mothers.

The release of a married daughter who has had a child takes the cooperation of her mother and a number of other women. Should a mother not be able to attend for some reason, the mother's sisters may go in her stead. For example, Iemba could not leave Nairobi to release her daughter living in the rural area. This daughter "grew" in Iemba's father's yard. Iemba asked her sister to perform the task and this sister requested that their mother also go along. The two women complained that they did not have the funds to accumulate the required gifts, and that Iemba's father would not assist. "He ate the cows from the marriage of Iemba; he should assist in releasing her daughter," the women reasoned. Women should carry clothing for the newborn, perhaps a towel, and appropriate food gifts. Mothers alone are responsible for "releasing" their daughters, but they expect the assistance of fathers. As Rebeka says:

> Children are the bridge for visiting even if children are born and die. I, as *guku* [grandmother] to the newborn must do this, else we may not receive the remaining uvukwi. *Guga* [the grandfather] will buy milk, tea, four live chickens, bread, sugar and firewood. I myself, I cannot give these items; he *must* assist; the payment [*uvukwi*] will go to him. I will travel with six other women [six is the ideal, however often only two or three women will go] to where my daughter is married. We will take the child away [to a private area in the yard], bathe it and examine it. We will sing meaningful songs and we will all handle it. After, we give the child back to those people [the daughter's affines]. Then we are fed very well; they [affines] all contribute to that [providing and cooking the food]. We take our containers back; they may not stay there overnight, but now [in this context] we do not give food with food. They [affines] must give an envelope with 100 or 200 shillings for us to take.[53] It is after this, if *uvukwi* has not been discussed, that the father of the daughter will go with some other men to ask. Every effort will be made to have this [releasing] done. The ladies I select know it must be done; they may even contribute to buying the gifts. They know an envelope will be returned [the women are aware they will retrieve some of their expenditure]. With each child this takes place until it reaches where the releasing of the daughter ends. When a daughter is in the middle of bearing children we take a bull, a well-decorated bull with flowers all over, horns, neck, the whole body. This ends the time of releasing.

Usually "the end of releasing" comes after the daughter has borne a number of children. In one case the daughter had eight children, in another, seven. A "celebration" to "finish" takes place in a number of contexts. Once *uvukwi* payments are complete and a woman is past child-bearing age, her sons ought to present her brothers with cows. Sarah tells us, "These can be sold and the money divided up, or they can keep them and give the calves to their children to use for *uvukwi*." This is a "final showing," in the context of *uvukwi*, of respect to the family who gave "a fine daughter to the family." In the case of a woman's death, her kin are responsible for providing a cow. A deceased man's affines are responsible for providing a bull for the funeral, to "finish:" a "final showing" in the context of the life of the deceased. Thus some of the cows supplied for *uvukwi* presentations might be returned in a number of contexts. *Uvukwi* discussions take these redistributive opportunities into account.

Once "released," the daughter can visit her natal home, bringing tea, sugar, and amounts of cash for both her mother and father. These gifts signify that she "comes from people, not trees," that she is highly regarded and cared for in the yard to which she is married. Her parents hope to see evidence that their daughter has literally and symbolically "grown fat." This is signified by the presence of material gifts and the "roundness" or plumpness of the woman's body, showing that she is well-fed. Both mothers and fathers "test" this plumpness by touching the daughter's body. The gifts the daughter brings allow her to receive maize, perhaps firewood, and the important chicken which is formally presented to her child. The pressure to produce the necessary items to give to the daughter falls on the women in her natal yard, but again, resistance might be encountered: even if chickens are in the yard, they usually belong to the husband. Should the husband choose not to assist, he will not be held responsible. Women see this as unfair, as he is the one to receive *uvukwi*. Women circumvent this constraint by obtaining cash through wage labour, or by maintaining a good reputation so that husbands or other relatives will assist them.

Death

In Maragoli, it is said that it is "impossible to have a funeral without women being present." On one occasion, many women in the village were to attend a Women's Meeting at Friend's Church. As people were coming from "all over" for the meeting (including women from affiliated churches), and it would be difficult to cancel the meeting, a man's funeral had to be postponed until the following day. It is said, "The funeral cannot be held without the women." Women not only produce the next generation of ancestors, but they also bury the last.

Women direct the procedures and decide when they should be carried out during funeral days. The signal of death comes from drums and from the wails of women in the yard where the death has taken place. The surrounding area is immediately alerted, and almost as immediately, neighbourhood women will stop work and gather in the yard of the deceased. A constant stream of women carrying chickens, eggs, beans, and perhaps even tea and sugar then files into the yard. Usually it is the responsibility of men to provide livestock for the funerals of close relatives and affines (a bull for men and a cow for women). Men should also supply market commodities: tea, sugar, milk, bread, and cash. Funerals tend to be very expensive in Maragoli. Hundreds, even thousands of people will attend for some part of the time. All must "take tea," that is, be given tea, and many will be fed *ovukima* with chicken or beef.

The body of the deceased is washed and dressed by women, and women direct men to begin building the coffin. Women fetch firewood, collect water, and begin to prepare the food for at least three days and nights of mourning which must occur prior to the burial of the body. Even after this has taken place, close relatives might stay on in the yard (sometimes for weeks), and they will have to be fed. All events, from the time of death until the religious ceremony and burial, are collectively called "funeral". *Luvago*, which takes place some time later, when the family is financially able to provide a bull or cow and feed large numbers of people, is translated as a "final wedding ceremony." The *luvago* provides the arena for a final reckoning, of what is owed to or by the deceased—not only materially, but also socially. For example, any insult or bad feelings must be resolved before the deceased is able to "rest" without bothering the living. Should a long time elapse between the funeral and *luvago*, a "comfort gathering" is often held for the deceased, and is attended by a number of the relatives and one or more elders from the deceased's area. Prayers, speeches, hymns, and "a very good meal" are the elements of the comfort gathering. It sends a message to the living and the dead, that the deceased has not been forgotten, and that eventually, the *luvago* will be held.

Women perform most of the work and meet the requirements to feed the hundreds of people who attend these events. At times, attendance figures run into the thousands. It is women who blow the whistles at funerals to alert those in attendance that a collection of cash for the deceased is about to be taken. Women collect money from both women and men during the days of the funeral, and decide how it should be allocated. *Ivani* (special money collected in small baskets at a funeral) assists women in feeding the people. During the burial, both women and men give *inguvu* (envelopes containing money given at a funeral). *Inguvu* literally means cloth. Aggrey explains:

> they do not say it is money. You can even buy the cloth to bury the person, but the dead body cannot use so much cloth, so today, money is given instead. After the burial the oldest child of the dead person is called forward, but if the oldest is a daughter she must call her brother up, to stand

with the mother or father. The two hold the basket [containing the envelopes] with both hands, one on each side. They pray over the money, then the family takes it. The money is divided: daughters who have paid *uvukwi*, sons, the unmarried get a share; the mother or the father [surviving spouse] receives the most.

No matter how destitute one is, some contribution must be made, if not immediately, then at some later point in time. Although I heard women complain of the difficulties in making the provision for funerals (considering the high population, endemic malaria and now AIDS), for the most part the responsibility is accepted without comment. One must have mourners at one's funeral; one must have one's history read. Otherwise the deceased does not rest peacefully and creates difficulty for the living. "If you do not mourn and bury your dead, who will mourn and bury you?" To say, "I will not attend [meaning contribute to] your funeral; I will not look on your dead body," is considered to be a very strong *olovo*. Refusing to contribute may invoke the wrath of the "gone soul." As "so many people die," reciprocal relations surrounding death are a frequent and never-ending requirement. Women must again rely on their influence to arrange for the necessary contributions. Once again, although the amount to be given is determined by how "close" or "distant" the deceased was to the living person, women are responsible for providing the appropriate tribute. Since funeral-giving is a requirement for "good Avalogoli," a woman takes pride and receives status by being seen as "one who provides well" for the dead as well as for the living.

State Politics

In the structures of state politics, women use their influence to add to their power. The political framework in which all Logoli people participate encompasses government officials on a national level—the President, Ministers and Members of Parliament—and nominated and elected candidates on the local level—the District Officer, Chiefs and Assistant Chiefs with their *amagutu* (headman), Kenyan police, and members of the local council.

Many women say that it is the government (i.e., men) that makes change. Generally, they consider that change to be "bad." Out of 64 women, 32 told me that it is the government that makes changes in their society. The question was not answered by two; 16 believe that people generally make change; five did not know; two believe it is the church; two answered men; four replied the government and people; and one woman believes it is the government and the church. "Bad" change is most often defined as an increase in prices for commodities upon which women rely. Government change is seen as bad by 36 out of 64 people. Change is thought to be both good and bad (good if you have money, and otherwise, bad) by 17; five see change as good; four did not answer; and two did not know.

Logoli women do not see themselves represented in state government. This is consistent throughout Kenya. In November 1987, a video conference made up of Kenyan and U.S. participants was held in Nairobi in order to determine, two years after the United Nations World Conference on women, if women's lot has improved. One of their reports stated: "Women are totally invisible in policy making." On a national level, since Independence, Parliament has had a maximum of three women MP's at any one time. During the 1983 general elections, seven women sought representation for the 158 parliamentary seats. Two were elected and one was nominated. In 1988, at least ten women vied for the 188 seats (there were 360 candidates overall); all except four were casualties of the nomination process. Of these four, one was nominated and one elected for a total of only two women Members of Parliament. This did not change in the 1993 elections.

In Maragoli, during the 1988 national election, one woman unsuccessfully ran for (council) office. When men and women were asked how they felt about women political candidates, invariably their first response was laughter. It was an amusing thought! After the initial reaction, some people said, "It's good for women to run," and a number of women said, "Women know women's needs." A few men believed women engaging in politics to be appropriate, and said, "It's just all right, times are changing." However, any comments they made could have been skewed by the fact that all knew my research interest was mainly in women. Two businessmen were advocating the woman contender, not because they were pro-women in politics, but because they were hoping she would defeat a particular man who was running against her. A pictorial presentation in *The Weekly Review* from the time of the election (March 11, 1988) seems to represent the popular attitude toward women engaging in political activity. It shows (in an undetermined location) women voters laughing, standing, and waving, with the caption "Prospective voters seem to have enjoyed the rare public drama to which they have been treated." The companion picture portrays a number of solemn, pensive, sitting men, and is captioned, "while some—though noticeably not the candidates—think it's still a serious business after all."

Government edicts are made with little electoral input, as people have limited means to act on the rights that government advocates. Maragoli women and men meet this lack of representation by deliberately misinterpreting government decrees for their own benefit. In the 1988 general election, President Moi's rallying call of *Nyayo* called upon the descendants of all ethnic groups to engage in *maendeleo* to help build the nation. According

ess. For example, if women were not "properly" provided for during the campaign, they loudly proclaimed the injustice. Common complaints were made: "I stayed there [at the candidate's house] for the morning without anything, not even tea;" the candidate "must give what it cost for the [KANU] stamps and add a bit more." It is women who gather at the homes of candidates they choose. They dance and provide information to support or gossip to oppose the candidates, influencing voters with the information they provide. The candidates in turn are aware of their influence. Assuring a "proper" supply of "tea and sugar" to women during campaigns is a significant measure of that awareness. This influence allows women to receive at least immediate benefits in the state political process. They loudly proclaim any injustice.

Following in the "footsteps of the ancestors" means for most Kenyans in positions of power (i.e., men) a retention of patriarchal sentiment. On the local level, it also provides a vehicle for the retention of traditional male power. Institutionally and ideologically, discussions and decisions in the political framework have always been men's responsibility. A complete acceptance of the underlying patriarchal sentiment similarly supported in the cultural rhetoric of the state is not in women's best interest. However, women recognise that they cannot afford to totally lose *Nyayo*, as it supports the collective sentiment upon which they rely. In today's patrimonial capitalist state, *Nyayo* provides yet another context within which women gain influence.

Abuse

On both the local and the state levels, women assure their continuing power through a cultural posture of ideological and institutional acceptance of male elder rule, while at the same time making decisions from the back door. This is particularly clear in the context of decisions made in the home. Even where it was obvious that women were making independent decisions, they said, "it is because I know how he wants the home to be run." Salome described herself as a "submissive wife," an attribute she considered to be the cultural ideal and in keeping with her Christian edicts. In contrast to the cultural ideal, Florah supervises her yard and the building of a new house independently of her husband. Given the effects of the capitalist market and the disadvantage this introduces for men, women's influence is actually growing. The power from the front door is being increasingly questioned by women as the power from the back door expands. Men often respond to these changes by retaliating. Florah's husband and his brothers referred to in the quote at the beginning of the section think women's "independence" has "gone too far."

It is becoming increasingly difficult for men to avoid the expanding range of power from the back door in Avalogoli daily life. The pressures from a capitalist system have confronted men with the reality of women's power. Abuse provides dramatic examples of the dynamics of reaction to the questioning of traditional male power. Both women and men say that abuse is more frequent today than in the past. Agnes has been "consistently beaten" by her husband for 20 years:

> He does not want me to have money, even my own salary; all money must go to him. When I ask for money, it is a war! This time he was taken to the police, but his relatives gave money for bond. He is out now, moving. This is called grievous harm, not assault. They say the case cannot come to court until I am healed. He is still trying to kill me; this is why I live behind the chained door. If I am able to testify it will be bad for him. Without me in the courtroom, he can make up stories. In Kenya the law is difficult. You tell them about a man and a wife and they take slow action, or they are given something little not to notice. Now my brother has gone one more time to the Chief to complain.

Agnes was barricaded in a small hut in her brother's yard. It took some time for her to undo the chains to allow me to enter. She had been severely cut with an *ubanga* and had more stitches than anyone could count. As I left her, I wondered if she would be able to unchain the door in time to escape should her husband decide to set fire to the thatched roof.

When interviewed on the subject of conjugal abuse, 43% out of 94 women said they were physically abused by their husbands. A further 52% said that although physical abuse was infrequently experienced, incidents of abuse were increasing. Men provided an economic rationale for this by saying that women "harass" men for support while they "only laze around." This assertion of failure of women to work and produce contradicts the evidence of women's actual output. An Assistant Chief in Maragoli describes the situation as follows:

> There are many cases which come to leaders in connection to domestic violence. The most difficult cases are those concerning fighting in families. It is difficult because many *avasatsa* [husbands] do not have employment; they do not work. Many leave early in the morning to go to groups with other people just to sit and talk; if they are drunkards they go to drink. They *kogotitsa lidiku* [lose the day]. When they come to their homes, because they have not brought any money or food they come home and begin beating their wives.

It seems that when husbands are unable or unwilling to provide, they strike out physically. Women say that the aspect of their lives they most dislike is being beaten by husbands. The women from Friend's Church agreed:

We cannot be happy if someone keeps doing that; we would rather have peace. Now, it is almost common, when there is not money to support the home, the mother wants money, she keeps asking, finally he gets angry and hits. But more and more she has no one else to ask.

Consider the case of Esta.

Esta

Esta's relationship with her husband appears to contain the characteristics of a classic double-bind situation:

My husband started beating me in 1947...unto this day he is still beating me. Even the [inyumba] people know. He comes home drunk and he asks a question; they all know how he beats me. After asking the question, you answer in one way he beats you; you answer in another way, he beats you. I ask for money; there is no resource to get money because he does not give me money. I came from a wealthy home. My father was rich. We never ground sorghum on the stone or anything like that; this is an example of how we lived [they always had cash to utilise the grinding mill]. I blame this [her situation] on the person who arranged my marriage, a school teacher. My mother died; when I got married my father said, look your mother is no longer here; to marry one person and move to the next one is no good. You marry this person you stay there. Also I had children. I could not leave the children. There is a woman here in [village name] who left her husband because he too used to make busaa and sell it, and drink. She left a number of children home. They grew, they are educated, they are teachers, they have other jobs. They are members here [in the village]; the problem is they do not want their mother because their mother left them. She has wanted to return but it is impossible to return. This is an example. I was beaten by slapping on the face and kicking. In 1949, he bit me on the nose. I bled and bled; that is why my nose is the way it is. I have tried everything possible; I have approached the church people. That did not work. After my mother died my father married again. I went to him and said I would like to get some job outside the home. Father said, "No. Your mother is dead; I have married again; you cannot get a job."[55] The [inyumba] is very sorry for me. Also, he blames me for not having enough children. I am not profitable. He is forever blaming me.

Conclusion to Part III

The conflict which occurs in Avalogoli society affects reciprocal relations. Within families, arguments take place between husbands and wives, children, parents, siblings and affinal relatives; these disputes spill over into the collectivity. Consanguines and affines debate about who should provide resources and how the resources should be distributed. Wives complain of husbands not sharing resources they receive from relatives and affines. Husbands complain that wives are hiding gifts, or that their provision of food to relatives and affines leaves the home yard without food. Women and men both complain that children do not provide them with support, or argue about how much each should receive if support is given, accusing each other of hiding the "real" amount provided. Children in contexts such as these accuse parents of having "big pockets that never get filled." In turn, parents hold up other parents in slightly better economic circumstances as examples; they say that the children's support has allowed these parents to "progress." Mothers argue that a portion of their daughters' *uvukwi* should be given to them: they say, "Who gave birth to this child, did he?" Daughters-in-law threaten to "walk" unless a part of their *uvukwi* is sent to their parents. Wives "push" husbands to "push" their fathers to send a cow to their parents.

In the midst of these conflicts, women "work hard" to accumulate the needed production so that their mothers may receive their gifts and their fathers may receive their cows. "My father *must* get his cows," they say, and become conscious actors in the economic sphere. Ritah, for example, removes herself from production and participation until *uvukwi* questions are answered. Logoli women contribute to paying their own *uvukwi* and also assist their sons in paying theirs. *Uvukwi* thus comes from women's production as well as men's. Florah and Alice, who have jobs, save money and buy livestock to pay their own *uvukwi*. Little if any mention of women's productive contribution to bridewealth is found in other research, where men's contributions and men's receipts are the topics of analysis.

The expectation that women should provide sustenance for their own families permeates the entire kinship network, and is enacted in the life cycle of marriage, birth and death. Superficially, it appears that cultural prescriptions about male power in Avalogoli life contain and restrict women's actions; however, women use these cultural rules and gain power over them. Women's ability to sustain and expand their cultural roles gains them considerable economic and political power in relationships with men. For most Avalogoli, domestic and wage labour production are inadequate. Women cannot depend on men for sustenance. Families are large and production is inconsistent. Notwithstanding the difficulties which patriarchal ideology and capitalist systems impose, women must take a central role in production. They are well aware of their added value as they perform not only with resignation but also with commitment.

Men are supposed to make all the important decisions in Avalogoli life. With the intrusion of a cash economy and the subsequent exacerbation of gender inequality, this has become increasingly difficult. Women continue to do what they have always done, even within the constraints of a patriarchal system. Women keep kinship networks working for them, fulfil their "home work" responsibilities, and engage in "outside work." Their ability to access avenues of reciprocity provides the economic basis for the survival of Avalogoli society. This represents a power for women which men fully recognise. Women are vigilant caretakers of patriarchal ideology to the extent that this sentiment is productive in their everyday lives. Today, women are beginning to speak of the unfairness contained in this sentiment. Traditional society limited male rule and the opinion of the collectivity was adhered to. But today, people say, "you may not interfere in the yards of others, they will have the law on you." Men attempt to control their yards, and in some cases attempt to curtail women's solidarity. In response to women gathering together, many men make the statement, "Women should stay in their own yards. Women who run to other yards make trouble in their own." Families are more nucleated and men are alienated. With their creativity, hard work and intelligence, women are questioning if the protection of male rule is worth the cost.

CHURCH GROUP: WOMEN GATHERING

Part IV

"POSTERITY" AND "PROGRESS," NEEDS AND MEANS

Introduction to Part IV

Part IV gives the detail on two related issues that directly affect Logoli people: "posterity" and "progress," or *maendeleo*. As mentioned, the cultural ideal of the "good life" in Maragoli requires land, cattle and children. Too little of the first, too few of the second, and what seems to be an overabundance of the third have placed Avalogoli in a position of risk.

"Overpopulation"—a tricky concept theoretically, politically and practically—stimulates endless "development" research. Poor economic conditions are often explained away with stereotypical and ethnocentric views that "African women have too many children."[56] Emic and edic approaches to what constitutes an acceptable population level collide, and at the moment of "truth," as we see in Maragoli, poverty reigns. What is analytically interesting is that there is confusion regarding over- and under-population on the macro level, and that (surprise!) attitudes on a micro level, although different, are equally confused.

There is an awareness that some aspects of the question of overpopulation are misrepresented in the research (cf. Chazan, Mortimer, Ravenhill, & Rothchild, 1992; Gordon & Gordon, 1992; Ahlberg, 1991; Acholla-Ayayo, 1988; Hartmann, 1987; Ndeti & Ndeti, 1980). Considering this, Kenyan indigenous research taking the view that overpopulation exists requires a hearing. In addition, an examination of the arguments that hold only women responsible for overpopulation is required. The chapter on population applies an anthropological perspective to the question of policy regarding overpopulation, which has as its basis the idea that overpopulation contributes to poverty, and as such is a major detriment to development. We briefly explore the general African context using mainly Western research and focus primarily on Kenya, extrapolating from Kenyan research. We move from an analysis of quantitative survey data on population to qualitative ethnographic data provided by Logoli women. Logoli women are provided with a platform to add their voices to the overpopulation predicament. Women's impressions of men's responsibility for overpopulation are thus displayed, as women discuss how they believe men influence their reproductive decisions. The information given by Logoli women conveys the opinion of one sex about the other, not the reality experienced by the other. While this does not provide a gender-balanced perspective, it does allow us to question assumptions about culture which are made when only a male perspective is taken into account. The technique is thus justified: "In order to counter-balance the monosexual tradition of Western thought, it will be necessary, for a considerable period of time, to conduct special studies of women which look at issues from a female perspective" (Eichler & Lapointe, 1985, 12). The addition of empirical data on the pivotal population-related question of fertility provides further insight.

Taking the population predicament into account, Chapter Eight concentrates on aspects of women's solidarity efforts in development, providing detail on Kenyan and Maragoli Women Groups. More than two decades of attention to women's place in African societies has forced acknowledgment of widespread diversity in women's roles and statuses. Much research has focussed on economic issues and development initiatives involving women who are embedded in sets of socio-culturally contextualised relationships. Models in current use arise from three basic critical strategies. First is the criticism of the optimism about economic progress of women through modernisation, which usually entails the imposition of a capitalist economic system. Second is the re-evaluation of the role of women to reflect their changing status in contexts where an underlying emphasis on patriarchal ideology has endured and expanded through changing economic practices and deliberate state policies. The third approach, connected to the second and crucial for this research, emphasises a topic which is absent or incipient in early research: the association of women's decision-making power in economic, social and political spheres with gender and class inequalities. Today's literature speaks about women's continuing hard work within changing systems of production and women's contribution to economics and development issues. It examines women's responses to economic restructuring (i.e. under structural adjustment policies) and issues of their empowerment via case studies (cf. Blumberg et al., 1994). Particularly salient in these examinations is women's solidarity, although there is a problem when solidarity efforts are assumed to provide economic betterment.

African women's efforts in women's groups are portrayed locally, nationally, and globally as a viable means for economically successful ventures which result in improved economic conditions. Researchers have recognised that Africa has a particularly rich heritage of women cooperating with women in secret societies, revolutionary groups,[57] official women's organisations that may be associated with a ruling party, employment and trade union organisations, voluntary associations, modern cooperatives,[58] rural work groups, and urban and rural groups mobilised for development purposes (cf. Chazan et al., 1992; Gordon & Gordon, 1992; Staunton, 1991; Stamp, 1989, 1986; Nzomo, 1989; March & Taqqu, 1986; Riria-Ouko, 1985; Wipper, 1984, 1975-76, 1975). As a result, women's difficult financial circumstances are often only responded to—if they are responded to at all by the government or other self-help enterprises providing economic assistance—through organised women's groups like the Women in Development (WID), (*Maendeleo ya Wanawake*) groups in Kenya (cf. Stamp, 1989; Moi, 1986). Unfortunately, the expectation that these groups will help women has been used to legitimise inaction on other fronts.

Chapter Seven

SHE EATS FOR NOTHING!

It is curious—if not unethical—that the Western concept of overpopulation (i.e., that in some sense usually pertaining to world systems economic theory, there are too many people) has been most frequently applied by outsiders to the situation in Africa. Western researchers, development workers, world financial organisations, foreign media, donor governments, and particularly these governments' taxpayers describe African reproductive behaviour as "irrational,"[59] as if ignorance were a variable. Many Africans are now convinced that they have too many children, and that if they have fewer in the future, their economic situations will improve. However, limitations exist in logico-deductive theoretical approaches that borrow from classical economic theory; such approaches inevitably involve the utilitarian assumption that people maximise the utility of their choices through rational assessment of their alternatives (cf. Nerlove, Razin, & Sadka, 1987). These "cost-benefit" models of decision-making provide the opportunity for ethnocentric assumptions regarding women's "non-rational" assessments of "costs" and "benefits". There is a failure to recognise that Western cost-benefit models may not be entirely compatible with culturally relative assessments of costs and benefits in other areas of the world. Although the capitalist economic model, with its emphasis on individual accumulation of wealth, is pervasive and even necessary for understanding, there are contexts in which it is not the best tool for analysis. Other models intrude. For example, in contexts where children are seen as "precious like coral" (Mazrui, 1986) or as "posterity" (Abwunza, 1985; and this book), the overwhelming costs of raising and educating them, even in situations of abject poverty, may still be counter-balanced by these ideological benefits.

It is also curious and unethical that "causes" of and "solutions" to overpopulation are most often directed at women rather than both sexes, as if men do not procreate. One of the reasons postulated for the "failure" of family planning programs is the dependent status of women, who see a large family as an economic and social necessity (cf. Ginsburg & Rapp, 1991; Handwerker, 1991; Population Policy Guidelines, 1984b, 17; Ndeti & Ndeti, 1980; Mott & Mott, 1980; Boserup, 1970). Thus, women are seen as not empowered to "pursue goals independently of their childbearing capacity" (Handwerker, 1991, 62). Handwerker is of course quite correct in his assessment that women are often excluded from areas that Westerners define as influential or powerful outside reproductive areas. However, this is not a comprehensive representation. In Maragoli, both men and women gain economic help and status from fertility. To assign the responsibility for overpopulation to one particular sex is plainly discriminatory.

Much research says women lack power in social, political and economic situations (cf. Handwerker, 1991), and that African women are often presented as subordinate (Stichter & Parpart, 1988, 14-23). However, it is even more curious that there is still an expectation that women will have—indeed, should have—the power to solve overpopulation and poverty by not having so many children. If we are to assume African women's subordinate position, then to say, "African *women* have too many children" can be little other than victim-blaming.

African Overpopulation

The African continent is in fact sparsely populated. Compared with Western European and Asian standards, it is underpopulated. In the eighteenth century, 20% of the world's population lived in Africa; by the year 2000, less than 13% will (Hartmann, 1987, 17). Underpopulation is given as an important factor that held back African economic development. There is even an argument that the emphasis on family planning may be an "ideological ploy" by capitalist societies to blame the poor (and "their overbreeding") for Africa's poverty, neglecting any investigation of economic and political inequalities in the global economy (cf. Gordon & Gordon, 1992, 135). Many African officials and a few anthropologists have maintained that in order to develop African countries' resources, a larger population is required. Research centred on demographic and social realities, rather than on simplistic notions of general overpopulation, has thus been advocated (cf. Gordon & Gordon, 1992, 134-35; Franke, 1981).

The United Nations Population Fund, development agencies, and family planning proponents from capitalist industrial nations appear to take a "neo-Malthusian" position on overpopulation. This holds that there is a correlation between high birth rates and low living standards in the so-called Third World, and that increasing demands for necessities, particularly food, will be overwhelming (cf. Sadik, 1991). They note that Africa is heavily dependent on agriculture, and that because much of the land base is unsuitable for intensive human use, increasing population exacerbates ecological damage and poverty (cf. Gordon & Gordon, 1992; Sadik, 1991; Timberlake, 1986). The philosophy of population control which has influenced the activities of most international aid organisations rests upon three basic assumptions: overpopulation causes the Third World's development problems (hunger, environmental destruction, economic stagnation and political instability); people must be persuaded or forced to have fewer children before conditions will improve; and birth control services can be provided for women and should be promoted, and pregnancy prevention should even take precedence over health and safety concerns. The overriding goal of family planning programs is to reduce population growth (Hartmann, 1987, xiii).

Yet some population experts are pointing out how the developing world is currently engaged in a "reproductive revolution;" family planning is regarded as the key factor. Fertility is declining, although the decline is not following the classic demographic transition theory which is commonly applied to industrial countries, where improved living conditions appear to be the key factor leading to the decline (cf. Robey, Rutstein, & Morris, 1993). Conditions in Africa are inconsistent with the premise that population decline follows development. Thus, the theory that overpopulation difficulties are associated with underdevelopment or poor living standards for citizens is called into question. Fertility rates are declining in Africa, even though living standards have deteriorated. Robey et al. point out that even in countries where few people use contraception, educated women no longer believe that large numbers of children provide them with economic and social status, or that fate decides family size. These authors say the idea that "development is the best contraceptive" is controversial: "The pace at which fertility will keep decreasing [depends] on three interrelated factors: how fast societies develop; how quickly new norms concerning small families and the use of family planning are accepted; and, perhaps most important, how well public programs and private suppliers can meet the need for contraception" (Robey et al., 1993, 60-67).

Disputes about the reason for population decline aside, we cannot doubt that overpopulation equals poverty: although droughts and wars leading to famines are also strong variables, excessive population growth does lead to hardship. By 1985, the number of absolute poor in Africa was 47%; this population constituted 16% of all the poor in the developing world. An additional 100 million poor is projected by 2000, which means that Africa will have 30% of all the poor in the developing world (World Bank, 1990, 5, 29). Africa's population growth rate is the highest in the world (cf. World Bank Reports, 1986, 1989, 1990; Chazan et al., 1992, 25, 232) and has been described as having "exploded" in the post-independence era (Gordon & Gordon, 1992, 76). The continent's population is 648 million, three times what it was in 1950. It may reach 2.6 billion by 2030, a five-fold increase which will result from high fertility and declining mortality rates.

Interestingly, the World Bank has predicted that replacement-level fertility (each woman giving birth to two children) will exist in Africa by 2035-2040 (1986, 10). It remains unclear how this is to come about when there is no prediction for such a severe drop in growth rates, which are projected at over 3% in 2000, and where fertility levels—the total number of children women have before the end of their childbearing years—are projected at 5.9 in 2000. Even if the revolution in family planning and development occurs and an ideological shift legitimises smaller family size, it would still be 80 to 100 years before population stopped growing (cf. World Bank, 1986, 10). It is doubtful that the media's presumptions that Africans continue to contribute to their own economic decline would change. It appears that catch-up time is not permitted for Africans: a "do it by next week" mentality exists.

The entire appraisal of overpopulation and population decline in Africa emerges as inappropriate. First, it is inappropriate to measure Africa against all other regions of the world where population rates have gone down since 1965, since those regions have generally moved from agrarian to industrial-based societies. For the most part, Africa remains agrarian. There is no good reason to assume that non-similar conditions will produce similar results, in particular that a smaller family ideology will occur in Africa because it has in the remainder of the world. Second, population growth as it has occurred in Africa is unprecedented, so comparison with the rest of the world is not practicable. In fact, we know only that fertility has declined in Africa and that smaller family ideology is being introduced. In what follows, we examine overpopulation as it has affected Kenya specifically.

Kenyan Overpopulation

Kenya has the highest natural increase in population ever recorded in the world for a single country. This was measured variously at 3.8% annually in 1980-88 (World Bank, 1990), 3.9% (Republic of Kenya, 1984a, 1),[60] and at present is 4% (Chazan et al., 1992, 25) or 4.1% (Staudt & Col, 1991, 246). Inconsistencies aside, the level and rate of fertility have been very high.

By 2025, the Kenyan population is predicted to be over four times larger than it was in 1980 (Gordon & Gordon, 1992, 124). In combination with a decreasing death rate (although it is still high according to world standards),[61] the expectation was that the Kenyan population would double every 17 years (Mott & Mott, 1980, 4). More recently, this number has been changed to every 15 years (Chazan et al., 1992, 25). Kenyan research confirms these predictions, reporting that should these levels of growth continue, the 1984 population of 19.5 million will be 39 million in 2002, 50 million in 2009, and 100 million before 2025, a five-fold increase in 40 years (Republic of Kenya, 1984a, 1).

Kenya has been a forerunner in family planning services since the late 1950s and early 1960s. The Family Planning Association of Kenya was organised by a private Kenyan colonial group in 1961 to provide information and education on birth control. It merged urban family planning associations in Nairobi, Mombasa and Nakuru which were initiated in the second half of the 1950s. In 1966, three years after Kenya's independence, a population council advisory mission was invited to study the population situation. As a result of this mission's report, the National Family Planning Programme was set up in 1967. By 1968, the Kenyan government had a policy to provide family planning services to all people of childbearing age via the Ministry of Health (Republic of Kenya, 1984a). The services were to be voluntary, respecting individual customs and values. Emphasis was placed on limiting family size and allowing adequate time between children. As Kenya's health infrastructure and trained personnel were then limited, the Ministry of Health depended on private organisations like the International Planned Parenthood Federation and the Family Planning Association of Kenya to carry out family planning programs (Population Policy Guidelines, 1984b, 2). The International Family Planning Foundation set up the African Regional Council in 1971, and Kenya became a member. At the 1974 World Population Conference in Bucharest, Kenya expressed a desire to slow population growth, and by the end of 1975, Kenya had an official policy to reduce population growth. In 1982-83, the National Council for Population and Development was organised via the Office of the Vice President and Ministry of Home Affairs. The Council was to co-ordinate the activities of the government ministries and non-governmental organisations involved in the Integrated Rural Health/Family Planning Programme. In 1984, a private sector family planning program was also established.

The goal of these organisations was to reduce Kenyan's population growth rate (Population Policy Guidelines, 1984b, 7). Much information did not reach rural areas such as Maragoli, but by 1985, President Moi and the then Vice-President Kibaki were making public statements in Kenya recommending family planning. At the United Nations International Conference on Population in Mexico in 1985, Kibaki discussed the need to "stabilise" Kenya's population. Family planning in Kenya has not progressed according to the standards set by developed countries. This situation has only recently begun to improve, in spite of the fact that the World

Bank holds that assisting Africa with plans to lower population is its highest priority in structural adjustment strategies supporting sustainable development (World Bank, 1986).

The population growth in Kenya highlights and exacerbates problems. The burden of dependents on workers is high: in 1979, statistics showed 113 dependents for every 100 economically active people. Even if all of the latter were constantly employed (and unemployment levels say that they are not) the ratio retards gains in living standards. Kenya's land space— 582,626 square kilometres (measured in 1979)—has approximately 17.5% cultivable land with an average density of 154 persons per square kilometre (Population Policy Guidelines, 1984b, 9). The availability of basic services, food, education, health care, and housing is impaired by rapid population growth.

The goals of the Kenyan National Council for Population encompass demography, education, and clinical services. Demographic goals include: reducing population growth by encouraging Kenyans to reduce both the number of children they have and ideal family size; helping people who want children but are unable to have them; reducing infant and child mortality; reducing rural urban migration; and (interestingly) motivating Kenyan men to adopt and practice family planning. The educational goals include promoting higher education, training and making available productive wage labour for women to improve their status, improving general education levels for men and women, and providing young people with information and education about population matters. The clinical services goals ensure the availability of contraceptives, counselling, and follow-up with contraceptive users. In addition, the Council promotes health and family planning through providing contraceptives and being aware of the type and quality of contraceptives which are distributed (Population Policy Guidelines, 1984b, 16-8).

The reality of the Kenyan overpopulation predicament is that family planning has experienced success according to both Kenyan standards and the mandate of international aid organisations (even if it is seen as lethargic by the latter). Fertility levels remain very high, but Kenya has recently projected a decline to 6.7 children per woman. The total fertility level has declined (cf. Bradley, 1991; Poole, 1991, 4) from 8.1 in 1977-78 to 6.7 in 1989 (Kenya Demographic and Health Survey, 1989). This is an amazing drop in slightly over a decade! Eighty-one percent of Republic of Kenya respondents (all women) knew of at least one family planning method (Republic of Kenya, 1984a, 65).[62] Contraceptive use, both modern and traditional, has a projected increase to 27% among married women of childbearing age in the year 2000 (Poole 1991, 4; Republic of Kenya,

1984a). In spite of these positive signs of change, Muganzi has stated that the influence of family planning programs on fertility is minimal, and that unless "drastic change" (meaning government intervention) takes place, this is unlikely to change in the next decade (1988, 35).[63]

Stronger government intervention is unlikely. Population policy in Kenya has rested on two factors: response to foreign donors who advocate, and even insist on, population decline, and Kenyan-inspired economic and health values influenced by contextual political vacillation. Part of this vacillation has to do with what has been called the government's "take it or leave it" commitment to family planning. In all likelihood, that strategy is motivated by the government's desire to avoid the appearance of targeting certain ethnic groups for family planning (cf. Ndeti & Ndeti, 1980, 144).

Muganzi cites information from KCPS (1984) showing that although 81% of the women surveyed know of at least one method of contraception, only 17% are using any method (1988, 35). Annual population growth is expected to be 3.4% between now and 2000. The overpopulation predicament is well-recognised in Kenya at government, research, and local levels. Ominde (1988, ix) discusses how the Kenyan nation has shifted from concentrating on the present to a deep concern about the future: "This transformation is part of a world-wide change from blind faith in material progress and in the product of Western technology." The change is reflected in "a concern with the future implications of our human numbers [as] a well established pattern of dialogue."

This dialogue must—and for Kenyan researchers who are insiders to the predicament, does—take into account the socio-cultural contexts which support the continuity of social systems, particularly as regards culturally-defined ideal family size. For example, the research of Ndeti and Ndeti pointed out that a higher acceptance of contraception will not be possible "until the Kenyan people cease to perceive strong economic and psychosocial benefits of having many children" (1980, 144). Knowledge about the interaction between cultural values and population requires "a more effective integration of development policies with people's values" (Ndeti & Ndeti, 1980, 3).

All agrarian societies value large families, but family size in Kenya and Africa generally exceeds that found in other developing regions. Hyden (1983) writes of the "economy of affection," a system promoted and sustained by ties to rural areas and a subsistence mode of production that depends upon large families. These ties are still in evidence, even though families today cannot withdraw from the market into autarky as Hyden posits they should. In Western Kenya, for example, 40 to 50 percent of households depend on purchased food. Men migrate to urban areas to seek work, or fail to help with "women's work." Agriculture and home work (women's work) are labour-intensive, and women thus need children to help them. Patronage relationships based on ethnicity and kinship are vital to gaining access to resources, jobs, schooling or money. Children are valuable assets even in urban areas *especially* because people face economic risk.

There is an actual relationship between population growth rates, birth rates, and desired family size (cf. Muganzi, 1988, 38; United Nations, 1984). Changes in population growth rates will depend upon lowering family size expectations or desires, which entails a change in cultural ideology. Acholla-Ayayo says, "although natural fertility variations are primarily determined by biological processes, they are also affected and modified by socio-cultural, socio-economic and behavioural factors" (1988, 57). Ayiemba (1988) points out how worldwide demographic research on the family is only a decade old and "underdeveloped." In Kenya, this research is described as being in its "infancy." The complications of families and households, inadequate databases, the lack of a suitable analytic framework, and the absence of relevant models predicting family transformations inhibit the research (Ayiemba, 1988, 48; cf. Bongaarts, 1985).

This "infant" research classifies family fertility levels in various areas of Kenya according to the average number of children per woman: very high, greater than eight; high, greater than seven, less than eight; medium, more than five, less than seven; and low, less than five (Ottieno, Osieo, & Acholla-Ayayo, 1988, 17). Family fertility levels are said to increase because of health improvement and in-migration; they are said to decrease because of education, place of residence and marital status. All variables are understood only as they refer to women.

Women who have primary school education have the highest fertility rates, greater than those with no education or those with secondary education. It is believed that women must have secondary education in order for change in family size attitude to take place (Njogu, 1991, 83; Republic of Kenya, 1984a). Education levels for women are rising (Ayiemba, 1988, 56).

Urban fertility is on average slightly lower than rural. Greater economic constraints in urban areas, as well as knowledge of and availability of contraceptives help in lowering levels. But internal migration and cultural norms are related to increasing fertility levels. People who manifest a cultural ideology favouring high fertility levels bring that ideology to settlement schemes and urban areas (Ottieno et al., 1988, 16-21).

Ayiemba provides models of transformation in patterns of marital status through analysing information gathered from Kenyan women. The results show that the proportion of women remaining single and the age of first marriage are rising, while women's desire for large numbers of children is lowering. These trends, combined with political campaigns to change "people's" perception of family size are leading to an expectation that fertility will decline (Ayiemba, 1988, 56).

Both marital and non-marital fertility contribute to high fertility levels. Acholla-Ayayo speaks of factors that contribute to higher fertility rates: norms, beliefs, and values; ideologies resistant to change; and even certain changes, like the shift from polygyny to monogamy. A deviation from the traditional practice of marriage, this change from polygyny to monogamy puts greater pressure on individuals to prove their fertility, thereby increasing fertility levels. There are research findings that reveal higher fertility levels in monogamous relationships in comparison with polygynous relationships (cf. Acholla-Ayayo, 1988; Republic of Kenya, 1984a, below; Mosley, Warner, & Brecker, 1982; Henin, 1980; but see Sheperd, 1984, for a counterview). Non-marital fertility is also significant in Kenya. For example, in 43 districts in Kenya, 14 have single women with an average of more than five children per woman; 19 have single women with an average of more than four children per woman; seven districts have single women with an average of more than three children per woman; and there are only two districts with single women with an average of less than two children per woman (Acholla-Ayayo, 1988, 57).

Acholla-Ayayo's interpretation of the research has moralistic overtones. For example, there is the statement that "if parents of the deviant girl [deviant being unmarried and pregnant] accept responsibility to assist the young mother and the child, many more examples will follow." The research commentary does not promote a return to the traditional polygynous arrangement to help lower fertility levels. This research describes maintaining polygyny as deviant and advocates an extensive alteration of societal attitude toward monogamy. Concerning family planning, the study reports that 40% of the female population of Kenya between ages of 15 and 49 must use contraceptives constantly for the next 14 years in order to reduce the population growth rate by 2.5% (Acholla-Ayayo, 1988, 63).

However, Ayiemba (1988, 56; cf. Republic of Kenya, 1984a, 119) warns that increased medical services to rural areas and increased primary education to females will cause fertility levels to remain high for some time, unless economic pressures and enforced government intervention of family planning services takes place. Hope lies in the projection that by the year 2000, educated urban residents will lead the way in reducing ideal family size norms.

Acholla-Ayayo's findings indicate that 15% of Kenyan women are using a method of family planning. Of this, 8.1% are using modern methods and 6.9% are using the traditional methods of rhythm, withdrawal and abstinence.[64] Elsewhere, the figures show more than a doubling in use, from 7% in 1977-78 to 17% in 1984 (Republic of Kenya, 1984a, 83; see also Muganzi, 1988, above). Acholla-Ayayo states that it is an unrealistic expectation that in slightly over a decade (the magic year of 2000) transformations will take place in socio-cultural ideology (1988, 57) if a "persuasive policy" alone is used (1988, 62).

For the most part, only differentials involving women are taken into account when Kenya's high fertility levels are examined, while factors involving men are largely disregarded (cf. Republic of Kenya, 1984a). In their 1980 publication, Ndeti and Ndeti criticised Knowledge-Attitude Practice surveys which purport to examine fertility behaviour. Ndeti and Ndeti argue that in African societies where the opinions of elders and husbands have more influence than those of young wives, it is ironic that the surveys depend upon the responses of women in their reproductive years. They say that this choice leads to a distortion in the presentation of the Kenyan family (1980, 3). For example, in the KCPS (1984a) survey, significant determining factors of levels of fertility, contraceptive knowledge and use, and desired family size were said to be the age of the mother, her place of residence, and her education. A "behavioural" difference exits between urban and rural women. Urban women marry later, have a smaller average number of children, smaller desired family size, and higher contraceptive knowledge and use. Yet rural women have longer durations of breast feeding and sexual abstinence, behavioural patterns that also lower their fertility level. KCPS research finds that women's education is positively related to smaller family sizes. Highly-educated women marry later, have smaller families, and desire two fewer children than women with no education. Contraceptive knowledge and use increases with the number of years of schooling. In measuring differences in levels of literacy for both sexes, the study finds that although illiterate women married to literate men had more contraceptive knowledge and use than literate women married to illiterate men, literate women married to illiterate men had a smaller desired family size. This does suggest that women's literacy has a positive effect on fertility reduction (Republic of Kenya, 1984a, 120). According to KCPS, contraceptive use is heavily influenced by husbands' reproductive intention. For example, 26% of rural couples have used contraception when only the wife wants to limit family size, as opposed to 40% when only the husband desires a limit (1984, 81). However, the husband's objection to contraceptive use is measured as a minor reason for not using contraception: only 9% of non-users cited husband's opposition (Republic of Kenya, 1984, 96).

Many people using contraceptives (58%) get their supply from government services, hospitals and clinics. Other sources include the Family Planning Association (27%), private sources, pharmacies and doctors (8%), and church organisations (6%) (Republic of Kenya, 1984, 105). Problems in getting services are listed as cost, distance, fear of speaking to young nurses at hospitals and clinics, poor services, and that preferred methods are not available. Cost is listed as a significant concern among three out of ten users (30%) in Kenya (Republic of Kenya, 1984a, 108). Interestingly, all government-supported services are distributed free (but see the section on Maragoli below concerning the issue of supply). The next greatest problem in getting services is fear of speaking to young nurses (25.4%), a full percentage point more significant than distance (24.4%) (Republic of Kenya, 1984a, 108; again, see Maragoli below).

When compared to the 1977-78 Kenya Fertility Survey (KFS), the KCPS of 1984 confirms many of the differentials given in the earlier research. The KFS found that Kenya was characterised by high fertility rates. This has changed very little in almost a decade. On the positive side, the number of pregnant women dropped, from 13% in 1977-78 to 11% in 1984. Use of contraceptives has more than doubled, from 7% in 1977-78 to 17% in 1984. This increase is a major finding of the KCPS and is considered a significant sign of success for the Family Planning Programme in Kenya. Other significant successes are connected to desired family size. Married women of childbearing age who said they did not want any more children almost doubled from 17% in 1977-78 to 32% in 1984. The average desired family size dropped from 7.2 children to 6.3. Although this is still quite high compared with countries where fertility is low, it is a marked improvement from previous desired family size. The KCPS recommends promoting still lower levels of desired family size.

In Kenya, provincial boundaries run along ethnic boundaries (except in Nairobi and Mombasa), and differentials caused by ethnicity follow. Ethnic group cultural structures and ideologies about marriage age, types of marital unions, postpartum abstinence, and breast-feeding affect the use of modern contraceptives (cf. Njogu, 1991). Cultural structures supported by ideologies surrounding "the good life" also have an effect. In Western Province, the area of this case analysis, the knowledge and use of contraception and knowledge of family planning outlets were low relative with the other Kenyan provinces (Republic of Kenya, 1984a, 120). The major ethnic group in Western Province is Abaluhya (Population Census Analytical Report, 1979), of which Avalogoli are a sub-ethnic group. Abaluhya cultural structures and ideology about the "good life" centre on having many children.

Western Province and Kakamega District

In the well-populated Western Province, the family fertility levels range from high (more than seven, less than eight) to very high (more than eight) (Ottieno et al., 1988, 17). At 5%, Western Province has the lowest current use rate of contraceptives in Kenya (Republic of Kenya, 1984a, 87; cf. Njogu, 1991, 91).[65] In the 1986 Kenya Contraceptive Prevalence Survey Provincial Report (KCPSPR), the average woman had more than nine births, the total fertility rate was 6.3, and 14% of the women were pregnant at the time of the interview. This was higher than the national average of 11% (see Republic of Kenya, 1984a above). The mean ideal or desired family size for women living in Western Province is 6.0 children; currently-married women desire 6.5 children, more than those never married, who desire 4.7. Where both wife and husband are illiterate, the mean ideal family size is seven children, averaging one child more than when both wife and husband are literate.

Knowledge of contraceptive methods is relatively low: 69% know one method. This figure varies with age: 82% of women aged 25 to 34 know at least one method, as opposed to only 60% and 71% among younger and older women respectively. Only 14% of the women have ever used any method of contraception and 9% of them report using a modern method. Use of contraceptives is higher among women over 24 years of age, among those with more than eight years of schooling, those who have worked outside the home, and those who did not want more children before their last pregnancy. Literacy also has an effect. When both husband and wife are illiterate, the one-time use rate is 6% compared with 22% among literate couples (KCPSPR, 1986, 27-29). According to the KCPSPR, the current level of contraceptive use in Western Province is the lowest in Kenya, at 4% (1986, 29; see KCPS above, showing 5%).

Approval of family planning and the intention among current non-users to use family planning in the future in Western Province gives a contradictory picture: 81% say they intend to use contraceptives in the future, but only 70% approve of family planning. The known methods of contraception are the pill (62%), injection (52%), the IUD (47%), and female sterilisation (37%). The method preferences among those who intend to use contraceptives in the future are injection (44%) and the pill (33%). Data on the perceived (rather than the actual) availability of family planning services show that 45% of non-users know a family planning outlet; 82% mentioned hospitals and 17% mentioned clinics as the preferred source. Only 20% of those women can reach the source within 30 minutes. Most would spend an hour or more to get there; 70% of them would walk. A small number of women, 11%, who know about contraceptives but do not use them, have been visited at home by a field educator. This report concludes that one out of every five women in Western Province is at risk of an unwanted or unplanned pregnancy. Among the women at risk, 21% do not know about contraceptives, 89% have never used any method, 65% do not know of a source, and 40% do not intend to use a method in the future (KCPSPR, 1986, 29-30).

In spite of these figures, provincial statistics for Western Province on attendance at family planning clinics show marked increases during the period 1981 to 1987. First visits increased from 3,625 to 31,371; re-visits increased from 13,336 to 127,677; and acceptors increased from 3,604 to 31,329 (Statistical Abstract 1990, 202).

In Kakamega District,[66] the mean number of children ever born per woman by selected ages are 5.0 for 25 to 34 year-olds and 8.8 for those 35 to 49; by level of education, this was 8.7 for those with no education, 8.9 for those with one to four years, 7.8 for five to eight years, and (8.7) for nine years or more.[67] Illiterate women had on average 9.0 children, while those who were literate had 8.1. The effects of a couple's literacy for currently married women show that where both are illiterate, the mean number of children ever born is 9.5; where both are literate, 7.8; where the husband is literate, and the wife not, 9.0; where the wife is literate, and the husband is not, 9.6 children. In polygynous relationships, for currently married women, those with no co-wife have 8.9 children, and those with a co-wife or co-wives have 8.2. Concerning currently married women's and couples' reproductive intentions, 26.2% of women want more children later and 21.2% want them soon; 16.9% want no more children. According to women interviewed, 36.9% of couples want more children, while in 17.8% of cases, neither want more. Although not discussed, husband's reproductive intentions have an influence. The difference appears statistically important between women who want more children (26.3%—later and 21.2%—soon) and couples who want more children (36.9%), as the sample includes the same women.

The mean ideal family size for Kakamega District is 6.0 children.[68] One contraceptive method is known by 70.4% of women surveyed; 3.4% are using a method. The largest clusters surrounding the small number of those who use family planning methods surround age (5.4% are 25 to 34); level of education (8.4% have nine or more years); working outside the home (11%);

and those with living children (5.9% with four and 5.7% with five or more). An amazing number of respondents in Kakamega District, 80.6%, say they intend to use family planning in the future, even though only 68.2% say they approve of family planning. According to women, husband approval of future family planning use in this area is low, 33.2% among these 80.6% future users. Consistently in the province (and nationwide figures), the highest future use clusters are in the never-married group, those aged 25 to 34, those with five to eight years of education, and those who already have one, three, or four living children.

Currently-married non-users (excluding pregnant women and women with no contraceptive knowledge) in Kakamega District provide their reasons for not using family planning: 8.4% want more children; 8.4% disapprove of family planning; 5.8% say their husband disapproves; 7.6% fear side effects; 13.6% cite a lack of knowledge; 3.3% say they do not know where to get contraceptives or find it difficult; 5.3% say they are too young to use contraceptives; 9.7% say they do not get pregnant easily; 19.3% say they are infertile or not sexually active; and 4.2% say they are postpartum. Women not using contraceptives say that if they used, they would prefer a hospital for their source; for the majority it would take more than one hour walking to get there. Only 11.8% of women in Kakamega District have ever been visited by a field educator in family planning. Of those who have never used contraceptives, 91.1% are at risk of unplanned and unwanted pregnancy: 17.7% say they do not know a method, 65.2% say they do not know a source, and 38.4% say they will not use a contraceptive (KCPSPR, 1986).[69]

Maragoli

The District is the smallest geographical area for which data were collected in the 1984 KCPS and 1986 KCPSPR. However, Maragoli Location has been and continues to be a resource for high fertility and overpopulation research. As we have seen, economic hardship is common in Maragoli. Wage labour positions are scarce and there is no sign of improvement. Agricultural land for personal subsistence is expensive and scarce. Since Ssennyonga's 1978 demographic analysis of a Maragoli sub-location, the "dangerous" and "frightening" population levels he predicted have come about.

Thirteen years after Ssennyonga's research, the anthropologist Bradley used participant observation to study the relationship between culture and fertility in the same Maragoli sub-location studied by Ssennyonga. Bradley's findings (1989, 1991) show a fertility decline in an area that has the distinction of having one of the highest rates of population growth in the world. As Bradley points out, "Although Maragoli is rural and has some of the most fertile land in Kenya, its population density is comparable to that of urban Kenyan provinces" (1989, 1). Bradley's research is focussed on the nature of demographic transition. She tests a theory of fertility put forth by Caldwell's (1982) "wealth flows" theory, whereby education results in the deterioration of collective ideology as the young gain individualistic values. In the course of her investigation, Bradley has also tested other perspectives, for example, those centred around modernisation, demography aspects, the economic value of children, and Handwerker's (1991) perspective that attributes a decline in fertility to women's improved opportunities in areas other than reproduction. Bradley's conclusions in a number of studies are that it is unlikely that only one factor may be isolated as contributing to the decline of fertility in Maragoli. Any number of factors may interact within a particular cultural context.

Cultural exploration in Maragoli has three aspects: an examination of the so-called traditional heritage that bears the weight of authority, recognising that Avalogoli have a history of migration involving contact with others long before their thirteenth century settlement in the Maragoli area; an evaluation of foreign factors; and an analysis of what those factors have influenced. According to Avalogoli tradition, children are seen as "posterity" (riches), and every living person is a child of the ancestors. Ideologically, individuality was and still is considered an illusion (see this book; cf. Abwunza, 1985, 1990, 1991). During the colonial period, Maragoli experienced population increases. For example, in his 1920s research, Wagner (1949) noted that the area had a very high population, as did Phillips (1930) in his report on land tenure, and Humphrey (1947) in his report on agriculture. The colonial government had a vested interest in ignoring the increasing population because the Maragoli Reserve was an important labour resource area (Abwunza, 1985). Overpopulation was not attended to by the colonial government until it became so difficult for people to feed themselves that it placed a burden on the government. Maragoli is not an area where population "exploded" in the post-independence era. Today, change has indeed occurred: the capitalist economy is pervasive. Even within the capitalist ideology of individual accumulation of wealth, the collective ideology prevails—indeed, must prevail for survival—and centres around richness in posterity where marriage "opens the way" and "children are the bridge for visiting."

Cultural norms in Maragoli encourage large numbers of children and sanction against small numbers of children, inhibiting state influence to lower birth rates. Gender relations are an additional factor affecting fertility. Avalogoli still practice patrilocality and bridewealth. Logoli women engage in marriage relationships structured by Abaluhya and Avalogoli marriage rules which specify their and their children's privileges via the patriline. A wife's kin receive cash, cows, and gifts from a husband's kin, who benefit from the children and labour a wife will contribute. As Staudt and Col point out, in Kenya generally, "A woman who leaves her own kin to live with those of her husband is celebrated for her reproductive capability" (1991, 246). In Maragoli, women are also celebrated for their hard work. An aspect of Logoli women's hard work, aside from the usual overwhelming activities related to providing food for the household and the community and all that entails, is found in their active participation in kin-based reciprocal relations. Reciprocal relations provide the *vika* for a "proper" Avalogoli way of life, and children provide the *daraja* (bridge) for "visiting" so that exchanges may take place. It is true that in Maragoli, "Childbearing continues to be an investment activity for women" (Handwerker, 1991, 75), but it is also true that children are an important investment activity for men, who also benefit from the exchanges. In what is to follow, Logoli women, experiencing a state-directed population planning program and economic risk, discuss the overpopulation predicament from within their own cultural context.

Logoli Women

"Aliza via vuza! (She eats for nothing!)"

In 1985, when President Moi and Vice-President Kibaki were making public statements promoting family planning for citizens, Amy, a farmer in her mid-thirties and her husband Gideon, in his early fifties, had eight children. Both Amy and Gideon have secondary school educations. Gideon, who holds a paid political position in Maragoli, was following "instructions" by making public statements advocating the government position. Embarrassingly, just as Gideon was championing the cause, Amy became pregnant with their ninth child. Shortly after the birth, Amy underwent a tubal ligation, a "TL." "She eats for nothing" is the euphemism neighbourhood Logoli people use to refer to Amy's sterility.

A male staff member of a local family planning centre promotes vasectomy for men to contain population growth. He uses himself as example. After he and his wife had four children, he had a vasectomy. He says, "Now there is progress [development] in my home." Avalogoli call him *kiziri* (eunuch), or *muradi*, meaning one who is castrated.[70]

Because the sample is inadequate, the following quantification can by no stretch be considered a "true" measurement, or be compared to the Kenyan statistics provided above; however, the results are interesting. Ninety-four women discussed specific questions concerning family planning.

Six (6.4%) of the women and forty (42.6%) of their husbands work in some (often sporadic) form of wage labour. Twenty-three (24.5%) women share their husbands in polygynous relationships. Seventy-eight (83%) of the women have some primary school education, and 16 (17%) have some secondary school education. Sixty-two women say 39 of their husbands have some primary school, and 23 husbands have attended secondary school. Thirty-two women thought their husbands had some schooling, but could not say what level of education they received.

Of the 16 women who have some secondary education, one has 11 children, two have eight children, two have six, three have four, three have three, one has two, two have one, and two have none in current marriages. All of those with three children and less say they will have more children.

In this group, all were aware of family planning (100%). Eight (8.5%) did not want to reveal if they used family planning, 74 (78.7%) did not use it, and 12 (12.8%) did. Among the 86 women who gave information, 22 (25.6%) were 50 years of age or older and described themselves as "finished" with having children. An additional ten (11.6%) women also said they were "finished," although none of them were using contraceptives, and all ten were still able to have children. Among the remaining women, the following were given as reasons for not using family planning: nine (16.7%) women believed it was for their "husbands to say;" three (5.6%) believed it was "God's will;" 17 (31.5%) women said they want more; two (3.7%) women do not yet have children in current marriage relationships; and one woman's husband was dead. Two women received contraceptive instruction from a magician; they have six and eleven children each, one having given birth to thirteen. Many of the remaining women provided "horror" stories surrounding family planning technology to justify their non-use. For example, they said, "The birth control pill destroys your insides, if you use it even for a little while you are finished;" and "You can still conceive with the coil, then it comes out with the child, in its eye, or somewhere inside;" and "The injections give me pains in my arms and I feel my head spin." Others complained of fluid retention and a general malaise when using modern methods of birth control.

Of the twelve users of family planning, two women—one over 60 with five living and three dead children, and one aged 52 with five children—use the rhythm method. Both had some primary school education. The remaining ten users have mixed characteristics: they range in age between 25 and 48. Eight have primary education, one has Form Two and another Form Four. Six use the birth control pill, three have injections (Depo-Provera) and one has a "coil" (IUD). Their family size ranges from nine to two children. A 26 year-old woman with Form Two has two children and takes the pill. She plans on having at least two more children. Another, a 25 year-old woman with primary school education, has six children. Three women with five, eight, and nine children are 48, 40, and 42 years old respectively, and have primary school education. The remaining women range from 30 to 37 with four and five children each. They all have primary school education. The total number of children for the 82 women who are non-users of family planning is 501, averaging 6.1 children each. Two women had the least number of children—none—and one had the most—19.

Some women provided additional details on the topic of family planning; through their information, we can examine the cultural structures, ideologies, and gender relationships that exist in Maragoli.

In Maragoli, some elder women, individually or in Women Groups, promote family planning for younger women. Tulukas and Mariam, elder women born in 1914 and 1910 respectively, discuss the difficulties of having many children. Tulukas gave birth to twelve children, but seven died. Mariam also gave birth to twelve children, five of whom died. Mariam says, "The problem is marrying land which has many sons. The land is gone." So why have so many children? Tulukas says, "God wishes."

However, it is clear not only God wishes for many children. Mariam says,

Look, say you get married to the first wife and you have twelve or thirteen daughters, this man is not satisfied. So a man begins to fool with other ladies, outside there, to get a son. He is stupid of course. It is possible he might end up with six other daughters before he gets a son and he may have to go on for a long time. But nowadays, today...women were older before, were older when they married, so the time for having children was not so long.

MARIAM   TULUKAS

Tulukas asks Mariam how old she was when she married. "How can we know? I have lived like that, I do not know," Mariam replies. She asks the other women around. Three women answer. Abigail, who is 44, says she was 19; Freda, who is 43, says 18; Fanesi, who is 37, says 17. "See, it is so," someone jokes (and everyone laughs). Mariam says, "Family planning had not come when I was having children, they just said go and get many children. We did not waste time, one after the other, one after the other." Mariam asks the younger women if they go to family planning. They assure her they all go. "Are you really sure you do that, go...and listen?" she asks. Freda responds, "When we go to family planning we are not instructed to stop having children, only to space, three or four years." Mariam asks her, "Do you say to your husband—do not touch me for the next three years?" Freda shrugs: "I take the tablets when they have them to give."

Another elder, Kagonga, who died in 1989, was 103 years old and "suffers from elderly disease and stomach ache." She gave birth to eleven children, three of whom died. She said,

> You are disturbing me. Here the person who stayed home with the children was a woman, so I made the decisions about children and growing up. If women do not take care of the entire house and yard, who is going to do it! Girls went to sleep with an old lady, not in a sack, for girls it was only banana leaves. The ladies teach you how to walk properly, where you get married and you have to grind well. Elder ladies made the cuts around the belly, it looked like what you write down [symbols] and an elder man removed the teeth. We girls went together, lined up and knelt down; young men laughed at you, to see if you were frightened, so you

dare not get frightened. We were totally naked. Only after marriage came the children, after *uvukwi* and marriage. And we needed many children, children are riches, the words of a childless man lack power and weight: *Ezingulu zitula kumwana.*

Another elder, Febe, likely in her eighties ("How do I know; how do I know the years?"), gave birth to ten children, five of whom survive:

Nowadays things have changed. Nowadays you find a fifteen year-old has a baby. The change is because of their own sense. When we were growing up, we had our own house where we all stayed, no boys went in there. We were well taken care of; we were well taught. Nowadays, where you have a girl's house the boys also stay in there, or they meet at school, and this is why they have children at fifteen.

Jonesi is 83, has only "a little bit" of "missionary" school, and has three surviving children. Her husband died in 1981. She lives with an unmarried daughter who has six children. The daughter digs for others, earning ten shillings a day, and another daughter sends money from Nairobi.

What happened was I would dig until dark, I would come home, the girls have gone to fetch water and my husband is cooking meat. All I cooked was *vukima*. During these olden days the children used to come and dig the land and help, during planting they come and help, during the weeding time they come and help mother. Nowadays if you have a child who is working somewhere, can send money sometimes, but you do not get the help of digging.

Rebeka was 78 when I spoke to her. She had given birth to 12 children, three of whom died. She had roughly three years of "old" primary school education. Rebeka shared her husband, and estimated that he has 29 "known" children. She passed on in May, 1994. She said,

Quite a deal! If you have so many children you cannot know the good ones and the bad ones. My reward is in food. Money comes from children. *Avana ni daraja yo kololana* [children are the bridge for visiting], even if children are born and die. [She reminds me of her statement made during another interview.] I as *guku* must do this, else we may not receive the remaining *uvukwi. Guga* will buy milk, tea, chickens, bread, sugar and firewood. We women will travel to where my daughter is married. We are fed very well, they all contribute to that. Here [in today's context] they do not give food for food, here they give an envelope with 100 or 200 shillings for us to take.

Esta is 62, attended the "old" primary school for four years, and has two children:

I do not know why there were no more. You marry this person, you stay there; I had children, I could not leave the children. People are sorry for me, he beats for everything, also he blames me for not having enough children, he says I am not profitable. He is forever blaming me.

Younger women also debate family size. Ritah and Aggrey decided to have only two children. Ritah has eleven sisters and brothers, and Aggrey calculates he has 23 siblings from polygynous unions. Ritah and Aggrey went to secondary school, estimating they achieved Form Two; their attendance was sporadic because of lack of fees. Both have experienced the difficulty of feeding and educating children in large families. In 1987, when they were 22 and 30 respectively, they considered themselves "blessed by God" in that they had the ideal family: a girl first, and then a boy. Aggrey says, "When the girl is older she can collect the water and the boy can care for the cows. The girl can assist in getting *uvukwi* to let the boy get a wife." Before the birth of the boy, they had "decided to stay with one child," as Aggrey already had a son "in another yard" who would need land. At that time, Aggrey himself had not been given land by his father. They visited a magician for help. Ritah tells how she followed his instructions:

I collected the blood after the birth, on cotton inserted in the vagina. Then I tied them on a long string and hung them over the cooking fire. From the time I did that we could not be together for the 17 to 23 days of my cycle. I do not know why it failed.

The fee for the magician's service was over 100 shillings. Both Ritah and Aggrey are aware of family planning and that contraceptives may be available at the local rural health centre: all their children were born there. Ritah talks of "one day going there to family plan."

Joyce is 26, with Form Three education. She has four siblings, all of whom finished Form Four. Joyce's husband has a job outside Maragoli. They have two children. Joyce does not "family plan from the clinic;" she says, "It is up to my husband if there are to be more children." She has the same information Ritah received from the magician, but if her husband "comes drunk at the wrong time, I could be pregnant."

Rosa is one of a number of *avakali vo mulugulu* (city women) who informed the research. Rosa is 23, with a primary school education and a few months of secretarial training. She has one child left at home in Maragoli with her many siblings, and one from her city relationship. She asks for help in "convincing" her husband to give *uvukwi*: "I have proved myself by having his child. He wants me to prove once more." Her husband gives her "trouble" and has a wife "at home," so "There is no land there for me to dig." She adds, "If I leave, people will say I just go from one man to another." Rosa describes her life as a "dead end," saying, "When the bird has sung, it has sung."

Rhoida is in her thirties, has secretarial training, and works in an office in Nairobi. She is a "second wife" and has five children. Rhoida has her own bank account: she says, "Women who have joint accounts with husbands will go there and find the money gone!" She has purchased a plot of land in Maragoli. She maintains that she was motivated to buy land because she is an orphan without parents to protect her, and because she is the junior wife. Rhoida's brother "ate" her *uvukwi* "down payment." She borrowed money, convinced her husband to contribute "a little," and bought the land. When it came time to register the title deed, Rhoida insisted the land be registered in her name. "My husband fought this, but I persevered. I gave 'tea' [a euphemism for "bribe"] and a worker in the bank assisted. People objected, but I explained that I was an orphan, the second wife with many children, and I paid most of the money. They said it was just all right. I am happy now." Rhoida and her husband separated in 1991.

Rubiah is in her thirties and has no children. She has primary school education and moves between Maragoli and Nairobi looking for work. She has been married several times, has gone to magicians and to clinics in Maragoli and in Nairobi for help in having children, but is "cursed." Her father favoured the younger house over the older in his polygynous relationship. Rubiah, a daughter of the younger house, was the recipient of the curse inflicted by the older house. "No one can assist me; there is not life for me," she says.

A nurse at a rural family planning clinic in Maragoli discussed how "the government" promised that "soon" contraceptives could be "given" to young people. It was her belief, thus the practice at this clinic, that only men and married women could be provided with contraceptives: "The government does not want to encourage sexual activity among the young." She believes denying contraceptives to anyone to be "wrong," but admits that young people would "fear to ask" in case their parents would be told. In an economic context where school attendance is sporadic, often "children" in primary and secondary school are in their late teens, even early twenties, and are certainly engaged in sexual practices: the proof lies in the birth rate among unmarried women. However, in terms of cultural norms, the unmarried are seen as "children," even though these children begin to have children of their own long before they are married.

SCHOOL CHILDREN

Violet is an example of this. She has limited primary education, but can speak and write some English. At 24, Violet says she is "finished" with having children. Out of her four children, two are from relationships during her school days: "One of the children is there [in the father's home], the other one is at home [with her mother]." The other two children, both boys, are from her marriage in 1984. She says,

I will not have more children. I have not gone to family plan but I will go. Right now the husband is staying far. My husband wants a girl first, to get the cows, then I will stop. If it is a boy then I will stop from there. Because maybe I continue I can go ahead and reach five boys. But here, if the husband wants more and you do not give, he will travel to another yard to get. You will have to feed the children he gets. There is not land for my husband, where would the sons find land?

Florah is a 45 year-old nurse at the rural health centre. She has six children and terms her last pregnancy (twins) as an "accident." She has used contraceptives "off and on" for years. Florah relies on first-hand experience to say that fertility levels are declining: "Many more people are attending family planning; the problem we have is supplies." In 1994, she added, "so many are now coming to family plan. We do not know how they are finding out" (meaning how they are gaining contraceptive knowledge).

A 40 year-old farmer and her husband, who is 47 and a teacher, have nine children, the youngest of which is five. The woman told me, "Since that youngest child was born we have not stayed together. We are too fearful of having more." I asked this woman why she did not get contraceptives from the rural health clinic. She said, "I would not like to go there. They have these young nurses. They talk. Everyone would know, all the neighbours will know." Quiet arrangements were made for her to have a tubal ligation at an urban hospital. As long as her "TL" remains a secret, she continues to give the appearance of eating for something.

Adherence to the ethos of the collectivity is at least theoretically intact in Maragoli. The necessity of capitalistic endeavours is dependent on the availability of cash, which, for the most part, is found in wage labour. However, it is also attained through the traditional system of reciprocity. Those who cannot work in wage labour may get cash and goods from other people. The demands are overwhelming: a constant stream of relatives expect some form of financial support from people who are barely eking out a living. But not giving means not receiving, and in times of difficulty having nowhere to turn.

Esta says, "Look men say, '*Mwana wovo ni mugingi vo mgongo, Mugingi vo mgongo.*'" Esta's comments refer to situations where children should adhere to cultural structures enforced by ideology. Logoli children should "buy this for me," and "build this for me." "Logoli sons are to know again their father;" Logoli daughters provide bridewealth and "think of and care for parents in their old age." Relations between parents and children are extended reciprocally throughout the community. All those in an ascending generation are parents and the young are their children. Kinship institutions organise the processes of distribution. All parents, not only women, must receive, most particularly those from *umuliango gwitu*, symbol of the *inyumba*. Relationships within *tsinyumba* (*inyumba* singular) give members a sense of affiliation and continuity, and provide the basis for individual security. This bond between the individual and the group is said to provide the "good life" of children, land, and cattle for men as well as women.

The magnitude of the difficulties involved in securing sufficient cash and land is largely influenced by population pressure. Many of these difficulties devolve on women, who are responsible for providing support and all that entails. Logoli people say ten children is the ideal family size. Along with support, ten children permit the carrying-on of ancestor names, allowing the lineage structure to continue. Yet people are beginning to question that ideal as the relationship between large families and economic stress is recognised. For now, the collectivity still provides crucial assistance, albeit sometimes with reluctance. Many women and men are still supplied with cash and other goods from relationships through the kinship structures of birth, marriage, and more birth. People who are members in good standing, following the ideological prescription of giving and receiving, continue to be supported, however meagrely, by the norms of exchange with children as the *daraja*. In Sarah's words:

It is the same as you people call banking. When I face problems I will send one of my children to the one I have given to and they will give to that child. It takes away my pain. We help each other like that, we give according to our heart and what we can, forever we have done that, we are forever exchanging.

Chapter Eight

"SILIKA—TO MAKE OUR LIVES SHINE"

Dedicated to the memory of Kagonga; may her songs live on.

In the early 1950s, Kenya's *Maendeleo ya Wanawake* (Women and Development) groups were a *harambee* effort. Women united to improve their social, economic and political status; to wage war against illiteracy and ignorance, poor health, poverty, and joblessness; and to call for government assistance to women's groups for technical, financial and other necessities for progress. Certainly no mean feat!

In 1977, at the foundation stone-laying ceremony for the *Maendeleo ya Wanawake* building in Nairobi, hopes were high. The building to come would accommodate national offices, provide space for vocational training programs for women and girls, and enable organisers to rent offices to raise income to finance educational welfare activities, extending these services to the rural districts. Symbolically, the very presence of a woman's monolith would "uplift the standards of living of the women of Kenya" (Kiano, 1977).[71] *Maendeleo ya Wanawake* and Licensed Women Groups were taken under the KANU government umbrella via the Women's Bureau of the Ministry of Social Services. This was done in order that "the women of Kenya maintain their faith in, hope and loyalty for, and co-operation with the Government, while raising their *harambee* self-help spirits and achievements to new heights" (Moi, 1986, 110).

By the 1980s, *Maendeleo ya Wanawake* groups were subsumed by *Nyayo*, calling for the Women's Decade focus on peace, equality, and progress to be "married" to the *nyayo* principles of peace, love, unity, and sharing (Moi, 1986, 117). No one can deny that *Maendeleo ya Wanawake* organisations all over Kenya achieved much through their efforts, with only minimal financial help from the government. But, as Stamp says, "[Kenyan] women become targets of development policy, problematic targets, where self-reliance is seen to be introduced from above and permits the paradox at the heart of the movement in Kenya to prod rural women into self-help groups" (1989, 152).

In 1992 and again in 1994, the *Maendeleo* building was relatively empty; the rooms set aside for the *Maendeleo ya Wanawake* organisation held a few desks and chairs, piled one on top of the other. A few books and pamphlets were laid out. A part-time secretary told how the Executive Director attended the office once or twice a week, and that an appointment was necessary to ensure her arrival.

The major difficulty is economic. Without seed or start-up funds (for of course it does "take money to make money"), the organisation and the other Women Groups in Kenya simply stagnate. Credit for start-up funds remains a severe problem: interest rates range from 30 to 40 percent annually; private money-lenders charge up to 240 percent. Kenya Rural Enterprise Programme (K-REP) is a pioneering non-governmental credit organisation in Kenya which provides groups with advice and loans. Recently, K-REP's emphasis has turned to individual entrepreneurial activity, with the hope that these individuals will create jobs for others through small-scale businesses. The point in mentioning K-REP is that women entrepreneurs have achieved an amazing 100 percent repayment rate in this group credit scheme (African Farmer, January 1994, 8).

Women's group activity, pervaded by a capitalistic ideology of progress and accumulation of wealth, requires a look into the practical as well as analytical sphere of economics, particularly when assuming a "women-in-development" (WID) approach. WID seems to presume the primacy of economic motivation in human life, at least in today's Kenyan state (including Maragoli), where development means progress and progress takes cash. I do not share this presumption in its entirety. Political motivations—who gets to lead and follow and who gets to criticise—and social motivations—women championing women and their families—appear to be subsumed by capitalistic motivations in WID constructs and many analytical approaches (see Stamp, 1986, 1989, for a refreshing divergent approach). However, this is to be expected. Anyone familiar with African situations and analytic presentations of those situations would not want to emphasise the political and social at the expense of women's economic contribution. To do so would allow for the suggestion that women's integral economic contribution is "marginal" or "petty." But Elson (1992, 40-1), for example, criticises the extension of self-help economic strategies to collective organisations, arguing that women's groups thus seem to be merely

women helping one another to meet their practical gender needs. They formalize the informal female support networks that women everywhere construct, but they perpetuate the idea that unpaid labor for the benefit of others is 'women's work' and they construct women's role in community organizing as an extension of their domestic role.

Her points are well-received. In the rural area of Maragoli, the "practical gender needs" of women involve the human needs of the entire community. Today, however, there is an additional expectation (a major point of this chapter) that women's collective organisations will also provide needed cash in an area where women's (and men's) opportunities for paid labour are scarce.

In Maragoli, Logoli women draw on a traditional sentiment of solidarity—*silika*—and now gather in "Women Groups" in an effort to realise both economic and social support. Women's group interaction is vital for community survival and development. Their interactions, sometimes in the guise of *harambee* or *Nyayo* efforts, include raising money through singing in choirs or by digging land, selling food and crafts, building schools or churches, or cleaning water resource areas. Women gather to provide these services, and have an acknowledged social power to influence communal action in aspects of development. In the words of one Assistant Chief: "You cannot have community development without women." On the other hand, in 1987, when I requested permission to investigate Women Groups in Maragoli, a District Officer in the area cynically informed me that there are no Women Groups in Maragoli. When I mentioned that so many were licensed to operate, he replied they do not exist as they do not make money.

WOMEN GROUP

There are over 200 government-licensed Women Groups as well as numerous unlicensed groups in Maragoli, an area of approximately 200,000 people. However, many are inactive and most are unsuccessful if measured in terms of economic accumulation. The sentiment on both local and national levels, that these groups are economically ineffective, underrates Logoli women's contribution and permits Logoli men and government officials to denigrate the productive benefits of women's solidarity. What is needed is an examination of some of these Maragoli Women Groups—both government-licensed and unlicensed—in order to offer something different: praise.

The tenuous economic situation in Maragoli has been recently further complicated by a structural adjustment program (SAP) which impacts on African women producers more than any other segment of the population (cf. Gladwin, 1993; Brown & Tiffen, 1992; Elson, 1992). The shift from project-oriented funds to conditional funds by the International Monetary Fund, World Bank, and bilateral donors has placed tremendous burdens not only on urban Africans, but also on the rural populations such schemes purport to assist. In brief, structural adjustment reforms are characterised by devaluation of currencies, increases in food prices and interest rates, alignment of domestic prices with world prices, an emphasis on tradable rather than subsistence crops, privatization of parastatals, reductions in public-sector employment and wages, decreases in budget deficits, and elimination of food and fertilizer subsidies (Economic Commission for Africa, 1989, 18-20). These prescriptions are all based on the neoclassical economic assumption that markets are good and that they work. The "positive sides" of SAP—for example, demanding that public service be efficient, reliable and honest, the divestiture of non-strategic public enterprises and one-party states, removing biases against exports to encourage entrepreneurial behaviour, and decreases in budget deficits—are all rules forcing a democratic market economy. The "benefits" of these policies, however, are often lost in the poverty of real life. A couple of examples are sufficient.

Improving the balance of trade requires that governments cut back spending, reducing imports while promoting exports. Along with the devaluation of an overvalued currency, this increases the cost of imported goods. The assumption is that this should in turn increase agricultural producer prices at home. Farmers are imagined to use few imports, thus their earnings should increase more than their costs. This should stimulate local agricultural production and promote exports, and all farmers should benefit. Urban consumers would lose, but the whole economy would be jump-started and in the end—so the story goes—everyone will gain.[72] But in some contexts, the SAP approach ignores power relations. This is the case in its failure to address the gap between urban elites and rural farmers, where urban elites have more influence over budget cuts. This can equally be applied to gender relations, where women producers neither own land nor have direct financial access to inputs of production such as credit, fertilizer and seed, and where they do not receive the income from cash or export crops that increase their labour and interfere with growing food for the family and community. High agricultural producer prices hurt women farmers, particularly in an area such as Maragoli, where households are not self-sufficient in food production and women are largely responsible for family food provisioning and community maintenance. Seed, fertilizer, transportation, and food prices increase markedly. Recently, a Logoli woman said, "In Kenya, 100 shillings is now worth 37 shillings."

Difficult local circumstances and imposed SAP create a situation of skyrocketing costs of food and other necessary market commodities, which in turn increase the costs of education and health care.[73] In the face of all this, Avalogoli economic risk is escalated. Much of the burden devolves on Logoli women who are active economic providers for their families and the community. A forced decline in living standards also drastically affects customary reciprocal assistance within the inter-household exchange networks that Logoli women are so dependent upon.

It is in this context that Logoli women say they engage in solidarity efforts to make "our lives shine." "Shining" is not only measured by the accumulation of much-needed cash, but also by food, a blanket, a lantern, utensils, a day or two days' work for one another, borrowing, lending, and providing support in times of need, whether the need is caused by unexpected guests or a death. Logoli women say the limited contributions of most men do not allow women's "lives to shine."

Silika

We called it .... yea, we called it silika*. Asande muno [thank you]. Thank you for reminding me.*

Febe is a respected elder, a community leader, "one who leads groups and gives advice." She discussed the importance of *silika*:
Thank you very much for asking me a question which reminds me that during those days there used to be a cooperation without money. Dig here one day, then go to my place and dig another day. All that each house had to do was give food for them to eat. No money. But that used to be here. Where the goodness was in those older days was this: women were helping each other, leaving one household to the next and what they were happy with was food; they would get a bunch of bananas, no maize then, millet was here, and they would eat plenty and they would go to the next

yard. Or we told the old stories; we sang and danced; we helped each other. I was a leader of young women. Today I am a leader of all women in the village, giving advice. People are happy with my advice. I am old; I wanted to stop doing leaderships, but women asked me to continue. I was always a singer; even today I sing. Nowadays, it is quite different. Each family thinks about their own household. There are those who have money and will progress. They only concern for themselves. They look at those who are poor and they do nothing. Their own progress is how they think, not about the *inyumba*.

Salome Kagonga also spoke on this topic:

And we sang. We young girls went to our house [traditional girls' house] and we sang the songs of the ancients. We used to plant vegetables and then they dried. And then an old lady would die; the vegetables would feed the people [at the funeral]. We said we will go sing for that one. Then we go to the grave; we picked up those dried shards; we didn't know that someone came from heaven. This is how we and the elderly women [grown-up and married] used to sing. The men sang too, but not with us. I did not know their songs. Or a woman would be sick or give birth, we would care for and feed. We made houses. We made rope, get shrubs and some trees, and tie ropes around. Then on top make the roof and that would be the house. Not mud houses, not then. That was in the land of my father and grandfather. We girls had incisions around the belly and then the teeth were removed. We went together. You lined up and you knelt and that was done. There were young men who were laughing at you, to see if you were frightened, so you dare not get frightened. We had no clothes, none at all. We were just walking around naked. A man could not touch those incisions, would never embrace, without giving a white chicken. If you did not do that every girl the same age laughed at you and was mean. When the teeth were removed you went to where your mother came from and her brother gave you a chicken. We girls all went together. When God came, we left this; people could not speak the English without the teeth. We left the incisions too. Then I came here [married] to Mahagira's land. I came with my grinding stone which my mother and father got for me. We women met and stayed together, at the back door; the kitchen was there. We helped one another. When there was a wedding we cooked bananas. And then the little girls who were born did as we did when we were young and when we grew. Men stayed at the front, they made decisions there. But the person who dug and stayed with children made the decisions about that. So I made the decisions about that. Now men go uplands and work there and we women stay and work. Men believe they are the commander [*omwene hango*], but if women do not take care of the entire house and yard who is going to do it? And we women work together to do that. My daughter-in-law [referring to me][74] that is finished, the rest of it has to rest. Now you tell about you. [One more question, Mama.]...Yes! In those old days, it was called *silika*. I remember that.

Traditional *silika* relied on elders instructing the young, mothers instructing daughters. Women's solidarity began early in a young girl's life: she would listen to grandmothers around the fire at the girls' hut, preparing to engage in the age grade rituals that permitted access to womanhood and marriage. After marriage, women retained solidarity and reciprocal relations with their natal relatives through visiting, as bridewealth was exchanged and children were born; *avana ni daraja yo kololana*. They formed new alliances with other wives where they married and with women affines who were married elsewhere. The network of "back door" support, women supporting women, expanded (and still expands) to enormous proportions. Women were and still are organisers and decision-makers. The function of *silika* was to provide assistance in work groups, but also to provide social support in marriage, birth, sickness, and death. And through it all they "enjoyed" by singing and dancing. Logoli women's group solidarity is yet another sphere that demonstrates the expansion of the "back door."

Maragoli Women Groups

Maendeleo *(development) has a lot of steps, many steps. One of them is to be able to have a number of cattle and chickens and it also means a different way of digging your land. If the harvest is good, from maize, bananas, you can sell. We try to do this alone and with women groups. It is money that makes you think and plan and change your life. (Finasi A.)*

Contemporary women's solidarity is quite different from traditional *silika*. Some groups are headed by respected community women, who serve as presidents or "chairladies," vice-presidents, secretaries and treasurers, and are licensed by the government of Kenya. Licensed groups have bank accounts to house the savings from dues and money raised from work or *harambee* efforts. A bank account is necessary proof of savings if the government arm that supervises women's groups offers the hoped-for financial support. A few women's groups have received some assistance and raised the expectations of all. Bank accounts have two or more members as signing authorities in an effort to control the narrow line between self-help and "help-self." Some groups are quite large, with over 100 members. Some are small, with 20 or 25 members. A function of women's solidarity today is cash accumulation. Women Group members work diligently to achieve economic success. Unfortunately, the economic results are often unreliable.

Women's efforts to organise and act through their groups are hindered by gender discrimination. Many Logoli men denigrate the benefits of women's solidarity, calling the groups nonproductive. They claim women's group activity only involves women gathering to gossip about men, and attempt to discourage women from joining. In response to women gathering in Women Groups, we once again hear the comment from men: "Women should stay in their own yards. Women who run to other yards make trouble in their own." Group activities are labelled economically ineffective, which is a way of saying that they take women away from what men consider more productive activity in their own yards. Many women, however, ignore the criticism and remain group members.

Today's Women Groups that are licensed by the government are organised to assist with women's development. What remains faithful to *silika* lies in the ideology of women supporting women for their own benefit and that of the entire community. Although active Women Groups are not always economically prosperous, they are always constructive. Women gathering in groups share information: for example, they pass on government directives in old and new laws, or discuss the wages for digging and the prices of commodities. They discuss agricultural assistance and innovations, and mourn the loss of kinship support. They pass on information about hygiene and health care. Together they learn a range of skills: from craft making to how to survive and act in difficult marriage relationships.

Women feel strength in Women Groups, and see them as a way to solve problems:

Before women were seen as weaklings, controlled, but government emphasis is on women and *Maendeleo*; the women have become productive. The President has announced this and also that the young should help their parents, some do—some do not. (Edelia)

Maendeleo is progress. Progress means being able to have something to eat at home and send to the market, but all we have is what we eat. Sometimes this is not enough. You only have a quarter of an acre and you plant. If the group [Women Group] could get money to buy a plot, we could assist, we could all benefit from what is sold. We cannot buy land from these small dues [membership dues]; there is no one to pay us to dig and the government has not given [money]. (Finasi B.)

A half dozen or so women are employed by the government to assist with Women Groups. Sarar Amadadi is a Location Women Leader. She describes her duties as primarily centred in community development, assisting with self-help projects, social welfare incidents including hunger and wife-abuse, and assisting those who are disabled. She also assists in educating women in child care, nutrition, and hygiene. Sarar believes that the best way to give assistance is through material goods, such as building supplies, cloth, or wool. Cash, she believes, is easily misused. All Women Groups or Community Development groups must assist the community rather than individuals if they want government support. Government regulations also say the group must have more than 25 members, pay 150 shillings for a licence (certificate), and submit a monthly report to the Women Location Leader. In 1987, only seven groups were provided with material assistance; in 1988, four; 1992, one; and by 1994, none. Sarar acknowledges that money is problematic:

The biggest problem is money. There is no money coming from the government, members are poor, and there is little help for them. So we suggest traditional ways of raising money, that is group efforts, but it's not successful. Sometimes leaders misuse, or do not account to members where money is going. The reports of this do come in, we get them, but how do we approach people like that [with high status in the community]. Still, these self-help programs are the only way to help the people.

Gideon, an Assistant Chief, agrees with the importance of self-help groups:

We must have self-help groups. So that members can dig, and invest money in digging, plant vegetables, plant trees, because there is not work for young people and some must learn the art of brick-making or building and sell to help themselves. This is to help people in the process of *maendeleo*; this is how we can get ahead. People can also get their livelihood from such projects. To say that I shall go to school and get a job is easy in thought, but even Form Six graduates are idle. They have no work. There is no work in Kenya for them. They are just at home.

Florence Vosolo, whose title is Community Development Assistant, supervises an area that covers 18 sub-locations, serving 74 Women Groups. Women Location Leader Beatrice Iganza trained to be a nursery teacher or nursery supervisor, but uses her training in nutrition, home management, and daycare centre management to assist with Women Groups. Her area covers nine sub-locations and serves 39 Women Groups. These women spend two days a week in their office at Mbale Market in Maragoli and three in the field visiting Women Groups. Florence and Beatrice discuss the problems they believe Women Groups face:

The goods Women Group members try to sell are not marketable. Knitting, vegetables, handicrafts: they are making things everyone makes, so no one buys. Leadership is always a problem, who should lead the groups. Often one person has all the power, becomes everything, and sometimes leaders take the funds for themselves. Women Groups are ignored by the administration, especially some Assistant Chiefs. The Chiefs do not let their wives join to give an example to other women. Men generally say, 'Why should women waste their time going to groups.' Some of the men and some of the elder women call women who join groups prostitutes. We hand in monthly, quarterly and annual reports which only get filed. No one reads them or provides any assistance.

MEMBERS OF THE VIGEZE WOMEN GROUP

The Women Group at Vigeze Village, with 40 regular members, bought a building plot in 1984 through a hire-purchase agreement. They are gradually constructing a cement block building which they hope to rent for income. Each member donates a bit of her own plot, and they rent land to grow and sell cash crops. They dig for others when others can afford to hire them and they pay dues if they can afford them. They also make and sell pottery—water pots, flower pots, and cooking pots—to pay off the land and finance the construction of the building. After they registered as a Women Group, Kenyan Social Services sent them 58 bags of cement. They have approached many people for financial assistance, the Assistant Chief of the area for example, as well as the "Women's Representative from the Government." In the past, they have written this women's leader many times, but she says there is no assistance for them. Once, through the Kenya Volunteer Development Association, people in Denmark sent a group of young men

and women to assist them with gathering stones for the building's foundation. They were also given a sewing machine from people in Sweden. The
members of the Vigeze Village Women Group discussed the benefits of the
group:

Having a group assists us, we can work together for food, for clothing. A
group must have trust in one another. We have three people who must sign
the cheques. Having the sewing machine is good, but it was difficult to
get. One woman travelled to Nairobi to carry it back. It took from Sunday
to Wednesday in Nairobi for her to receive it. [The woman slept on the
floor at the airport.] The duty on the machine was very high. We have to
depend on ourselves. We counsel one another.

The Lugaga Women Group formed in January, 1977 and "since then we
have never faltered:"

We were fifteen ladies who sat and began to plan the lives, to know how
these ladies can help themselves in their own homes. We sewed tablecloths, sweaters, made pottery, and began to dig and plant vegetables for
sale. We decided making tablecloths was not a good idea, no one would
buy. Then we made pottery and crafts with materials that are free [banana
fibre], making baskets, trays, bags, and place mats. We can make so many,
but few sell. But sitting idle is not the way for us. We now are fifty-two
members. When we get money, we buy food to sell. In different villages,
twenty [are] in one village selling maize, twenty-two [are] in another village selling fish, in another village ten sell beans. We have a building but
the plot is not ours. We have a nursery school in that building. We had
harambees to build that building. In 1981, the government gave us 7000
shillings and we used that money to plaster the building and some to invest in the business of selling food. We buy maize for five shillings and
sell for 5.50 shillings.[75] The same for fish, we add a bit, the same with
beans. Choir is one of our activities; in November 1987, we travelled to
Nairobi and sang for the radio. We sang about family planning. We sat
down and thought, the best way to teach is to sing. 'We are the women
from Lugaga—a good example for Kenya of family planning. Plan the
family—don't have too many children. This will improve your life and
your family's life. We will have happiness and a decent country. Listen to
our plan of bearing children. Follow *Nyayo* for bringing family planning.
Go to the hospital. You cannot bear children like tomatoes. There is no
progress without family planning.' We do not have conflicts; if we did, we
would not remain together. We will continue to work and save for our own
plot. (Lugaga Women Group Members.)

A member of the Nadanya Self Help Group says that originally their group was a Women Group. It began as a choir group in 1983. However, many of the husbands "disagreed" with women's membership, so in 1986 they opened the membership to men and registered as a self-help group. Twelve of the 42 members are men. Group members make pottery, sew tablecloths, and knit. They rent land to grow vegetables for sale, and they want to purchase a plot and build on it in order to "further develop." They would like to have a carpentry shop to build furniture, but they are unable to sell much of what they produce. In December, 1986, they sang for President Moi and he presented them with 10,000 shillings. In 1987, they sang as they escorted the visiting Member of Parliament. He gave them 5,000 shillings. They used some money to give each member 30 shillings, some to support community churches, and they used some more to entertain guests. The remainder was used to purchase uniforms, believing that they could earn money through their choir activities. Financially, the group is floundering, but socially, they remain together, lending their labour to the community by helping to build churches.

The Chambaya Women Group was established in 1984 and has 20 members. The Chairlady and Vice-Chairlady maintain they were required to pay 800 shillings to register their group. They have received no assistance from the government. The group's members say,

> We have approached the Women Group leader a number of times; she does not help. She says the government will help but they don't. We pay dues, 25 shillings every month on the 5th, the day we meet. We rent a plot to grow beans and maize to sell. We bought a building plot, we paid 5000 shillings and the man is hounding for the remainder, but we have prayed with him to wait. We thought it was easy [to raise money], but it is not. We want to construct a flour mill, but it is very costly.[76] In Maragoli, if your group is too large you end up with conflict. There is a lack of trust with money. We will do well if we are small and trust one another. The Woman Leader needs *ichai* [tea, euphemism for bribe]; she's hungry. Life has problems; you try and solve them. If you have ten shillings, you give her five, you remain with five, and perhaps you get help.

The Mmadanga Women Group is large, with about 100 members from surrounding sub-locations. They are licensed by the government, pay one-time 30-shilling dues, and engage in agriculture and knitting to raise money. The founders of this group are men, and the group was given money by the government to buy a plot on the tarmacked Kisumu/Kakamega road, a prime location. Mmadanga Women Group Members say,

We are trying to convince the government to give us 200,000 to 400,000 shillings to build a single-family, income-generating home on the land. For this, we will receive 1000 shillings a month rental. What can we do? We need someone to give us money. We need partners from overseas.

The Mmadanga Group is criticised by other groups: they are called "Those who sit on gold and wait for gifts."

The Digoi Women Group initially began in 1980 when five people met together and formed a group. They decided to contribute two shillings a month; after three months they raised this to seven shillings. They were licensed in 1981; the fee was 200 shillings. They dug to raise money—"we all love digging", they say—charging very low rates. The oldest member of the group, Diriya, decided to join because she was afraid of being alone and weak: "Now with these children [group] I am not lonely and I get strength from these children. When they talk I am part of them and them of me. I get hope from that." The group members characterise their organisation:

We were just helping people. We charged so little to dig, but when you are together you help each other. Now we have 35 members and four are men. Once we had 40, others saw us meeting and came one by one, two by two to join. At the beginning we made 800 shillings and we added 500 to open a bank account. Now we do membership digging only, and we ask members to give part of their plot to the group. We grow maize, peas, beans and cabbages to sell. We sell to everyone, but members get it a bit cheaper. If we have a good harvest, we also buy to sell more. KENGO [a corporation] gave us 5000 shillings in 1982. We will buy a plot and build a building for our transactions. The Horticultural Department gave us seeds and fertilizer. It is difficult; many people sell [crops]. The plot and building will be so expensive. We formed a group so that we could help one another. Belonging to a group is worthwhile. We assist when death comes or a baby is born. We loan money to our members; they pay 10% interest. Two members have not returned the money. They paid a bit, since then nothing. So now we are careful who we trust. We also give food to those who are without.

Asega is a former school teacher. He discusses the difficulties he sees in women's development groups:

Women do not have anyone to lead them. The women leaders do not have any more knowledge than the people they are leading. They need someone from outside the area who has knowledge, an expert. The women will follow his example. He will mobilise and instruct them. Our women will work if they have someone to teach them and mobilise them. The Assistant Chiefs must see that this is done.

Benson is an unemployed carpenter. He says,

Women Groups always want money. Women take money from home to
give there. Then they want women to work for them. We see nothing from
all that at home. If you tell me to move from here to there and I can be told
how that will help me I will move. If there is no help for me why should I
move [i.e., allow his wife to join]?

The comments of these two men—as well as many others— fly in the face
of women's actual activities.

GROUP OF WOMEN

Other women in Maragoli gather in small, unlicensed groups, often
without the knowledge of men. These women are involved in rotating work,
or contributing cash or goods on a rotating basis. In their words:

I work with two other women. We dig, plant, weed, and harvest together.
This has been going on for some years. We work two days at one place
and move on to one of the others. The person whose home is dug supplies
and cooks the food. Three others have asked to join us, but we have refused them entry. Its better to remain small and work with people you can
trust. My husband does not know we work together. Husbands do not approve of women being together; they want wives to stay in their yards. He
asks me, "Who did this building or digging for you?" I say, "I did this
myself." (Joyce)

Life is difficult but I persevere and we women assist one another, my co-
wives [sisters-in-law] and the groups [Women Groups]. We [her Women
Group] do not belong to the government; that way is too expensive and
you receive nothing. Even if the government gives, the leaders keep; the
groups get nothing and the leaders expect the groups to pay them "tea"
[bribes]. (Jerida)

We are four in our group. We are just beginning. We meet and discuss. We knit and embroider for sale. We do not save yet, we sell to get sugar, tea and vegetables for home. It is not good to try and grow food to sell. There is not land and who can tell about the climate. We want to begin a business that sells clothes [second-hand]. The big problem with Women Groups is that people stand for one another; they do not help others. They cannot trust one another. They steal from one another. Some do more work than others and want more. The old women corrupt the group. (Gladys)

Our group is small [18 members], but we work hard. We pay dues, 18 shillings a month. Sometimes we dig to raise money. Sometimes we cook food and sell it on the market. We loan our members money and we pay back with 15% interest. You see, I bought these utensils from one who was leaving. I borrowed the money to pay from my group. (Salome M.)

We are 15 members in our Women Group. We are not part of the government. We pay dues, 15 shillings a month, and we work with one another and for others during planting, digging, and harvesting. We all give a piece of our land for crops to sell for the group funds. We do not tell our husbands we do this. They would not want the land to be used for a Women Group. If we are able we buy fertilizer or seed, or rent oxen to plough. Sometimes we cannot afford so we go in the group and hoe. Our purpose is to uplift our members. If one experiences a death in the family, we do not visit bare-handed: we take sugar, milk, tea leaves, flour, or maize. We look into our welfare by keeping company and we help in disagreements in marriage. If our daughter has a child, we go there to know the home, to see the mother-in-law and the newborn. We take chickens, maize flour and some money in an envelope; this is to uplift the mother [group member] and the daughter, so the daughter does not look poor. If visitors come to one member's yard, the group is invited to help serve them, fetch water and firewood. We are close; we are aware what a member is missing. We meet and decide who will contribute what and it is carried to the member that month. We meet and decide who is the next member to visit. The person who is to be visited is told the month before. The treasurer keeps the money; the person tells what they need; and the group shops. We buy utensils, cups, kettles, dishes, put nicely in a bundle and give to her as a present. She serves us as visitors with tea and perhaps food. The woman this month chose a kerosene lantern, *sufuria* [pot], blanket and a basin. With these gifts, she gets to shine. We help one woman to shine every month. We have done this since 1984. Many people want to join us, but instead we advise them how to start their own groups. Many have. We are successful: we have assisted members to buy iron sheets, water tanks, and pipes. Sometimes it is clothing for children. Now we are working hard to get water close to our homes. We will work hard to raise money for this. (Florah)

FLORAH AND FRIEND

Conclusion to Part IV

Logoli women face difficult circumstances on a daily basis as they are confronted with an overwhelming number of children and obstacles to "progress." The ideas and practices surrounding women's fertility and their involvement in Women Groups require analysis, as they appear to operate as forces of both power and subordination. As examined in this research, fertility relationships may be viewed as intrinsically political locally, nationally, and globally. The local political scene in Maragoli until very recently promoted large family size. Even today, this structure is legitimised by ideology, as children are still perceived as "posterity," the "bridge" for support for both women and men, especially during these risky economic times. Commodities and education are the greatest causes of financial burden in Maragoli, but benefits from children still accrue for both women and men.

The Kenyan state's promotion of family planning depends on controlling population through a redefinition of desired family size through a change in cultural fertility ideology. This is promoted by adopting a global ideology that explicitly links economic development or a decline in poverty to population control. Overpopulation is assigned a negative economic value by the Kenyan government and the global community which offers financial support. Women's contribution to overpopulation through high fertility is seen ethnocentrically by the global community as their non-rational assessment of "costs" and "benefits." It appears that culturally-relevant costs and benefits are not recognised, for although costs in Maragoli may reconcile to Western notions, benefits are more aligned with Avalogoli notions of "posterity." This initial error in judgement leads to an error in expectation as the global community holds African women generally responsible for carrying out a decline in fertility.

I would suggest that because overpopulation as a detriment to development is treated as a given, we fail to recognise the beliefs that may have led certain African people in an opposite direction. Indeed, some groups may still see an increase in population as a *solution* to some of their social, political and economic (thus development) difficulties, rather than as a disadvantage. For these groups, even under conditions of social change leading to poverty, stabilising at current levels or even continuing increases in population may be a solution for supplementing not only personal status but general survival. Up to a point, parents see children as assets, helping in work and future security. In today's Maragoli, women and men still want children, not only to help in daily chores and provide support in old age, but also to sustain and enlarge kinship networks of reciprocity, especially during these times of economic risk. This promotion of fertility is pronounced in Maragoli, even though there is no man or woman, young or old, who does not recognise the economic difficulties associated with having the ideal family size of ten children. To think otherwise is an insult to their intelligence. Once there are enough children to meet their needs—and this must take infant mortality rates into account—women and men do want to limit family size. They are the ones after all who face the economic challenges of supplying food plus all the other expenses on a day to day basis for their "posterity." To say ignorance is a variable standing in the way of contraceptive use is not only a misrepresentation: it is unethical.

Family planning is promoted almost exclusively to women. Availability of contraception and privacy are of prime importance, but are not always guaranteed. Add to this the indiscriminate use of contraceptive technology— placing women on the pill, injecting Depo-Provera or inserting IUDs without adequate medical screening—and it becomes likely that women will experience negative side effects and discontinue use.

Although it is sometimes the case that men expect women to be sexually available without the consequence of pregnancy, it is also true that men may expect or even demand that women become pregnant. Men are decidedly influential in women's assessment of pregnancy. Women in Maragoli live with men and ancestors; every living person is a child of the ancestors. Under these circumstances, individual autonomy is a myth. The question must then be asked: why is population research and family planning only focussed on women? This flaw also creates a context in which an error in judgement creates an error in expectation.

In a state marked by pervasive gender inequality, women are particularly vulnerable to the promotion of family planning, which in turn is legitimised by the "overpopulation" predicament. Family planning programs set out to regulate women's fertility behaviour more than men's. Very little attention is given to men's cultural fertility attitudes, even in the Kenyan research cited above. This is astounding in a country where many people adhere to normative cultural structures defined by patriliny and a corresponding patriarchal ideology. Women also bear a disproportionately large share of the burden for change. The family planning schemes add to women's burden of responsibility, as only women become the data for statistics and are held responsible for using or not using methods of birth control to "family plan." The final error in expectation is that women alone must somehow empower themselves to challenge the cultural structures and ideologies in which the actions of both women and men are embedded.

Listening to women's narratives on membership in groups raises the issue of whether or not Women Groups are economically "developmental." But more importantly, this analysis questions if they should be expected to be economically successful. Our Western construction of economics assumes that women's development groups ought to "develop". Stamp (1989) calls this the "hidden assumption" of WID. Development means "increased productivity" resulting in an increased cash flow, whether through large-scale intensive commercialisation or through the efforts of the small women's group. Indeed, the emergence of these groups is seen as positive economic development, whereby Women Groups are portrayed as an economic risk management strategy.

Women's voices illuminate the fact that their solidarity efforts through licensed groups are currently not financially viable for individuals. The group itself may accumulate a little capital, but all groups continue to work and save for what members hope to be individual economic assistance in the future. Once the plot is owned and the rental building is finally constructed, the proceeds can be divided up. This seems to be the future plan for many groups. However, land and building materials are so expensive that the necessary financial investment, when measured against the future financial benefits, makes it appear that one's grandchildren are likely to be the only beneficiaries. The expectation that women's collective organisations will provide cash for the capitalistic measure of success—individual accumulation of wealth—remains unfulfilled; economic theories are largely inadequate in this case. Yet all people, including Women Group members, hold to this capitalist belief that success equals individual financial "progress."

The opportunities for groups to make money are extremely limited. Certainly, most members now recognise that crafts are not a viable economic strategy and that it becomes increasingly difficult to sell food when many people are attempting to do so yet few can afford to buy. Former members of groups maintain they can no longer belong: the investment of time and money for dues is something they cannot afford when there is no immediate return. Many groups in Maragoli disintegrate for these reasons. Still, those group members who are active tell us how they receive much more than just economic support. This seems to be particularly salient in the smaller, unlicensed groups, which follow their own agendas, and devise their own support strategies.

When the "modernising" tactic implicit in capitalism did not improve women's circumstances, the responsibility for women's economic betterment was placed on their own heads through women's group work. This criticism is not to deny the benefits of women's solidarity, only to point out yet another situation in which women are expected to (and indeed do in many circumstances) better their own economic lots. If the money does not appear—and it does not in most cases in Maragoli—economic theories are shown to be insignificant. Today, "traditional" groupness is transformed into an entity with capitalistic intention as its hallmark. Thus, when group effort by women in development is judged an economic failure, women are disempowered. An unintended consequence is thus produced. In their history, Logoli women have politicised their roles in society through their solidarity, exercising their power and influence from the "back door." Today, gender tension is activated as women, exercising community leadership, recount their confrontations with men, often husbands. It is as if women's efforts somehow confront the weaknesses and failures of men's support. Indeed, this is why men think women only gather to talk about them in the Women Group meetings. Women's solidarity is not only seen as counterproductive, but also as counter to the ideological patriarchal stigmatisation of women. But women's voices in this context tell a different story.

The problems and opportunities, complications and consequences surrounding Logoli women's groups have been examined. Success is relative, and is perhaps best measured by identifying common group needs, some of which appear fulfilled even without individual economic improvement. Is it the hope of riches to come that keeps some of these groups functioning, or is it the security and comfort found in solidarity? "Shine" takes different forms. Cash may be one form, but "helping one another" is another. In these times of economic risk, traditional economic ideologies may be on the increase rather than decrease, particularly when elicited by a state edict such as *Nyayo*, that calls for peace, love, unity, and sharing. *Silika* is actively reconfigured both from the inside and the outside as capitalism invades. Yet *silika* remains a symbol inspired by the efforts of group work for and sharing with one another. Women's insistence on gathering in groups against the wishes of some, even when their efforts are denigrated as non-productive, may be viewed as women's reclamation of what the invasion of capitalism violated: women's solidarity. Women's efforts of "gathering at the back door" undeniably turn men's denigration into praise, allowing their lives to "shine" through.

Part V

BURYING THE PATRIARCHAL WORLD?

Chapter Nine

OMWENE HANGO DEFAULT

The story of Avalogoli, particularly Logoli women, is now told— for the most part by the women themselves. Their voices are no longer muted. The elaboration of a single, significant idea—that of women's power in recognising their needs and achieving the means to meet those needs—is what constitutes this book. In discussing the reality of gender relationships in Maragoli, women have told how people posture in their interactions. Just as men posture patriarchy, women posture obedience to patriarchy. In many contexts of power, 'real' power is assumed to be men's, so that when women exhibit power, it is frequently labelled something else, perhaps strategy or informal power. It is obvious that men posture in interactions, yet we label them powerful. But we cannot for some reason associate 'real' power with women, and instead assume their postures to be powerless. Logoli women's voices have provided the evidence of 'real' power, even as they posture an adherence to patriarchy. I suggest that although in many ways the situation of Logoli women is unique, we are able to draw parallels between them and other African women, and extend these parallels to women worldwide who live in patriarchal societies.

In the past in Maragoli, acceptance of patriarchal ideology had benefits for Logoli women: "commanders" "provisioned" in their best interests. "Commanders" provided land and *uvukwi*—women's means of production and the recognition of women's vital role as producers. In these days of decreasing land supply, limited employment and neglect of *uvukwi*, Logoli women question if they should continue to posture an adherence to the rule of "commanders." Logoli women believe that changes in Avalogoli society have placed them in a marginal position, even as they recognise that they are the main producers. Logoli women see that gender inequality has increased and is subsequently placing them in a disadvantageous position. They see this change as detrimental to family and community survival and progress.

It is an active social assumption in Maragoli that women's labour has productive value. Neither men nor women see women as subordinates in the productive process. Men's means to productive value are now more limited in the contexts of land and wage labour. They recognise that much production comes from women. Many men blame women for inadequate prodution, but women have increasing power over their own production, decisions about which crops will be grown, and what to do with them, as well as power over their available cash.

Avoiding men's voices, women use their apparent agreement with patriarchal ideology to accrue power. They make creative efforts to use capitalism to their advantage as a replacement for the loss of their traditional power. Instead of further disadvantaging them, capitalism better enables women to use their authority in the kin-based collective. "Women with reputation"—as mothers, sisters and daughters—call upon their own resources and the resources of the collectivity to perform their cultural role and engage in a limited capitalistic effort.

Because of the analytical reliance on economic analyses which value cash and individual wealth, and the view that gender inequality was generated after communalism as a direct consequence of private property, women's power has been hidden from view. In contemporary African societies, an assumption has been made that the imposition of capitalist economics heralds the deterioration of collectivities. If economics is redefined to better fit actual social circumstances, then it must also include production that re-enters the system in direct benefit to its producer. Women are thus workers and producers of not only "use value" but also "exchange value," even within a communal system. In any society, whether communal, collective, or capitalist, women are likely to be producers of labour and production which generates a profit. A necessary community reputation that constitutes their influence is thus accrued to them. This production is vital to human survival and development. Maragoli society is not communal; it is an idealised collectivity articulating with capitalism. It is crucial to recognise women's participation and influence in this society, as they are the prime actors in the movement of goods, services and cash. Women's work and decision-making in Maragoli provides the economic base for the individual family as well as for the community. This could be construed as true in any African society.

Today in Maragoli, men use patriarchal sentiments to challenge the means by which women accumulate influence. Logoli women recognise this as seriously detrimental, not only to economic progress, but to actual personal and family economic survival. This book shows that women's work and decision-making translates into the ability to generate value in the collective cycle of reciprocal rights and obligations, a value that gives them the influence that has an effect on others. Women's work is also not exclusively confined to the domestic sphere: economic activity necessitates women's involvement in the public sphere. The proceeds from "home work," "outside work," and group efforts are employed in generating value in reciprocal rights and obligations. Making the reciprocal obligations of the collectivity work takes effort: members do not appear in needy yards with a donation. Those who require assistance must travel the network, walking or perhaps scraping up the money required for transport. Women do this work while carrying babies on their backs, baskets in their hands, or perhaps stalks of bananas on their heads. They call on the yards where they hope to get support, waiting, sometimes for most of the day, and then return home, hopefully with the needed cash or commodity.

Women generate political value, thus influence, on both local and state levels. It is mainly the women in Maragoli—the mothers, sisters, and daughters—who keep the networks of the collectivity animated. It is women who trek from yard to yard giving and receiving, mediating and placating situations even as they politicise them, recognising their own reliance and that of others on resources available through reciprocal relations. On the state level, no serious political candidate in Maragoli could survive a hostile proclamation by groups of women. The consciousness of women's social, economic, and political effects provides women with the influence necessary for their power.

The organisation and dynamics of Avalogoli society provide empirical support for the realisation that women have public power on two levels: productive—accruing and moving goods, services and cash—and reproductive—giving birth to the next generation of actors in reciprocal relations, productive and otherwise, as well as the next generation of ancestors. Women's decision-making in reference to aspects of fertility is a viable, if difficult, topic for research in Maragoli, particularly in the light of the area's natural increase in population. All women interviewed are aware of the government's stance on "family planning," but family planning in Maragoli does not mean having fewer children; it means spacing children over a longer period of time so that elder siblings will (hopefully) be in an economic position to assist younger siblings. Many women view certain forms of birth control as "dangerous." The "pill," "coil," or "injection" can "finish" a woman's insides, even when used for a short time. Amy's "TL" was supposed to be an "example" for the community, but instead caused her to be labelled one who "eats for nothing." Ten children is still the ideal for many women, and they are influenced in this regard by husbands and other members of their families. This will continue as long as posterity is seen as coming from children. Questions surrounding fertility decision-making and birth control procedures in the past and today must be put forth carefully, as many people see information of this sort as a helpful tool to engage in witchcraft. For example, the usual question directed to a pregnancy in the Western world—"When is the baby due?"—is not an appropriate question in

Maragoli. Why would you want to have this information? It is not important when the child is due to be born, only that the child is eventually born and survives.

Despite the recognition of Logoli women producing both "use" and "exchange" value in both private and public spheres, the ideology of male rule remains pervasive. This remains true even when changes in the patriarchal structure are consciously acknowledged. For example, many women advocate owning their own land, yet few women do own land. Information from this study permits our awareness that the pervasiveness of an increasingly threatened patriarchy in this Kenyan society may in fact be a hallmark of women's increasing power in decision-making. Maragoli provides an example where we may examine women's intelligence as well as their hard work. In Maragoli, women move between collective and capitalist modes using the same cultural avenues for accessing resources and amassing power. Gender relations are politicised by patriarchal values which both men and women posture. Women posture an acceptance of patriarchy for men's benefit as well as their own because it provides them with the ideological basis for structuring their own reputations. "Good Logoli wives" adhere to patriarchal ideology. Gaining a reputation as "good wives" permits their access to the collectivity. Access to the collectivity permits survival in today's stressful economic situation, and even "progress" in some cases. Although women's cultural posture of submission in fact denotes a recognition of the avenues of their power, it is generally this posture which is analysed in research. As a result, women's power has been identified as informal or as mere strategy, second orders of power, rather than categorised as what it rightly is, a primary order of power. Additionally, not recognising that women posture an acceptance of patriarchy as an astute social action may have provided the mistaken contexts in which some research has portrayed African women as "oppressed," "under-valued," or as a "dependent class."

In today's Maragoli, women are conscious that their best interests may no longer be served by assuming a posture of ideological and institutional acceptance of patriarchy. A reduction of value in men's labour and a recognition of its ineffectiveness reveal that men are impotent rulers who do not act in the best interests of those they rule. The assumptions of patriarchal sentiment are symbolic statements for the way things used to be for both women and men. Participation in the cultural expression of patriarchy still provides women with some benefits, but also with increased gender inequality. Thus, women may change the way they relate to the structures of patriarchy. The increase of back-door decisions points to an increase in the degree to which men are unable to maintain patriarchal control. Men's increased violence on the home front speaks directly to the demise of patriarchy.

Women still draw on the tradition of the back door and gather in groups, even as they confront men's authority. Women's *silika* is vital. Women gather to provide services and have an acknowledged social power to influence communal action in respect to needs and the means to acquire them.

Studying Logoli women from a gendered perspective, watching them act, as well as listening to their voices, forces a reassessment of theoretical perspectives in regard to productive and class relations. Using this case as an example allows us to see that the direct effects on women and their resistant responses to patriarchy and capitalism may not be assumed by generalised theoretical perspectives. From the early research of Boserup (1970) on African women and the research of all those who followed, it was recognised that women's economic role is skilful and vital in African societies. It was also recognised that women have skills not only in production, but also in the redistribution of that production for individual as well as community benefit. Yet it appears that the latter contribution, community benefit, is only recognised when it is economically productive. The question of women's status did not accurately reflect their skilfulness and vitality until dynamics between gender relationships were examined and extended to show how state structures were impacting on these local contexts. Local studies showed that the social and economic positions of African women were at risk, and that their position was reflected in the lives of all African people. Local studies permitted an awareness of the necessity to include women, at least as the actual producers of the family food supply, in development programs. Additionally, as shown by the Avalogoli example, "family" requires cultural definition, spilling over as it does in African contexts to the entire community.

Gender-focussed research also permits awareness of the pervasiveness of traditional patriarchal ideology as it articulates with the patriarchal ideology contained in capitalism, both on local and state levels. We see that women have been relegated to a 'private' domain and placed in a category of 'dependent class.' But this book and other research provides evidence that previous views did not accurately reflect women's actual production in both 'private' and 'public' domains. Additionally, women's actual power in collectivities—as well as their increase in power through capitalism—has been underanalysed, with a few notable exceptions (cf. Stamp, 1975-76, 1989; Presley, 1986; Bujra, 1986).

This book has focussed on Logoli women's power and resistance and their effect on issues of economic survival and "progress," and on their needs and the means to achieve them. It has examined the increase and decrease of gender inequality in Avalogoli socioeconomic and political organisations and how that impacts on issues of local development. Although it is recognised that the collective mode is integrated and articulates with capitalism, the Avalogoli case questions the subordinate status usually applied to tradition. The producers in Avalogoli society—for the most part women—rely so heavily upon that traditional mode for the goods that permit all Logoli people to hold on, if not to "progress."

Finally, this study of Avalogoli women directs attention to women's intelligence in political spheres. Logoli women posturing an adherence to patriarchal ideology is an intelligent and significant political decision, and is representative of their power. In Maragoli, power has traditionally been in the hands of men, but a metamorphosis is taking place. The social and economic experience of half of the caretakers of traditional power do not see their interests being maintained by that authority. However, rather than organising against patriarchal oppression through revolution, Logoli women use resistance, politicising gender relations from the back door by accruing information and using their influence. The importance of their influence for community survival has been evident throughout this study. We have heard women's dissenting voices in regard to male power and observed women's powerful productive, political and social resistance.

In this study, theoretical frameworks have been extended to focus on women's power, rather than on their powerlessness. Today in Maragoli, with the authority of patriarchy resting on tradition, men's provision of the *vika* to a "proper Avalogoli" way of life is shown to be falling off. The irrational aspects of male authority are exposed as women question to what extent men are ruling in women's interests.

Today, Logoli women and some men say that both men and women must work together to "progress." Hermann tells us, "The women do the best they can digging, but the men sit and talk; they need to help dig. The men are lazy; the women have too many responsibilities to dig properly." Imposing patriarchal ideology as well as assuming a posture of adherence to it takes energy, which is perhaps better directed toward more productive goals. As is true worldwide, Maragoli society can no longer afford to support the doctrine of separate gender spheres. Logoli women see that men must recognise women's work and decision-making as productively superior to that of men. Most men have sufficient access to neither a traditional (land and cows), nor capitalist modes (cash) of support. Although their actions are limited, women operate at the intersection of both modes. Their production from both modes is what permits some in the society to hold on and others to progress.

Today in Maragoli, women's critique of men suggests they are not avoiding, circumventing or even negotiating patriarchal control. They are no longer convinced that abiding by men's rule is in their own or their community's best interest. Some Western research has been skewed by a misinterpretation of women's posturing in the face of patriarchy. This is a failure to acknowledge women's power in decision-making. When posturing an adherence to patriarchal ideology no longer serves women's interests, as is the case today in Maragoli, the value in men's power, also based on a postured patriarchy, loses its foundation. This is a significant change which may permit the death and burial of Avalogoli patriarchy, assigning to women a 'real' power that more appropriately reflects their efforts.

"Progress"—indeed, survival—cannot occur without due regard for women's contribution to the economic, political and social systems. Women's power is the organising principle around "progress," just as it is the organising principle around survival. African women's hard work has been recognised by researchers. With a few exceptions, their intelligence in political processes has not. In Maragoli, patriarchal posturing is a significant intellectual action that has politically served women's best interests in the past. Today, Logoli women are conscious that many Maragoli men are interfering with survival and progress.

Theoretical approaches that omit women's voices and gender inequality from analysis lack access to the truth. The situation demands that serious attention be given to what women actually do and say, a principle that is particularly clear when we reflect on Avalogoli society. Men sit and reflect on strategies to make do; women accrue information and utilise influence to produce. The situation requires that men follow women's lead. Women are the main actors who provide the resources, gained from both women and men, that allow the society to carry on. While men are traditionalists with situational power, women look forward and their power is everywere. Women's actions begin first thing in the morning, when, leaving their back doors, they begin to think about the day's supply of food. A cynical statement made by Violet reveals the trend of change indicated by the actions of many Logoli men and women: "Men think; women dig as they think."

FLORAH

Chapter Nine: Omwene Hango Default/ **187**

Glossary

Terms are Luragoli unless otherwise noted.

aliza via vuza: she eats for nothing
amagutu: headman
ambihu: gift for the person on whom the child first excreted (usually the mother)
asande muno: thank you very much
askari: police (Kiswahili)
avadaka: poor people
avakali vo mulugulu: city women
Avalogoli: people of Logoli
avana: children
avana va: children of
avana ni daraja yo kololana: children are the bridge for visiting
avasatsa: husbands (singular *umusatsa*)
bhang: marijuana (Luragoli and Kiswahili)
"big pockets": greedy (local English)
busaa: local beer made from millet
chandangu: back door
chang'aa: alcoholic brew distilled from maize (Kiswahili)
"commander": ruler or owner of the home (local English)
daraja: bridge
"dowry": bridewealth (local English)
ezingulu zitula kumwana: power comes from children
"grow fat": literal, weight; symbolic, material wealth (local English)
guga: grandfather
guku: grandmother
harambee: working together (Kiswahili)
ichai: tea with milk and sugar; in context, bribe (Luragoli and Kiswahili)
ichoo: latrine
Imungu: traditional deity
inasoli: opium (Luragoli and Kiswahili)
inguvu: cloth (at a funeral, money in envelopes)
inyumba: house (segmentary lineage; plural, *tsinyumba*)
itama: excessive sexual desire
itulungi: tea without milk and sugar
ivani: money collected in small baskets at a funeral
kiziri: eunuch
kogotitsa lidiku: lose the day (waste time)
koteva: to ask

kotsa: aunt or uncle and respective spouses

kutulitsa mukana: release daughter

kuvahira: elopement

kuvumba ha chandangu: gathering at the back door

luvago: final wedding ceremony (death)

maendeleo: development (**"progress"** in Avalogoli context)

Maendeleo Ya Wanawake: Development of Women Group (Kiswahili)

matatus: buses or taxis (Kiswahili)

mfundi: workmen

mugingi vo mgongo: my name to go up (support)

misiri: Egypt

mugenda gendi: a woman having children with different men

mugitsi: yard, homestead

muharikwa: sister-in-law

mukafu: tea with milk and without sugar

mukali: wife

mukali gwa: wife of

mukaye: wife (elder woman)

Mulogoli: ancestor of all Avalogoli (contextually, people of Logoli)

mulimi: land for crops

muradi: one who is castrated

Musungu: European

mwana wovo ni mugingi vo mgongo: your child is the supporting stick of your back

ngonya: help me

nindio: that is all; the end of a discussion.

Nyasaye: God

Nyayo: footsteps; political slogan, footsteps of the ancestors, peace, love unity and sharing (Kiswahili)

olovo: curse

omwene hango: ruler or owner of the home, **"commander"** in local English

ovukima: a porridge made from maize flour

"posterity": children

"provisioning", "to provision": providing food or food-related goods (local English)

"run": in context, improper sexual behaviour (local English)

shamba: land or garden (Kiswahili)

silika: reciprocal group work

sufuria: pot (Kiswahili)

"tarmacking": looking for work

"tea": in context, bribe

"tea and sugar": idiomatic expression for market goods (local English)

tsimbago: traditional hoes

tsinyumba tzinene: great houses (lineage)
ubanga: machete (Kiswahili; *panga* Luragoli)
uhuru: freedom (Kiswahili)
umumenya: one who is not Avalogoli (outsider; plural, *avamenya*)
umulaya: prostitute
umuliango gwitu: from our door
urukali: marriage
uvukwi: bridewealth (Avalogoli translation: **"dowry"**)
va: of
vika: steps
vivuni vye chandangu: back door decisions
vuche, vuchee: morning greeting
vukima: maize porridge (Kiswahili)
"walked": in context, separation of spouses (local English)
"with blood": pregnant (local English)
"yard": compound (local English)
yatigala nalinda misanga gia mulogoli: caring for father's land (Mulogoli, in context)

Endnotes

Introduction to Part I

1. In Bantu languages, the prefix 'ava' or 'aba' transforms the meaning of the morpheme 'Logoli.' The morpheme 'Logoli' always occurs with another element. It should be prefixed, as in 'Avalogoli;' however, in English translation it may be realised as Logoli people, Logoli women, etc.

2. Most people who informed this research asked that their real names be used. However, I consider that use to be contextually dependent on degrees of sensitivity. I believe it unwise to identify those who candidly offered their opinions in certain circumstances. In addition, the composition of the area is such that people within the area, and to some extent outside the area, have an awareness of where and from whom data are gathered. To compound the problem, the use of pseudonyms is not appropriate in Maragoli, as the names of people and places are for the most part lineage-derived or otherwise identifiable. I have attempted to resolve the ethical problem by referring to "the sub-location" or to "the village." In sensitive areas, I refer to people by what is considered their more common first names. They will be able to recognise themselves in my text, but will not be easily identifiable to others. Photographic images are authorised.

3. Logoli women considered my work, constant writing day and night, to be extremely taxing. They often suggested I put my pen away as they put their hoes away after digging was finished for the day. At some point, they began to call my pen, the tool associated with my work, a hoe.

4. Total population of the sub-location is given as 7615: 3495 males, 4120 females (Republic of Kenya, 1982).

5. Names are symbolic and Avalogoli are careful with them and to what end they may be used, for example, in witchcraft. When I asked their husbands' names or their children's in the process of collecting census information, women would say to me, "I am wondering what you will do with his/her name."

6. The English term used by some Logoli women was "thick."

Chapter One

7. Ogot (1967, 72) and Were (1967a, 64-65; 1967b, 7-8) provide historical aspects of the Logoli people. Also, Whiteney (1960), Ochieng (1978), Osogo (1965) and Barker (1950) give histories of the settlement of the area that includes Avalogoli. Wagner (1949) engaged in fieldwork in Western Kenya in the 1920s and 1930s. The Avalogoli are included in his ethnography of the "Bantu Kavirondo." For a more detailed treatment of Avalogoli history, as well as ethnographic particulars, see Abwunza (1985).

8. Mwelesa (undated) has recorded the circumcision sets of Avalogoli and includes on this chart these deaths and places of the deaths.

9. For example, the Avalogoli and the Avakisii consider themselves brothers. The Kisii people are said to have split off in this manner.

10. This provides the explanation for similarities in language and customs among Abaluhya.

11. Barker (1950, 3).

12. Dates are not provided in Avalogoli sources until the first circumcision in the area of present day Maragoli. This is recorded as 1750 (Mwelesa, undated).

13. Mulama's Maragoli Map containing the names has been printed within the last five years.

14. Published statistics (Republic of Kenya, 1982) show the Maragoli population as 142,205; however, the census taken in 1987 gives 197,324 as the population count (Provincial Office, Kakamega, private communication).

15. Republic of Kenya 1979 Population Census Analytical Report. Until 1979, the Luo group was second in population size. The Baluhya have now overtaken the Luo. The Baluhya province of Western Kenya has the highest rate of natural increase in population in Kenya (cf. Ssennyonga, 1978).

16. See Abwunza (1985) for a more detailed investigation of independence, along with the analyses of other researchers.

17. See Abwunza (1993) for a more detailed analysis of ethnic politics.

Chapter Two

18. The words of a very old woman at an early morning Assistant Chief's *barazza*. This "Mummy" refused me permission to "take her name to Canada."

19. Robertson is criticising the attitude of some western researchers, in particular western women, who have assumed a superior or privileged knowledge position in their investigations of African women. Hence her phrase "matriarchal attitude." See also Stamp (1989); Davison et al. (1989); Lyons (1988); and Wipper (1972, 1988) for similar criticism, as they suggest western researchers and development workers listen to rural women, write *their* words, and take heed of their experience and suggestions.

20. Definitions of power and patriarchy are taken from Weber; in one adaptation or another, these classic presentations appear to be the most used in contemporary analyses. Weber sees power as "The probability that one actor within a social relationship will be in a position to carry out his own will despite resistance, regardless of the basis on which this probability rests" (1968, 1, 53). Patriarchy refers to "...a form of traditional domination characteristic of the household group or clan organized on kinship and economic terms," granting "the authority of the father, the husband, the senior of the house, the sib elder over the members of the household and sib" (Weber, 1958, 296; Sydie, 1987, 56).

21. "Review of Steven Goldberg, *The Inevitability of Patriarchy*" (Leacock, 1981, 264).

Chapter Three

22. The following "day in the life" is taken from interviews and observations.

23. Foreign exchange rates fluctuate. During 1987-1988, there were ten to twelve Kenyan shillings in a Canadian dollar; in 1994, the shilling ranged from 80 to 32. Consider the following 1988 prices when a woman receives ten shillings a day digging for others: a two-ounce packet of tea sells for 3.80 shillings; a kilo of meat sells for 29.50 to 33 shillings; washing soap sells for five to ten shillings; bread, 4.20; sugar, 11.40 a kilo; kerosene, three shillings for six ounces. Government price controls were in existence for many commodities: for example, meat, sugar, tea, bread, maize, and kerosene, as well as some building materials—but these controls were removed in 1993 as a result of structural adjustment policies. The people believe the government controls all pricing.

24. Hermann, a businessman in the area, says that with proper use—by this he means using hybred seed and chemical fertilizer—people could get enough maize to last from harvest to harvest (as he does). They would not have to buy. According to him, there are two reasons for the very expensive import of maize from the Nandi area to fulfil Maragoli needs: "First, people are lazy here; second, they do not receive instruction. The agricultural officer does not do his job; he writes false reports...he does not walk the land; he is afraid to get his shoes muddy. The women do the best they can digging, but the men sit and talk; they need to help dig. The men are lazy; the women have too many responsibilities to dig properly."

25. At a seminar on "Women, water supply and sanitation," the Minister for Water Development, Kyale Mwendwa, amused the audience when he said that a sociologist he talked to opposed the idea of providing water in every home, since trekking for water provided "women with an opportunity for gossip, and the girls with an opportunity to meet their boyfriends and possible future husbands." The women I talked to stated that collecting water might be enjoyable, say once in a week, but other than that it was simply difficult, time-consuming work. Also, they said girls are able to meet enough boys in the schools. Girls who develop relationships with boys at rivers and springs soon acquire a "bad" reputation, and likely another mouth for their family to feed.

26. On one occasion, we fed a young man meat, rice and vegetables, a very large plateful. Leaving our house, he went to the kitchen hut and complained he had not eaten. We had not given him *ovukima*.

27. For example, on one occasion during planning for a congregation work group to assist in building their church in a village, extra days were allowed ("We never know who will die."), as the death would necessitate a work stop. An incident took place during the building of this same church. *Mufundi* (workmen) from another village not realizing a death had occurred in the village broke into the locked church and continued with the construction. A number of people believed the work performed that day should be "undone" as a curse might ensue. It was decided to let the work "sit" and a signal system was set up to alert the *mufundi*, should the incident be repeated.

28. Husbands' fathers supply the four main posts for a house, and designate the area where it is to be built by placing the four posts. Husbands and other men should put up the frame and either collect thatching grass or buy roofing material. Wives assist in filling in the frame with mud and in "plastering" or smoothing the mud. Wives make the cow-dung floor. "Women do not build houses; it is men's work." See also Flora (below) in terms of building her own house.

29. Unfortunately for Joyce, in 1988, the rains began and stopped, allowing the army worms to invade the soil and eat the seeds. Those who were "lazy" and put off planting did not lose their seed. Planning ahead does not always pay off when nature dictates the terms.

30. Marrying a relative results in *olovo* that inflicts the entire family. Logoli mothers-in-law complain bitterly about these *avamenya* (outsiders), saying they do not know how to work as Logoli women do. They are called "lazy" and "disrespectful," even as these same women under discussion are cooking, fetching water, and digging. One young wife from Bunyore, whose mother-in-law was berating her, said (under the guise of teasing), "Maragoli people are all crazy!" Another gave the following advice: "You must laugh and forget (what they say) or you cannot survive here."

31. These statements were made during the initial interview with Ritah, in the early stages of our relationship. As time went on, it became impossible for her to maintain the facade of mutual respect.

32. At this point, Ritah is providing a more realistic assessment of her situation.

Chapter Four

33. This selling is actually an illegal activity, as anyone supplying a service in Kenya—that is, operating a business or selling market wares—is required to purchase a licence. One person said angrily: "In today's Kenya you cannot even sell a pencil without a licence" (Waiter, in a Nairobi hotel).

34. I found this contrast very interesting, as I visited with Estella in 1976 and again in 1979, during the time she was market selling in the Eldoret area. In fact, they had a very small garden, with sparse stocks of maize and a one room mud hut. What was most startling was the lack of an *ichoo* or latrine, signifyng their transient status, even though they lived on that plot for over 20 years. Outwardly, there was no sign of affluence, although she is correct in saying that the children were attending school. On the occasion of both visits, I found her husband in the local bar; he did have a drinking man's reputation.

35. Recently, the government has provided the means for those with enough land to engage in growing and selling French beans. The procedure is as follows: government workers assess the size of the land and its suitability, give instruction, and provide the seeds. Twice during the growing period, government workers spray insecticide and chemical fertilizer. During harvest, which requires a morning and evening picking, the beans are taken to a collection depot where they are weighed. During the first harvest in the area, which was very scant, these depots were some distance; however, they have now made available more depots to facilitate faster collection, thus less walking and less

spoilage. At the end of the season, the cost of seed, fertilizer, insecticide and administration expense is deducted and the remainder paid to the grower. Most people said it is too soon to assess if French beans will be a viable cash crop. The second crop was underway during 1988, and most of the growers, who were paid four shillings a kilo, shared their apprehension that others—i.e., those who sell them fresh or can them—will be making lots of money, while those who grow will get very little. Mariam says, "They killed us; they received much higher prices." Growers also felt too much work was involved, most particularly the morning and evening picking. Maragoli people do not eat French beans; they are sold fresh to hotels, and canned for supermarket sale— that is, for urban areas and for export to Eurpoe. Using land for this cash crop will take land away from subsistence crops.

36. Erika underestimated the money and overestimated the hours for digging. She insisted she only received five shillings for a day that began at seven a.m. and ended at four in the afternoon. In fact, these are the hours and wages based on rates in the early 1970s, which gives some idea of how long ago she engaged in digging for others.

37. Erika cares for one cow, which belongs to a relative. She has no chickens or other livestock in evidence.

38. Florence, along with the Women Location Leaders and the Nursery Supervisor, was instrumental and extremely helpful, setting up appointments and accompanying me, thus assisting with the research on Women Groups and nursery school education.

39. This information was given by Benjamin Magwaga, Executive Secretary, Kakamega Branch, Kenya National Union of Teachers, December 23, 1987.

40. Currently, this is only for men, the expectation being that men will supply the living accomodation for their wives, unless it can be shown that female teachers' husbands are dead or "incapacitated." However, the Commission's point is that all teachers should receive a house allowance, and that to not provide one for female teachers is discrimination: "she is employed as a teacher, not as a woman; a worker is a worker" (Magwaga, December 23, 1987).

41. Turkana was the example given.

42. In examining the records for 1985 for Kakamega in Western Province, 535 primary teachers (not sexed, and no total) were fired for desertion, which means they simply walked away from their jobs, losing all benefits. To be reinstated, they must apply through their Chief, their church, and the TSC Disciplinary Committee. Apparently, reinstated teachers are few. It would seem that teaching, although a secure position for some, may not be perfect. Teachers list

the following reasons for job dissatisfaction: low or non-existent wages; lack of promotional opportunities; unjustifiable criticism of parents who expect teachers to provide an image the teachers cannot afford (i.e., manner of dress); singling out teachers in the issue of drinking as this is a nationwide problem; overwork; harassment by officials and inspectors; and unfairness in handling disciplinary cases. Some say their commitment to the profession per se soon becomes lost in the above problems and many only remain teachers or engage in teaching "because of a lack of alternatives" (*The Kenya Teacher*, 1987, 18).

43. This regulation, if passed, will affect only the very few women who have positions in the government sector.

Introduction to Part III

44. Febe tells how God, prior to missionaries and the intervention of Christianity, was *Imungu*. "Today God is *Nyasaye*. *Nyasaye* came when Jesus Christ died; *Imungu* had to leave." Muwg'oma is a place name in the Maragoli Hills. The ancestral caves—the caves people lived in when they first settled in the area prior to building houses—are at Muwg'oma. Up until mid-century, Logoli people made pilgrimages to the caves (although "at eighteen years, girls could not go close; men made the sacrifice"): "They gave food for the ancestors, medicines and herbs in the calabash. This gave us a good crop; the storms could not spoil the millet."

Chapter Five

45. Finasi has four daughters and one son. However, the son was born some years after the death of her husband and after the dispute over his land. Finasi describes her young son as "being from the bush"—that is, from a temporary liason. This means that she may not send the boy to his biological father's yard when it is time for his circumcision—further meaning he will inherit the land where Finasi lives. On the other hand, the boy's father could, if he wished, call for the boy to come to his yard, have his head shaved, be circumcised, and be given land from there.

46. Finasi was not asked to be involved in the system of levirate.

47. Finasi, her husband, their children, and her husband's mother all lived in one hut. After her husband's death, Finasi's brother built a house for her and her children in the same yard.

48. People who work in wage labour and use a banking system to deposit and withdraw cash.

49. As a result of population expansion, it is said that cows are no longer a major part of *uvukwi*; people have no money to buy them and no land on which to graze them. Additional money takes into account the price of cows. At a market in 1988, Zebu cattle were selling for 2000 shillings; half-bred, 3000, and a purebred cow sold for 4000 shillings.

50. *Uvukwi* discussion was to begin, and part of the money paid. In a symbolic sense, "the way is opened" for reciprocal relations to commence among affines.

51. This means the parents are able to decide how much is seen as coming from their daughter's husband (to be) and how much from their daughter, if the designation is not made during the discussion. The designation is important, as the money from the daughter is given to the mother. In this case, the daughter's husband made the decision (see below).

52. An interesting aside to this interview was that women are not able to be leaders in the church if *uvukwi* is not paid. The payment allows for their marriage in a church (a requirement for leadership), for both husband and wife to be "properly dressed" (long dress, shoes, hat, and a suit for the husband), and food for the guests, usually tea and bread with butter. A decorated car is hired, flowers...but no sheep for virginity! Florence says, "My mother and father were married last year; they are over seventy years. These weddings are in plenty—they are very common. To be truly Christian this has to happen." For many years, missionaries attempted to force church weddings, and were, for the most part, ignored. However, it is at present "voluntary," as women seek a viable position in Christian patriarchy.

53. Containers exchanged through this presentation are returned empty, as food is not to be exchanged for food. However, what actually was provided prior to giving cash has been "lost:" some assume it may have been the traditional hoes, while one older woman thought it may have been water pots or containers. In any case, all agree that the exchange never took the form of food for food.

54. See Abwunza (1990a) for a more detailed analysis of *Nyayo*.

55. This has to do with Esta's natal family providing care for her children while she worked.

Introduction to Part IV

56. Hartmann (1987, 1) says a great deal by providing the following citation by the anthropologist Levi-Strauss as a preface quote: "Once men begin to feel cramped in their geographical, social and mental habitat, they are in danger of being tempted by the simple solution of denying one section of the species the right to exist" (*Tristes Tropiques*). Recently, *Issue: A Journal of Opinion* (1994) criticised press coverage of Africa: "It appears that they exercise no reflection on the way...news will interact with stereotypes of Africa.... We see the consequences of press coverage in the beliefs of our students, societal attitudes toward Africa [see Note 3 below]." One of these stereotypes centres around the overpopulation predicament, even though it is statistically ascertainable by demographers and other population experts (cf. Bradley for the area of this case study and other Kenyan research cited throughout the chapter) that fertility rates are dropping. Unfortunately, the population experts appear not to realise that the stereotypes remain, not only for the "general public," but also for many researchers outside their area of expertise. Thus, this chapter not only provides a forum for Logoli women to speak, but also for scholarly research inside and outside the area of expertise to be portrayed.

57. In February, 1992, a group of women, The Mothers of Political Prisoners, along with hundreds of supporters, engaged in a hunger strike and demonstration in Uhuru Park, Nairobi, Kenya. The Mothers were violently dispersed and arrested by Kenyan police. Many Mothers displayed their naked bodies to the arresting police, inflicting an extreme curse. After their release, the Mothers took up a stand in a Nairobi church for most of 1992.

58. Modern cooperatives with membership drawing from both sexes may take the form of organised Rotating Savings and Credit Associations, and Savings and Lending Associations (cf. Levin, 1988; Bouman, 1979). In 1994, many urban people I spoke to were cooperative members, some belonging to more than one privately-organised group. What I found interesting in Nairobi was that membership in private cooperatives appears to be sexed. When I asked one man why women did not belong to his cooperatives (he belongs to six), he replied, "They have their own." After a pause, he said, "You know groups belong to women. They had them first. We men are just beginning." Stimulated by these remarks, my future plan is to extend research inquiry to urban people's economic and social resilience as these are evident in the contemporary development of private cooperative enterprise in Nairobi.

Chapter Seven

59. The December 21, 1992 edition of *Time Magazine* presented a report on Somalia called "Restoring Hope." A response in the Letters section (January 11, 1993, 3) "stressed the necessity for birth control.... Until we can put reliable birth control measures into every Somali woman's hands, we are spinning our humanitarian wheels" (Betty Eschuk, Parma, Ohio). How bizarre, in a situation where thousands of children have died and continue to die, leaving an entire generation drastically underpopulated, that an American taxpayer should believe and that *Time Magazine* should publish such a misrepresentation. Even if the U.S. government was to cast ethics aside and tie population control to their aid in Somalia, the logistics of such a manoeuvre are inconceivable. For example, Alberg writes of the difficulties existent in condom supply both for family planning and HIV/AIDS prevention in Africa. In the case of Uganda, which is experiencing problems of supply, a donation of two million condoms may "look enormous, but if all Ugandans use them, this is the supply for only one night. Furthermore, major donor agencies such as USAID have already indicated they cannot ascertain a regular supply" (Ahlberg, 1991, 216-7; cf. Watson, 1988; *The Lancet*, 1989).

60. Calculated as the difference between the crude birth rate of 52 and the crude death rate of 14 per 1000 population (Republic of Kenya, 1984a). Funding for the KCPS was provided by USAID and the Government of Kenya.

61. Infant mortality rates in Africa began to rise between 1985 and 1986, from 107 to 113 per 1000 births (World Bank 1989, 146, 165).

62. In terms of knowledge of scientific methods, the pill is the most widely-known method (73% of all women, 78% of ever-married women), followed by injection (59% and 65%), intra-uterine devices and female sterilisation (55%), and finally, a low of 18% knowledge of male sterilisation (Republic of Kenya, 1984a).

63. I agree with Hartmann (1987) that no matter how perilous the population problem is thought to be, coercive incentives by a national or foreign government power to impose or deny access to contraceptive technology are unethical and unjustifiably intrusive. This thinking is in line with the United Nations World Population Plan of Action, which endorses the principle that population policies should be consistent with "internationally and nationally recognized human rights of individual freedom and justice" (1984, xiii). In recognising International Women's Day, March 8, 1993, the Canadian International Development Agency reminds us that "Women's Rights are Human Rights," and that international human rights were defined and officially adopted by the United Nations in 1948. Among women's rights as humans is the right to reproductive

choice. As CIDA says, "While many people may assume that these human rights laws and treaties cover both genders equally, global reality sadly proves them wrong" (Canadian International Development Agency, 1993b, 2).

64. On a national basis, the most widely-used methods are the pill (3%), abstinence (3%), IUD (3%), and female sterilisation (2%) (Republic of Kenya, 1984a, 85). In urban areas, the most popular methods are ranked as the pill, IUD, and then rhythm, while in rural areas, the ranking shows rhythm, abstinence, and then the pill. When non-users were asked their preference for use in the future, the pill and injection are the most preferred. In rural areas, 36% prefer the pill and 31% prefer injection; in urban areas, those preferring injection is lower (25%), while the pill is higher (38%). In rural areas the rate of those who would select an IUD is 7%, and in urban areas, the rate of those who would use female sterilisation is 8%. The rate of preferred condom use is 2% in rural areas and 4% in urban areas. Rural non-users are twice as likely (5%) to want to use abstinence as urban non-users (Republic of Kenya, 1984a, 97-99). Other methods, either modern or traditional, are used by less than 1% of Kenyan women (Republic of Kenya, 1984a, 86). Contraceptive use by men—i.e., their preference for contraceptive use or male sterilisation—is not measured.

65. The sample used for the Kenya Contraceptive Prevalence Survey 1986 Provincial Report (KCPSPR) for Western Province included 1001 women with the following characteristics: 90% rural, mean age 28, with 47% less than 25 years old, and 28% 35 years or older; one-third illiterate with a decrease in educational level with age, 22% of women aged 35 to 49, 37% of those 25 to 34, and 77% aged 14 to 24 have more than four years of schooling; three out of four have never worked (outside the home); one in seven is currently working; and one in ten worked only in the past; six out of ten are currently married, almost all before their 25th birthday (more than 50% were less than 18 when they married for the first time). Polygyny is quite prevalent: 28% of the women are in polygynous relationships; more than one in five women in the age group 15 to 24 have one or more co-wives; and one-third of the women aged 35 to 49 are husband-sharing (Republic of Kenya, 1986).

66. Western Province has been divided into three Districts: Bungoma, Busia and Kakamega. At the time of the KCPS and KCPSPR studies, and until 1992/93, Maragoli Location was included in Kakamega District. Vihiga Division was given District status in 1992/93, and includes Maragoli Location and sub-locations. The selected KCPSPR sample for Kakamega District shows the following characteristics for women aged 15 to 49: 94.8% rural; 33.5% illiterate with 32% having no education, 15% having one to four years, 32% having five to eight years, and 20.8% having nine or more years; 15.2% are working, 8.6% worked in past, and 76.2% have never worked (outside the home). Husbands' characteristics (wives were interviewed) show husbands' level of education as

none, 19.0%; one to four years, 22.4%; five to eight years, 34.9%; and nine or more, 20.5%; with a 19.4% illiterate rate; 69.7% own a farm (13.6%), are otherwise working in farming or business, and 30.4% are not working. Couple literacy for Kakamega District shows 13.1% both illiterate, 46.5% both literate, 34.1%, he literate, she not, and 6.3% she literate, he not. The marital status statistics for Kakamega District show 61.1% of women currently married, 33.2% never married and 5.7% married in the past. Of the currently-married women, 41.1% state their husbands are away, and 18.3% say their relationship is one of husband-sharing. The highest cluster for women's age at first marriage is in the 15 to 17 age group, at 43.0%. Only 8.6% remain unmarried after age 25 (Republic of Kenya, 1986).

67. () signifies fewer than 20 cases.

68. Ideal family size statistics are differentiated by the following characteristics: never married desire 4.7 children; married in the past, 5.6; currently-married, 6.5; currently working outside the home, 6.4; worked in the past, 5.9; never worked, 5.9; husband's work status—own farm, 6.3; other farm, 7.0; own business, 6.4; other business, 6.4; not working, 6.6; couple's literacy status—both illiterate, 7.0; both literate, 6.1; he literate, she not, 6.8; she literate, he not, 7.0 (Republic of Kenya, 1986).

69. Explanations are not offered for statistics totalling less or more than 100%.

70. *Murade* is sometimes used to refer to women who have a "TL," tubal ligation. However, in a literal sense, only male animals can be castrated.

Chapter Eight

71. Introductory speech, *Maendeleo* building site.

72. Interestingly, the Western world attempts SAP "with a human face," implementing a graduated correction of imbalances within their own economies. In addition, the United States and Canada have yet to create, out of numerous political rhetoric, any viable policy for deficit reduction. Paul Volcker, past chairman of the Federal Reserve Board, is cited in Gladwin (1993, 103-4): "We say to all kinds of countries, "Fix up your budget deficit and do it by Tuesday. We ask them to do all kinds of things we are not prepared to do ourselves." Gladwin calls SAP "draconian measures." Gladwin's comments are emphasised in the recent edition of *African Farmer*, where further criticism is directed to the World Bank's efforts to expand "safety nets" to alleviate supposedly short-term hardships affecting "vulnerable groups" such as women. Gladwin calls these efforts "paternalistic." Rural women are regarded primarily as victims, rather than as the core of the continent's food-production system (1994, 44).

73. For example, health costs in Kenya have shot up by 250% since structural adjustment was renewed in 1991. "As earning power has not risen, the inevitable result is wide-spread and growing malnutrition" (Ngotho in *African Farmer*, 1994, 43).

74. The use of "daughter-in-law" here signifies my relationship to Avalogoli.

75. In 1994, the same amount of maize was selling for 40 shillings on a local market.

76. In 1993, this group purchased the equipment (through hire-purchase) and began the grinding mill operation. The equipment has "refused"—that is, broken down—on three occasions. In March 1994, the members were trying to accumulate the money to buy spare parts, as the "machine has refused" once again.

Works Cited

Aboud, F. E. (1981). Ethnic self-identity. In R. C. Gardner & R. Kalin (Eds.), *A Canadian social psychology of ethnic relations* (pp. 37-56). Toronto: Methuen.

Abwunza, J. M. (1985). *Mulogoli's 'posterity': Fathers and sons living the land.* Unpublished master's thesis, The University of Western Ontario, London, Canada.

Abwunza, J. M. (1986, November). *Overpopulation as a male oriented strategy for status and survival: The Avalogoli of western Kenya.* Paper presented at the African Studies Association 29th Annual Meeting, Madison, Wisconsin.

Abwunza, J. M. (1990). Nyayo: Cultural contradictions in Kenya rural capitalism. *Anthropologica*, 32(2), 183-203.

Abwunza, J. M. (1993). Ethnonationalism and nationalism strategies: The case of the Avalogoli in western Kenya. In M. D. Levin (Ed.), *Ethnicity and Aboriginality* (pp. 127-153). Toronto: University of Toronto Press.

Abwunza, J. M. (1995). Conversation between cultures outrageous voices? Issues of voice and text in feminist anthropology. In S. Cole & L. Phillips (Eds.), *Ethnographic feminisms: Essays in anthropology* (pp. 245-257). Ottawa: Carleton University Press.

Acholla-Ayayo, A.B.C. (1988). Cultural codes and population change in Kenya. In S. H. Ominde (Ed.), *Kenya's population growth and development to the year 2000* (pp. 57-65). Nairobi: Heinemann Kenya.

African farmer: A quarterly publication of the hunger project, 10. (1994, January). New York.

Ahlberg, B. M. (1991). *Women, sexuality and the changing social order: The impact of government policies on reproductive behaviour in Kenya.* Philadelphia: Gordon and Breach.

Amadiume, I. (1987). *Male daughters, female husbands.* London: Zed Books.

Armstrong, P., & Armstrong, H. (1983). Beyond sexless class and classless sex: Towards feminist marxism. *Studies in Political Economy*, 10, 7-43.

Ayiemba, E.H.O. (1988). The Kenyan family and attitudes towards family formation. In S.H. Ominde (Ed.), *Kenya's population growth and development to the year 2000* (pp. 48-56). Nairobi: Heinemann Kenya.

Barker, E. (1950). *A short history of Nyanza*. Nairobi: East African Literature Bureau.

Barth, F. (1969). *Ethnic groups and boundaries*. London: George Allen and Unwin.

Begler, E. (1978). Sex, status and authority in egalitarian society. *American Anthropologist*, 80, 571-88.

Blumberg, R. L., Rakowski, C. A., Tinker, I., & Monteón, M. (Eds.). (1995). *EnGENDERing wealth and well-being*. Boulder, CO: Westview Press.

Bongaarts, J. (1985). Demographic and other factors of the family life cycle. *Proceedings of the International Population Conference*, 3. Liege, Belgium: I.U.S.S.P. Publication.

Boserup, E. (1970). *Women's role in economic development*. New York: St. Martin's Press.

Bouman, F.J.A. (1979). The RoSCA: Financial technology of an informal savings credit institution in developing economies. *Savings and Development*, 4.

Bradley, C. (1989, June). *The possibility of fertility decline in Maragoli: An anthropological approach*. Population Studies and Research Institute, University of Nairobi.

Bradley, C. (1991, July). *Declining fertility & wealth flows in Maragoli, Kenya*. Population Studies and Research Institute, University of Nairobi.

Brown, M. B. (1980). *Women's oppression today*. London: Verso.

Brown, M. B., & Tiffen, P. (1992). *Short changed: Africa and world trade*. Boulder, CO: Pluto Press with the Transnational Institute (TNI).

Bujra, J. M. (1975). 'Women entrepeneurs' of early Nairobi. *Canadian Journal of African Studies*, 9(2). 213-234.

Bujra, J. M. (1986). "Urging women to redouble their efforts...": Class, gender and capitalist transformation in Africa. In C. Robertson & I. Berger (Eds.), *Women and class in Africa* (pp. 117-140). New York: Africana Publishing.

Burstyn, V. (1985). Masculine dominance and the state. In V. Burstyn & D. Smith (Eds.), *Women, class, family and the state* (pp. 45-89). Toronto: Garamond Press.

Caldwell, J. (1982). *Theory of fertility decline*. New York: Academic Press.

Canadian International Development Agency, Women in Development (CIDA). (1993, March). *Women, human rights and democracy: Making the connections*. Ottawa: Author.

Canadian International Development Agency (CIDA). (1995a). *Engendering development: Women in development and gender equity*. Ottawa: Author.

Canadian International Development Agency (CIDA). (1995b). *Creating a world of equality: CIDA, women and empowerment in developing countries*. Ottawa: Author.

Charlton, S. E. M. (1984). *Women in third world development*. London: Westview Press.

Chazan, N., Mortimer, R., Ravenhill, J., & Rothchild, D. (1992). *Politics and society in contemporary Africa* (2nd ed.). Boulder, CO: Lynne Rienner.

Comaroff, J. (1987). Of totemism and ethnicity: Consciousness, practice and the signs of inequality. *Ethnos, 52*(3-4), 301-323.

Coward, R. (1983). *Patriarchal precedents*. London: Routledge & Kegan Paul.

Daily Nation Newspaper. (1988, 28 Jan). Nairobi.

Davison, J. (Ed.). (1988). *Agriculture, women, and land: The African experience*. London: Westview Press.

Davison, J. with the women of Mutira. (1989). *Voices from Mutira: Lives of rural Gikuyu women*. London: Lynne Rienner.

Economic Commission for Africa. (1989). *African alternative framework to structural adjustment programs for socio-economic recovery and transformation* (E/ECA/CM.15/6 Rev. 3). New York: United Nations.

Edholm, F., Harris, O., & Young, K. (1977). Conceptualising women. *Critique of Anthropology, 3*(9-10), 101-130.

Eichler, M., & Lapointe, J. (1985). *On the treatment of the sexes in research*. Social Sciences and Humanities Research Council of Canada.

Elson, D. (1992). From survival strategies to transformation strategies: Women's needs and structural adjustment. In L. Beneria & S. Feldman (Eds.), *Unequal burden: Economic crises, persistent poverty, and women's work* (pp. 26-48). Boulder, CO: Westview Press.

Emeagwali, G. T. (Ed.). (1995). *Women pay the price: Structural adjustment in Africa and the Carribean*. New Jersey: Africa World Press.

Foucault, M. (1980). *Power/knowledge: Selected interviews and other writings*. New York: Pantheon.

Fox, B. J. (1988, May). Conceptualizing 'patriarchy'. *The Canadian Review of Sociology and Anthropology (CRSA)*, 25(2), 163-182.

Franke, R. W. (1981). Mode of production and population patterns: Policy implications for west African development. *International Journal of Health Services*, 11(3), 361-387.

Gardiner, J. (1975). Women's domestic labour. *New Left Review*, 89, 47-58.

Ginsburg, F., & Rapp, R. (1991). The politics of reproduction. *Annual Review of Anthropology*, 20, 411-43.

Gladwin, C. H. (1993). Women and structural adjustment in a global economy. In R. S. Gallin, A. Ferguson & J. Harper (Eds.), *The women and international development annual* (Vol. 3, pp. 87-112). Boulder, CO: Westview Press.

Goldberg, S. (1973). *The inevitability of patriarchy*. New York: William Morrow.

Gordon, A. A., & Gordon, D. L. (Eds.). (1992). *Understanding contemporary Africa*. Boulder, CO: Lynne Rienner.

Handwerker, W. P. (1991). Women's power and fertility transition: The case of Africa and the West Indies. *Population and Environment: A Journal of Interdisciplinary Studies*, 13(1), 55-78.

Hartmann, B. (1987). *Reproductive rights and wrongs: The global politics of population control and contraceptive choice*. New York: Harper & Row.

Hay, M. J. (1988). Queens, prostitutes and peasants: Historical perspectives on African women. *Canadian Journal of African Studies*, 22(3), 431-447.

Hay, M. J., & Stichter, S. (Eds.). (1984). *African women south of the Sahara*. London: Longman.

Henin, R.A. (1980). *Population, development and economic planning*. PSRI Research Series Publication.

Heyer, J. (1975). The origins of regional inequalities in smallholder agriculture in Kenya, 1920-1973. *East Africa Journal of Rural Development*, 8(1-2).

Howell, J. T. (1973). *Hard living on Clay Street*. New York: Doubleday Anchor Books.

Humphrey, N. (1947). *The Liguru and the land: Sociological aspects of some agriculture problems in north Kavirondo*. Nairobi: Government Printer.

Hyden, G. (1983). *No shortcuts to progress*. Berkeley: University of California Press.

Isajiw, W. W. (1975). The process of maintenance of ethnic identity: The Canadian context. In P.M. Migus (Ed.), *Sounds Canadian: Languages and cultures in multi-ethnic society* (pp. 129-138). Toronto: Peter Martin Associates.

Isajiw. W. W. (1979). *Definitions of ethnicity*. Toronto: The Multicultural History Society of Ontario.

Issue: A journal of opinion, 22(1). (1994). Editor's introduction.

Kariuki, P. (1985). Women's aspirations and perceptions of their own situation in society. In G.S. Were (Ed.), *Women and development in Africa* (pp. 22-29). Nairobi: Gideon Were Press.

Karl, M. (1995). *Women and empowerment: Participation and decision making*. London: Zed Books.

Kenya, Republic of. (1979). *Population census: Volume 2*. Analytical report. Nairobi: Central Bureau of Statistics, Ministry of Finance and Planning.

Kenya, Republic of. (1982). *Population census: Population by sex and sublocation*. Nairobi: Central Bureau of Statistics Western Province, Provincial Commissioner's Office.

Kenya, Republic of. (1984). *Kenya contraceptive prevalence survey*. Nairobi: Central Bureau of Statistics, Ministry of Planning and National Development.

Kenya, Republic of. (1984). *Population policy guidelines Sessional Paper No. 4.*, Nairobi: National Council for Population and Development, Office of the Vice-President and Ministry of Home Affairs.

Kenya, Republic of. (1986). *Kenya contraceptive prevalence survey 1984 provincial report*. Nairobi: Central Bureau of Statistics, Ministry of Planning and National Development.

Kenya, Republic of. (1989). *Kenya demographic and health survey*. Nairobi: Central Bureau of Statistics, Ministry of Planning and National Development.

Kenya, Republic of. (1990). *Statistical Abstract*. Nairobi: Central Bureau of Statistics, Ministry of Planning and National Development.

Kiano, J. M. (1977, October 17). *Introductory Speech*. Given at the Stone Laying Ceremony, Maendeleo Ya Wanawake Building, Nairobi, Kenya.

The Lancet. (1989, August 26). *Indeterminate western blots and HIV*.

Leacock, E. (1981). *Myths of male dominance*. New York: Monthly Review Press.

Leacock, E. (1986). Preface. In E. Leacock, H. I. Safa & Contributors, *Women's work* (pp. ix-xi). Massachusetts: Bergin & Garvey.

Levin, M. D. (1988). Accountability and legitimacy in traditional co-operation in Nigeria. In D.W. Attwood and B.S. Baviskar (Eds.), *Who shares? Co-operatives and rural development* (pp. 330-342). Delhi: Oxford University Press.

Levy, M. F. (1988). *Each in her own way: Five women leaders of the developing world*. London: Lynne Rienner.

Ligale, A.N. (1966). Some factors influencing the pattern of rural settlement in Maragoli, Western Kenya. *East African Geographical Review*, 65-68.

Lisingu, S. J. (1946). *Kitabu kya Mulogoli na vana veve (The Mulogoli history and family)*. Nairobi: Colonial P. Works.

Lyons, H. (1988). Introductory Note. *Canadian Journal of African Studies*, 22(3). 422-426.

March, K., & Taqqu, R. (1986). *Women's informal associations in developing countries*. Boulder, CO: Westview Press.

Mazrui, A. A. (1986). Preface. In A. Mazrui & T. K. Levine (Eds.), *The Africans: A reader*. New York: Praeger.

Mba, N. E. (1982). *Nigerian women mobilized*. Berkeley: Institute of International Studies.

Mbilinyi, M. (1989). "I'd have been a man": Politics and the labor process in producing personal narratives. In *The Personal Narratives Group, Interpreting women's lives* (pp. 204-227). Bloomington: Indiana University Press.

Meillassoux, C. (1981). *Maidens, meal and money: Capitalism and the domestic community*. Cambridge: Cambridge University Press.

Mies, M. (1986). *Patriarchy and accumulation on a world scale*. London: Zed Books.

Mirza, S., & Stroebel, M. (Eds. & Trans.). (1989). *Three Swahili women: Life histories from Mombasa, Kenya*. Indianapolis: Indiana University Press.

Mmbulika, L.M.E. (1971). *Resistance and reaction to agricultural change and development in Maragoli, 1946-1962*. Unpublished Bachelor's Dissertation, University of Nairobi, Nairobi, Kenya.

Moi, D. T. (arap). (1986). *Kenya African nationalism: Nyayo philosophy and principles*. London: Macmillan.

Moore, H. L. (1988). *Feminism and anthropology*. Minneapolis: University of Minnesota Press.

Mosley, W.H., Warner, L.H., & Brecker, S. (1982). The dynamics of birth spacing and marital fertility in Kenya. *World Fertility Survey Scientific Reports*, No. 30.

Mott, F., & Mott, S. (1980, October). Kenya's record population growth: A dilemma of development. *Population Bulletin*, 35(3).

Muganzi, Z. (1988). Fertility and mortality trends in Kenya. In S.H. Ominde (Ed.), *Kenya's population growth and development to the year 2000* (pp. 34-39). Nairobi: Heinemann Kenya.

Mulama, D. J. (no date). *Maragoli: Cultural map*. Private Publication.

Mwelesa, G. W. H. (no date). *Amita ga vaguuga ne vikevo Mulogoli; Amina na makula ge vikevo via Mulogoli*. Kenya: Private Publication.

Nasimiyu, R. (1985). Women in the colonial economy of Bungoma: Role of women in agriculture, 1902-1960. In G. S. Were (Ed.), *Women and development in Africa* (pp. 56-73). Nairobi: Gideon S. Were Press.

Ndeti, K., & Ndeti, C. (1980). *Cultural values and population policy in Kenya*. Nairobi: Kenya Literature Bureau.

Nerlove, M., Razin, A., & Sadka, E. (1987). *Household and economy: Welfare economics of endogenous fertility*. Boston: Academic Press.

Newbury, M. C. (1984). Ebutumba bw'emiogo: The tyranny of cassava a women's tax revolt in eastern Zaire. *Canadian Journal of African Studies*, 18(1). 35-54.

Njogu, W. (1991, February). Trends and determinants of contraceptive use in Kenya. *Demography*, 28(1), 83-99.

Nzomo, M. (1989). The impact of The Women's Decade on policies, programs and empowerment of women in Kenya. *Issue: A Journal of Opinion*, 17(2), 7-8.

Oboler, R. S. (1985). *Women, power, and economic change: The Nandi of Kenya*. Stanford, CA: Stanford University Press.

Ochieng, W. R. (1979). *People round the lake*. Hampshire: Evans Brothers.

Ogot, B. A. (1967). *History of the southern Luo: Vol. 1*. Nairobi: East African Publishing House.

Ogutu, M. A. (1985). The changing role of women in the commerical history of Busia District in Kenya, 1900-1983. In G. S. Were (Ed.), *Women and development in Africa* (pp. 74-90). Nairobi: Gideon S. Were Press.

Ominde, S. H. (Ed.). (1988). *Kenya's population growth and development to the year 2000*. Nairobi: Heinemann Kenya.

Osogo, J. (1965). *Life in Kenya in the olden days: The Buluyia*. Nairobi: Oxford University Press.

Ottieno, J.A.M., Osieo, A.O., & Acholla-Ayayo, A.B.C. (1988). Demographic models applied at the population studies and research institute. In S.H. Ominde (Ed.), *Kenya's population growth and development to the year 2000* (pp. 12-21). Nairobi: Heinemann Kenya.

Pala Okeyo, A. (1980). Daughters of the lakes and rivers: Colonization and the land rights of Luo women. In M. Etienne & E. Leacock (Eds.), *Women and colonization* (pp. 186-213). New York: Praeger.

Patterson, O. (1977). *Ethnic chauvinism: The reactionary impulse*. New York: Stein and Day.

Personal Narratives Group (Eds.). (1989). *Interpreting women's lives: Feminist theory and personal narratives*. Indianapolis: Indiana University Press.

Phillips, A. (1930, October). *Report of native land tenure in the North Kavirondo reserve*. Colonial Archives.

Poole, V. H. (1991). Fertility drops in some countries of Sub-Saharan Africa. *Population Today*, 19(3). 4.

Presley, C. A. (1986). Labor unrest among Kikuyu women in colonial Kenya. In C. Robertson & I. Berger (Eds.), *Women and class in Africa* (pp. 255-271). New York: Africana.

Reiter, R. (1975). Men and women in the south of France: Public and private domains. In R. Reiter (Ed.), *Toward an anthropology of women* (pp. 252-282). New York: Monthly Review Press.

Rey, P. (1975). The lineage mode of production. *Critique of Anthropology*, 3, 27-79.

Richardson, L. W. (1981). *The Dynamics of Sex and Gender (2nd Ed.)*. Boston: Houghton Mifflin.

Riria-Ouko, J.V.N. (1985). Women organizations in Kenya. In G. S. Were (Ed.), *Women and development in Africa* (pp. 188-197). Nairobi: Gideon S. Were Press.

Robertson, C. (1988a). Research on African women since 1972: A commentary. *Canadian Journal of African Studies*, 22(3), 427-428.

Robertson, C. (1988b). Never underestimate the power of women: The transforming vision of African women's history. *Women's Studies International Forum*, 11(5), 439-453.

Robey, B., Rutstein, S. O., & Morris, L. (1993, December). The fertility decline in developing countries. *Scientific American*, 269(6), 60-67.

Romero, P. (1988). *Life histories of African women*. London: The Ashfield Press.

Rubin, G. (1975). The traffic in women: Notes on the "political economy" of sex. In R. Reiter (Ed.), *Toward an anthropology of women* (pp. 157-211). New York: Monthly Review Press.

Sacks, K. (1979). *Sisters and wives: The past and future of sexual equality*. Westport, CT: Greenwood Press.

Sadik, N. (1991). World population continues to rise. *The Futurist*, 25(2), 9-14.

Sanday, P. R. (1974). Female status in the public domain. In M. Rosaldo & L. Lamphere (Eds.), *Women, culture and society* (pp. 189-206). Stanford: Stanford University Press.

Schegel, A. (Ed.). (1977). *Sexual stratification*. New York: Columbia University Press.

Sheperd, G. (1984). *Responding to the contraceptive needs of rural people: A report to Oxfam of Kenya*. Nairobi: A.G. Chambers.

Shitakha, T. (1985). Opening Address. In G. S. Were (Ed.), *Women and development in Africa*. Nairobi: Gideon S. Were Press.

Ssennyonga, J. W. (1978). *Maragoli's exceptional population dynamics: A demographic portrayal*. Nairobi: University of Nairobi, Institute of African Studies, Paper No. 8.

Stamp, P. (1975-76). Perceptions of change and economic strategy among Kikuyu women of Mitero, Kenya. In A. Wipper (Ed.), *Rural Africana*, 29, 19-43.

Stamp, P. (1986). Kikuyu women's self-help groups: Toward an understanding of the relation between sex-gender system and mode of production in Africa. In C. Robertson & I. Berger (Eds.), *Women and Class in Africa* (pp. 27-46). New York: Africana.

Stamp, P. (1989). *Technology, gender, and power in Africa* (Technical Study 63e). Ottawa: International Development Research Centre.

Staudt, K. (1985). *Agricultural policy implementation: A case study from western Kenya*. West Hartford: Kumarian Press.

Staudt, K., & Col, J. (1991). Diversity in east Africa: Cultural pluralism, public policy. In R. S. Gallin & A. Ferguson (Eds.), *The women and international development annual: Volume 2* (pp. 241-64). Boulder, CO: Westview Press.

Staunton, I. (1991). *Mothers of the Revolution*. Bloomington: Indiana University Press.

Stichter, S. (1988). The middle-class family in Kenya: Changes in gender relations. In S. B. Stichter & J. L. Parpart (Eds.), *Patriarchy and class: African women in the home and the workforce* (pp. 177-203). Boulder, CO: Westview Press.

Stichter, S. B., & Parpart, J. L. (1988). *Patriarchy and class: African women in the home and the workforce.* Boulder, CO: Westview Press.

Sydie, R.A. (1987). *Natural women, cultured men.* Toronto: Methuen.

Sylvester, C. (1993). Riding the hyphens of feminism, peace and place in four- (or more) part cacophony. *Alternatives: Social transformation and human governance,* 18(1). 109-118.

Tadesse, Z. (1982). The impact of land reform on women: The case of Ethiopia. In L. Beneria (Ed.), *Women and development: The sexual division of labor in rural societies* (pp. 203-222). New York: Praeger.

Thomas, J. (1988, July). Women and capitalism: Oppression or emancipation? A review article. *Comparative Studies in Society and History,* 30(3), 534-549.

Timberlake, L. (1986). *Africa in crisis: The causes, the cures of environmental bankruptcy.* Washington, DC: Earthscan.

Time Magazine, 140(25). (1992, December 21). *Restoring Hope.* 28-35.

Time Magazine, 141(2). (1993, January 11). *Letters.* 5.

United Nations. (1984). *United Nations world population chart.* New York: Department of Economics and Social Affairs.

Van Allen, J. (1972). "Sitting on a man": Colonialism and the lost political institutions of Igbo women. *Canadian Journal of African Studies,* 6(2). 165-181.

Van Allen, J. (1976). 'Aba riots' or Igbo 'women's war': Ideology, stratification and the invisibility of women. In N. Hafkin & E. Bay (Eds.), *Women in Africa: Studies in social and economic change.* Stanford: Stanford University Press.

Vock, J. (1988). Demographic theories and women's reproductive labor. In S. B. Stichter & J. L. Parpart (Eds.), *Patriarchy and class: African women in the home and the workforce* (pp. 81-96). Boulder, CO: Westview.

Wagner, G. (1949). *The Bantu of western Kenya* (Vols. 1-2). London: Oxford University Press.

Walby, S. (1986). *Patriarchy at work*. Minneapolis: University of Minnesota Press.

Watson, C. (1988, November/December). Uganda: An open approach to AIDS. *Africa Report*, 33(6). 32-35.

Weber, M. (1958). From *Max Weber: Essays in sociology* (H.H. Gerth & C. W. Mills, Trans. & Eds.). New York: Oxford University Press.

Weber, M. (1968). *Economy and society: An outline of interpretive sociology* (Vols 1-3, G. Roth & C. Wittich, Eds.). New York: Bedminster.

The Weekly Review. (1988, 11 March). *Plenty of personality clashes and a marked lack of issues* (Nairobi). 4-5.

Were, G. (1967a). *A history of the Abaluyia of western Kenya c. 1500-1930*. Nairobi: East African Publishing House.

Were, G. (1967b). *Western Kenya historical texts*. Nairobi: East African Literature Bureau.

White, L. (1980). *Women's domestic labour in colonial Kenya: Prostitution in Nairobi*. Working Paper #30, African Studies Center, Boston University.

Whiteney, W. H. (1960). *The tense system of Gusii*. Uganda: East African Institute of Social Research.

Wipper, A. (1972). The roles of African women: Past, present and future. *Canadian Journal of African Studies*, 8(2). 143-146.

Wipper, A. (1975). The Maendeleo ya Wanawake organization: The co-optation of leadership. *African Studies Review*, 18(3), 99-120.

Wipper, A. (1975-76). The Maendeleo ya Wanawake movement in the colonial period: The Canadian connection, mau mau, embroidery and agriculture. In A. Wipper (Ed.), *Rural Africana*, 25. 195-214.

Wipper, A. (1984). Women's voluntary associations. In M. J. Hay & S. Stichter (Eds.), *African women south of the Sahara* (pp. 69-86). London: Longman.

Wipper, A. (1985). *Riot and rebellion among African women: Three examples of women's political clout*. Working Paper #108. Women in International Development. Michigan State University.

Wipper, A. (1988). Reflections of the past sixteen years, 1972-1988, and future challenges. *Canadian Journal of African Studies* 22(3). 409-421.

World Bank. (1986). *Population growth and policies in Sub-Saharan Africa.* Washington, DC: World Bank.

World Bank. (1989). *World development report.* New York: Oxford University Press.

World Bank. (1990). *World development report.* New York: Oxford University Press.

Young, G., Samarasinghe, V. & Kusterer, K. (Eds.). (1993). *Women at the center: Development issues and practices for the 1990's.* West Hartford, CT: Kumarian Press.

Index

wage labour 18, 19, 29, 30, 46, 60, 61-63, 72-81, 92, 93, 108, 113, 144, 147, 159

wages 62, 75-76, 108, 160, 164

empowerment (see power, women's)
women's 4, 34, 128

Erika 69-71

ethnicity 16-18, 138, 141-142

ethnic identity 3, 16-17, 18
inequality based on 17, 137

Esta 120, 150

Estella 63-65, 104

exports 160

"exchange value" 43, 182

family
definition of 13, 185
ideal 48, 134, 136, 137-138, 139, 140-141, 142, 143, 146, 151, 154, 183
relations 20, 37, 90-91

family planning 131-134, 135-137, 139-141, 142-144, 147-155, 167, 173-174, 183,
barriers to 137, 140-141, 144, 146-148, 153-154
clinics 141, 142-143, 152
decision making 127, 131, 136, 140, 143, 147, 151, 174, 183
ideal family 48, 134, 136, 137-138, 139, 140-141, 142, 143, 146, 151, 154, 183
men and 43, 136, 147

Febe 91, 96, 103-104, 150, 161

fertility 132-146, 173-174, 183
and polygyny 139, 143
rates 19, 32, 133, 134, 135, 136, 138, 142-143, 145, 153

Finasi A. 163

Finasi B. 94-95, 164

Florah 6-7, 78-81, 87, 118-119, 121, 153

Florence 65

food
prices 92, 160, 161

production 43, 45, 52-53, 83, 90, 146, 161
sale of 15, 50, 167, 168, 169, 171, 175
sharing 98-99, 121, 150, 161
supply 46, 49, 52, 61, 136, 137, 185

Gideon 146

Harambee 157, 159, 163, 167, 189

Hawa 71-72

health care 133, 136, 138, 157, 161, 164
access to 12, 136

housing 3, 13, 51, 55, 136, 162

Iemba 112

illiteracy 73, 140, 142-143, 157

IUD 142, 147-148, 174

Jayi-Nora 103

Jerida 67-69

Jonesi 150

Joyce 54-56, 106-107, 151

Kagonga 43, 87, 91, 103, 149-150, 157, 162

Kenya African National Union (KANU) 117, 157

Kenya Rural Enterprise Program (K-REP) 158

kinship
and residence patterns 13
networks 53, 63, 73, 93, 100-101, 121-122, 138, 154, 174, 175

labour (see also work)
children's 13, 14, 42, 45, 48-49, 52, 150-151
division of 25-26, 29-30, 45-83, 138
double day of 74-75
men's 45-83, 92, 184
women's 30, 32, 45-83, 89-93, 109, 114, 158, 182, 183, 186-87
wage 18, 19, 29, 30, 46, 60, 61-63, 72-81, 92, 93, 108, 113, 144, 147, 159

land 93-98
appropriation 12